The Navajo
and the Animal People

*Native American Traditional
Ecological Knowledge and Ethnozoology*

Steve Pavlik

Foreword by William B. Tsosie Jr.

The Navajo
and the Animal People

Native American Traditional
Ecological Knowledge and Ethnozoology

Steve Pavlik

Foreword by William B. Tsosie Jr.

Library of Congress Cataloging-in-Publication Data

Pavlik, Steve.
  The Navajo and the animal people / Steve Pavlik.
    pages cm
  Includes bibliographical references.
   ISBN 978-1-938486-64-7
1. Navajo philosophy. 2. Traditional ecological knowledge--Navajo Nation, Arizona, New Mexico & Utah. 3. Human-animal relationships--Navajo Nation, Arizona, New Mexico & Utah. I. Title.
  E99.N3P39 2014
  979.1004'9726--dc23
                               2014017209

Printed in the United States of America
0 9 8 7 6 5 4 3 2 1

Illustrated by Benton Yazzie
Designed by Ken Lockwood

Fulcrum Publishing
4690 Table Mountain Dr., Ste. 100
Golden, CO 80403
800-992-2908 • 303-277-1623

www.fulcrumbooks.com

 # Contents

# Preface

This is a book about the orthodox traditional Navajo relationship to the natural world. By *orthodox,* I mean Navajo traditional lifeway before it came into significant contact and subsequent influence from outside forces, most notably the Judeo-Christian religious tradition. This was a time when the Navajo people followed only the teachings of the "Holy People," the *Yeis.* It was a time when they saw themselves intimately connected to, and a part of, their sacred land and the other living beings with which they shared that land.

Specifically, this is a book about how the Navajos once related to the Animal People, and particularly a category of animals that they collectively referred to as *naatl'eetsoh*—"the ones who hunt." Western science and society classify these animals as carnivores or more often simply as predators. The predators discussed here, like Native Americans themselves, were once viewed as standing in the way of progress. They were considered a threat to ranching interests and even to public safety. Consequently, the federal government launched wars of extermination against them—as it also did against Native Americans. But both predators and Native American people like the Navajos proved resilient, and both survived the efforts to destroy them. Sadly, the war to exterminate predators continues to this day.

Each of the chapters in this book began its life as a paper presented at a professional conference between 1996 and 2004. Most were presented as part of the Native American religion and spirituality panel of the

American Indians Studies section at the yearly Western Social Science Association conferences. My mentor and close friend, the late Vine Deloria Jr., Tom Hoffman, and I comprised this panel over the years, from time to time joined by other invited scholars.

In time, several of these papers found their way into publication in various journals or anthologies. The others remained buried in the document archives of my computer. Over the years I received requests for copies of these published and unpublished papers, some of them from authors who were writing books on the wildlife species in question and who wanted to include a Native American background to their more scientific or popular writing. Increasingly, I was receiving requests from college students, most often Navajo students, who needed information for research papers or who simply wanted to learn more about their culture's traditional view of the natural world and wildlife. Eventually I decided the time had come to bring these papers together in book form. Readers are reminded that each of the chapters was originally written as a "stand-alone" essay. It is my goal in this volume that they remain so. Consequently, although I have edited the chapters to remove redundancy and have expanded each of the original essays, most often for the purpose of updating the material, the chapters remain much as they were when I first presented them at the various conferences.

The main source of information for these essays is early anthropological writing. No actual "fieldwork" was done on my part; rather, I have simply brought to light that which has been previously published. This is reflected in the extensive citations included in this book. The Navajos have always been—for better or for worse—the most anthropologically studied people in Native North America. Religion, spirituality, and ceremonialism have been the primary focus for most of the anthropologists who have studied and written on the tribe. Unfortunately, most of the resulting publications are books long out of print or articles that appeared in obscure or very early journals not readily accessible to most people. My task has been to dig out these sources and make the information in them more available to a wider and new universe of readers, especially to young Navajos who want to learn more about the early traditional ways but who do not have access to the tribal resource people to teach them.

A word about anthropology and anthropologists: historically, the field of anthropology has been much criticized by Native people due to its exploitative nature. Many early anthropologists would leave their ivory towers each summer to rush onto an Indian reservation, hire a favored "informant" who told them what they wanted to hear, perhaps observe a few ceremonies, then rush back to their host institutions to write the "definitive" account of that tribe's culture and traditions. More often than not, what they wrote was pure trash. Even worse, their shoddy scholarship often came to form the basis of ill-conceived federal Indian policy. The 1969 publication of Deloria's groundbreaking *Custer Died for Your Sins: An Indian Manifesto*—and its seminal chapter "Anthropologists and Other Friends"—served to blow the whistle on such practices and eventually changed forever the face of American anthropology.

But Deloria's criticisms of anthropologists did not blind him to the fact that the body of work they recorded often remains the best source of information available for those trying to learn about traditional knowledge and how early tribal people related to the natural world. He lamented the fact that tribal elders of today—products themselves of the boarding school era, or perhaps a generation removed from that time—had little intimate knowledge of the stories, ceremonials, or values of their ancestors. He wrote:

> The possibility that we do have, however, is the sense of the knowledge of the old people as recorded by non-Indians, beginning with first contact and continuing until the 1930s and in some cases the 1950s. . . . People may claim to have this same knowledge today but such claims are mostly wishful thinking. The task today is that of intensive research and study to enable people to project what the various tribal peoples probably meant when they described the world around them. (Deloria, 2004: 4)

The Navajos' experience with anthropologists was somewhat different from that of most tribes. Although there were a few early anthropologists who might be considered little more than charlatans, most who came to study the Navajos were dedicated people who generally conducted themselves well and produced important and useful scholarship. Many learned the language—indeed, one, Father Berard Haile, a Catholic priest by profession who lived among the Navajo for more than fifty years, not only developed a written form of the Navajo language, but also invented a typewriter to type it. Other anthropologists established personal relationships with collaborators and families that spanned decades. A common reservation joke has always been that the typical Navajo extended family was composed of the mother and father and their children, the grandmothers and grandfathers, aunts and uncles, nephews and nieces—and at least one anthropologist. There was certainly a measure of truth in such witticism.

The most important contribution of these anthropologists was their careful recording of the Navajo stories—often in the Navajo language itself. Thanks to their efforts, the Navajo people have been able to retain a nearly complete record of their sacred history—far more so than any other tribe in the Americas. These stories, at least to me, represent the single greatest epic ever told and recorded in the history of civilization by any people.

The second great contribution of the anthropologists who studied the Navajos was their highly detailed accounts of the tribal ceremonial practices that were based on their stories. Although some Navajo ceremonies have gone extinct over the years, most have not. And while some have become greatly diminished over time, some, like the Nightway, remain strong and vibrant.

I might add that I lived on the Navajo Reservation for nineteen years, and during that time I had the opportunity to meet and talk with many medicine men. I found it interesting that a number of these traditional ceremonialists had themselves read—and I presume learned from—the old anthropological books and papers.

It is impossible to talk about the anthropologists without talking about the many Navajo collaborators who provided them the information that went into the books—including the information now appearing in this book. What were their motivations? Of course they received financial compensation, welcome money in a cash-poor economy. But they had a deeper motivation. To begin with, Navajo orthodox traditional society was far more open than most people tend to acknowledge. Although there were lines that could not be crossed and thresholds that could not be breached, many early Navajo singers and others with ceremonial knowledge were eager to share their beliefs with the outside world. This was especially true by the middle of the twentieth century, when traditionalists saw the world they knew begin to slip away. As these individuals witnessed firsthand the decline of their traditional culture, they valued sharing their stories and ceremonial knowledge with anthropologists as a way to keep it from being lost forever. In telling his version of the Navajo origin story to Aileen O'Bryan, Sandoval stated:

> In time to come my people will have forgotten their early way of life unless they learn it from white men's books. So you must write down all that I tell you; and you must have it made into a book that coming generations may know this truth. (O'Bryan: vii)

Or consider the words of Claus Chee Sonny in explaining why he shared his Navajo hunter tradition with Karl W. Luckert—knowledge that he wanted preserved "for young people from all over the world" (Luckert: 6):

This is all there is to the story and the ritual. I thank you for asking about my tradition, my way of life. You have asked about these things and about the way I live. You came to me, and I gave it to you. And now you take it to others. And I appreciate this. I thank you for it.

. . . By asking your questions you have renewed my prayers, my songs and story. Now it is up to the young men and women, who wish to learn this and take it seriously, to carry on. And this is all. (Ibid.: 21)

I think that the rationale used by Sandoval and Sonny Claus Chee was shared by many other orthodox Navajos who were seeing the stories being forgotten and the ceremonies being replaced by what I have called the "new traditionalism"—the peyote ceremonies of the Native American Church (NAC)—and, to a lesser extent, the services of the various Christian churches that were emerging to challenge traditionalism. In sharing their stories and ceremonies, they desired to leave behind a written record of a way of life that they feared was vanishing and yet remained important. I think that most of the so-called informants—as they were unfortunately referred to by the anthropologists with whom they collaborated—would be pleasantly surprised to see that many of the old ways are still alive, and that there is a revival of interest today in traditional religion among many young Navajos.

Historically, the stories that were told to the anthropologists and the ceremonial knowledge shared with them were individually owned by the collaborators—they did not belong to the tribe. Indeed, the very concept of a "tribe" would have been something unfamiliar to early Navajos. Consequently, this information was a gift of the most personal kind. It is for this reason that wherever possible I have provided the names of the Navajo sources. In the truest sense, their knowledge is the heart and soul of this book. I hope the book is an opportunity for them to speak again.

In addition to the anthropological record, I have relied heavily on the stories and insights given to me by my own Navajo associate—my good friend and other mentor, William Ben Begay Tsosie. Will is *Ma'iideesh-giizhinii* (Coyote Pass People), born for *To'aheedliinii* (Where the Two Rivers Meet People). His grandmother clan is *Bit'ahnii* (Folded Arms People), and his grandfather clan is *Tl'aashchi'i* (Red Streak-Cheeked People). After a Catholic high school education, Will turned away from Christianity, rejected the NAC, and followed the ways of his traditional ancestors. He participates fully in the traditional ceremonies of his people and, most importantly, lives his life in a manner prescribed by the Holy people. Will, who is now a field archaeologist, in the truest sense is an orthodox traditionalist, one of very few on the Navajo Reservation today. I can't remember when I first met Will—it seems like I have known him forever. But we have traveled together for more than twenty years. Very early on, he cheerfully accepted the almost impossible task of trying to teach this *biligana* about Navajo traditional culture. Often over a cup of strong coffee at my house or his, or perhaps while driving along some long, lonely stretch of Navajo highway, or sometimes very late at night inside the cab of one of our vehicles while waiting for a *yei be chai* or Fire Dance to begin, Will talked and I eagerly listened.

I never recorded anything, and I seldom took notes, although I would often later write down what I remembered or even call and ask him to elaborate on some of the finer points of his earlier discourse. In many ways, Will, through his generosity and willingness to share his culture, is a reflection of those early orthodox traditionalists who have gone before him. I will forever be indebted that he has done so, and I am honored that he has written the foreword to this book.

This book itself is a study in the traditional ecological knowledge (TEK) of the Navajo people in regard to how they viewed the natural world, their relationship with the Animal People, and very specifically, with the carnivores or predators. Fikret Berkes, the scholar who might very well be considered the "father" of TEK, defines this field as being the "cumulative body of knowledge, practice, and belief, evolving by adaptive processes and handed down through generations by cultural transmission, about the relationship of living beings (including humans) with one another and with their environment" (Berkes: 8). In this definition, the operative word is *relationship*. Native Americans maintained intimate relationships with all other life with whom they shared the Earth. Unlike western society, whose relationship with all life is based on competition and exploitation, the tribal relationship with all life—including the Animal People—was based on cooperation and reciprocal exchange.

When looking closely at Berkes's definition, several separate but intimately related aspects of TEK emerge. The first is what might be considered the acquisive component—how the people acquired their knowledge. For the Navajos, knowledge generally came in two ways: the sacred (spiritual) knowledge handed down to them through the creation stories, and the experiential knowledge acquired through centuries of observation, inventiveness, and practice. The second part of TEK might be referred to as the *utilitarian* component—how the people utilized what they learned about the natural world, specifically in regard to the acquisition of food, the development of shelter and clothing, tools and weapons, and the countless other examples of technology that allowed a tribe like the Navajos not only to survive but to actually thrive in a landscape that would prove challenging to most other people. The third part of TEK is the *psychological* or, to use the term that I prefer, the *emotional* component— how the people *related* to the land (place) and all it comprised. In the case of the Navajos, this emotional aspect focused around the creation stories that take place within the borders of the four sacred mountains. To me, it is this third element that is most important, because it accounts for the value system—the ethical foundation—upon which everything else rests and that ties everything together.

In recent years, increased attention has been given—at least in some quarters—to the TEK of tribal people. In part this stems from the realization that western society has largely destroyed and despoiled the natural world, and that we need to find a more life-enhancing way of relating to and living on the Earth. In general, however, the western scientific community continues to dismiss or disparage indigenous wisdom. TEK is often rejected because it is often not "testable" in a scientific sense and consequently does not rise to the level of acceptable scientific standards. In addition, western science steadfastly tends to not take seriously any spiritual knowledge—the foundation of TEK. Although one sees a degree of patronizing lip service given to TEK (at least while the grant money lasts), published reports tend to be greatly underutilized. This is truly unfortunate because TEK has much to offer the modern world. We are belatedly beginning to recognize this as we finally acknowledge and confront the large issues that face our contemporary societies, most notably climate change and the need to establish a sustainable lifestyle.

TEK is generally divided into various subfields, including the focus of this book, ethnozoology—the study of documenting, describing, and explaining the complex relationships that exist between specific cultures and animals. Other subfields of TEK include ethnoastronomy (the cosmos), ethnogeology (geological features), and ethnobotany (plants).

One key aspect of the psychological or emotional component of Native American ethnozoology is the knowledge that humans and animals are related—that they share a very real kinship with one another. Animals are simply fellow beings in a different form, and as such share common traits and are deserving of the same rights as humankind. Native Americans have always known that a very fine line separates humankind from the animals. This knowledge serves as a foundation of the Navajo relationship to the Animal People and, consequently, for this collection of essays.

Western society is just now starting to grasp this concept. Consequently, a new field of science—or a recently rediscovered field of science—has emerged: cognitive ethology, which studies the emotional and the consequent behavioral lives of animals (see Bekoff). It starts with the premise that every animal is an individual and that animal behavior is largely the product of two separate but related processes: thought and emotions. In sum, cognitive ethologists believe that animals possess conscious, rational thought processes—including self-awareness. In the world of cognitive ethology, the concept of "instinct" plays only a minor role in understanding animal behavior, because it explains almost nothing. Cognitive ethologists also generally believe that animals are capable of experiencing emotions that are in many ways comparable to those enjoyed by humans: love, hate, joy, sadness, fear, jealousy, and compassion, to name a few. The first western scientist whom we might now consider a pioneer in cognitive ethology was Charles Darwin, who in 1872 published *The Expression of Emotions in Man and Animals.* In this book, Darwin discussed no fewer than thirty emotions possessed by animals that most people generally associate only with humans.

The field of cognitive ethology languished for more than one hundred years largely because mainstream western science refused to accept the fact that animals could think rationally or possess emotions. A new era of interest in the field began with the publication of *The Question of Animal Awareness: Evolutionary Continuity of Mental Experiences* by Donald R. Griffin in 1981. In recent years, the writings of Marc Bekoff and others have contributed to making the field a legitimate and recognized branch of scientific study and research.

In reality, Native Americans have always been cognitive ethologists. They have always known that animals are conscious, rational, thinking beings endowed with a wide range of emotions. The creation stories of the Navajos, for example, presented the Animal People in such a manner, and orthodox Navajos *knew*—they did not merely believe—that these qualities persisted after the final emergence into the present world. The fact that Navajo TEK stems from the sacred creation stories—from the spiritual realm—distinguishes it from mainstream cognitive ethology that accepts only a scientific evolutionary cause for animal behavior. Because it is more inclusive, this indigenous cognitive ethology offers what I believe to be a deeper and more comprehensive understanding of animal behavior than that offered by western science.

Sadly, the orthodox traditional understanding of the natural world is largely lost. Today the average Navajo is as far removed from his animal relatives as are his non-Native counterparts. We all live in a human-made, artificial universe of computers, iPhones, iPods, iPads, and e-books. We tend to view the natural world and its inhabitants as alien, sometimes even threatening. What we think we know about the animal world is largely a product of the "reality TV" programming on the Animal Planet, Discovery, and even the National Geographic channels, programming that more likely focuses on animal attacks rather than animal-human understanding. Edward O. Wilson's biophilia hypothesis—the belief that we are innately drawn, in a positive and protective way, to our animal kin—has already given way to what seems to be an era of cultural, media-driven biophobia: a fearful, threatening, adversarial view of animals and the natural world in general.

It is my hope that those who read these essays will not view the stories found within as being merely quaint and interesting vestiges of the past, but rather as vital knowledge that has value for today's world and beyond. I hope this book rekindles an interest in the old ways so that they might be used to form the foundation for a different way of relating to and treating all life around us—a new beginning based on traditional knowledge, not only for the Navajo people, but for all of us.

In closing, I would like to thank a number of people who have made this book possible. First and foremost are my two friends and mentors, Vine Deloria Jr. and Will Tsosie, to whom I have dedicated this book. I would also like to acknowledge Tom Hoffman and Daniel R. Wildcat, who shared the WSSA panels with me and whose insight and suggestions were invaluable; Rick Wheelock and especially David E. Wilkins, for their encouragement along the way; Barbara Deloria, for allowing me to spend the summer months finishing up this project at the Deloria home in Tucson; my brother and sister-in-law, Rick and Judy Pavlik; my nephew Steve and his wife, Carla, and the kids—Chelsea, Jon Ross, Andrew, and Molly—for their love and support over the years; and finally to my Navajo students, especially Etta, Sophie, Tara, Willie, Lisa, Denise, and Vera, who always served as a source of inspiration.

References

Bekoff, Marc. 2007. *The Emotional Lives of Animals: A Leading Scientist Explores Animal Joy, Sorrow, and Empathy—and Why They Matter.* Novato, CA: New World Library.

Berkes, Fikret. 1999. *Sacred Ecology: Traditional Ecological Knowledge and Resource Management.* Philadelphia: Taylor & Francis Publishers.

Darwin, Charles. 1872/1998. *The Expression of Emotions in Man and Animals.* New York: Oxford University Press.

Deloria, Vine, Jr. 1969. *Custer Died for Your Sins: An Indian Manifesto.* New York: The Macmillan Company.

Deloria, Vine, Jr. 2004. "Philosophy and the Tribal People," in *American Indian Thought: Philosophical Essays,* edited by Anne Waters. Malden, MA: Blackwell Publishing Company: 3–11.

Griffin, Donald R. 1981. *The Question of Animal Awareness: Evolutionary Continuity of Mental Experience.* New York: The Rockefeller University Press.

Luckert, Karl W. 1975. *The Navajo Hunter Tradition.* Tucson: University of Arizona Press.

O'Bryan, Aileen. 1956/1993. *Navaho Indian Myths.* New York: Dover Publications.

Wilson, Edward O. 1984. *Biophilia.* Cambridge, MA: Harvard University Press.

✻ Foreword

These pages hold the voices of a kinship that once existed between my people and the natural world, one that has been silent for some time now. The perspective of the Navajos' connection with nature has been changing under the pressure of living in a modern world. At the beginning of the twenty-first century, the natural world has been forgotten along with the Navajos' traditional worldview. Few are the Navajo homes where the language is still spoken and the traditional Blessingway spirituality is practiced. The majority of Navajo people no longer see nature as once our forefathers and foremothers did. But there is still hope. There are still pockets of orthodox Navajo traditionalists who resist the onset of Christianity, the Peyote religion, and a pan-Indian identity.

The natural world people like the *Ch'osh, Na'ashoii, Tsidii, and the Naldlooshii*—the insect, reptilian, bird, and animal people—have long been absent from the

Navajo conscience. These people of the natural world and the Five-fingered People—humans—had a long shared relationship in the past. They lived together, interacting with and needing each other, looking out for and helping each other. The natural world people gave of themselves to nurture our human physical, mental, and spiritual health. They have been our food, healers, teachers, and spiritual guides. The natural world is a reflection of human existence, and our lives are a reflection of the natural world. How we choose to treat the natural world is how we choose to treat ourselves. Without a connection to the natural world, we as humans are disconnected and not complete. In modern times we have emptied our souls by not having a connection to the natural world.

Our oral tradition is called storytelling, but our wonderful stories are very important to us because they form a template as to how we see our world. People of the natural world have human characteristics, or, conversely, perhaps we have the characteristics of the beings of the natural world. In our oral traditions, humans were able to talk and have kinship with the people of the natural world. Navajo ceremonial stories tell of humans being healed of sickness by these natural people so that we could regain our balance and walk again in beauty. It should be said that the illness we experience is brought about because we are no longer in balance with the natural world. This healing came about through songs and prayers. In our ceremonies, stories of the natural world formed the foundation of our healing practices.

My father, William B. Tsosie Sr., is an orthodox traditionalist. He told me that when First Man and First Woman emerged into this world, "the composite of all the different colors of light," we emerged with the Insect People, the "ones who were close to the ground" (the reptiles), the "ones with wings who could fly" (the birds), the "ones who traveled on all fours" (the animals), and other special beings. The beings of the natural world lived in this world long before the Navajo people did. They prepared the world for us and thus influenced our own creation. Our stories have been told and retold over many generations. It is said that our stories are living. We do not consider our stories "myths" or simple children's stories. Our stories have many dimensions containing a wealth of knowledge and wisdom. The oral tradition defines who we are and how we are to exist. Our oral tradition has many versions, and that is good. There were probably many people who bore witness to what occurred, not just one person. When we retell our stories, we are also acknowledging those who witnessed the events. When recounting our stories we begin by saying *"Jii ne,"* which is the Navajo word for "it is/was said." When we retell our stories we also say that they, "the ones who witness," are telling the story, not us. My father went on to say that we should remember this when we are listening to someone telling a Navajo story, that we should listen to as many versions as we can to get the best perspective of what is being told. Everyone has a story that deserves to be respected and honored. The day our stories become one story, it will be sad, and we will then have a limited view of the world.

Steve Pavlik has spent much of his life in a scholarly quest of what has been preserved in the archival text of the ethnographers, anthropologists, and others interested in the Navajo way of life—what some call "culture." His special interest has long been the traditional relationship between the Navajo people and those beings of the natural world, the Insect, Reptile, Bird, and Animal people. Over the many years that I have known and worked with Steve—through his countless questions regarding Navajo ceremonialism and worldview—I became very interested in his research. At times I felt like I was taking a child by the hand and walking with him, pointing out the wonders of a beautiful world through the Navajo senses. I cannot help but feel that I have molded some of his concepts and helped him understand what was most respectful and honorable to the Navajo perspective. I have also tried to communicate carefully what is most important, being careful not to burden him down with too much detail, and cautioning him that it would take a lifetime to truly understand the deep complexities of the knowledge he sought. There were times that I asked him to not include in his writings certain things that I shared with him, things that were meant for his reference only and that could not be given to the outside world. I trusted in him, and then let him do what he needed to do. He did not disappoint me. I might add that Steve was a high school and college teacher who lived among our people for twenty years. In this capacity he saw the beauty and richness of Navajo culture. He was allowed entry into our traditional lifeways and in time became a literary scholar of our culture. The Navajo way of life called to him, and he has caringly answered it. With this book and through his writings, he is giving back.

Nearly all anthropological and ethnographical works from the past have been from the edited perspective of non-Navajo scholars. Their ability to use Navajo associates—most of the times called "informants" (a term I never liked)—to record information was extraordinary. Few non-Navajo scholars were able to "go Native" by learning the Navajo language or by spending their lives living among the people (although a notable exception was Father Berard Haile). Their efforts to collect documentation amount to "snapshots" of the Navajo people. I am certain that many of the Navajo associates had their influence on what was recorded and/or translated by the way they communicated the information gathered. I am also willing to venture a guess that the Navajo associates were thinking of the future of their people when they worked with the non-Navajo scholars. This certainly motivated my own work with Steve. Future Navajo anthropologists and ethnographers will have the luxury of utilizing these past works and then including their own perspectives to provide additional clarity to benefit later studies.

On a more personal level, I have known Steve as a friend for almost thirty years. He once told me that he was invited to attend a Navajo *yei be chai* his very first week on the reservation. This experience began his lifelong interest in Navajo traditionalism. Since then he and I have attended many Navajo ceremonies, from Blessingway's *kinaalda* to Mountainway Fire Dances. Most of the time, Steve was the only white person in attendance. One time we were at a Mountainway Fire Dance held far out in the reservation wilderness. When the white clay fire dance clowns made their appearance, I could not help but to say to him, "Hey, Steve, here come your people!" He just smiled. I am thankful that our paths crossed and for his interest and involvement in our traditional way of life, even to the point of helping out my mother with my Nightway *yei bi chai.*

In closing, I think that Steve's book will serve to break that before-mentioned silent voice of kinship between the Navajo people and the natural world. As someone concerned with the loss of Navajo traditional culture, I hope this beautiful collection might help in some small way to contribute to a renewed interest in Navajo youth about their traditional culture and ultimately to begin a Navajo traditional renaissance. *Ahehee'* Steve Pavlik *shi k'is.*

William B. Tsosie Jr.

Navajo traditionalist/anthropologist
Shiprock, Navajo Nation

I am one with all those who give me life, keep me company as I travel upon our mother the earth and fly in the sky carried by our father sky's breath. My kin of the natural world are all the other beautiful beings I dwell with upon our mother the earth and our father the sky.

These I have become again

These I have become again

These I have become again

These I have become again

It has become beautiful again

It has become beautiful again

It has become beautiful again

It has become beautiful again.

—Navajo Blessingway prayer

 # Introduction

The Navajo Universe and the Natural World

The Navajos are the largest tribe of Native Americans in the United States. Numbering more than 200,000, they inhabit a 27,000-square-mile reservation in the Four Corners area of the American Southwest. Most of the contemporary Navajo Reservation is located in north-eastern Arizona; the remainder is in northwestern New Mexico and southeastern Utah. Historically, the Navajos occupied a much larger area than they do today. The mountains of southwestern Colorado, for example, must also be considered historic Navajo Country.

In a traditional sense, the Navajo homeland is bounded by four sacred mountains: Mount Blanco, the sacred mountain of the east, near Alamosa, Colorado; Mount Taylor, the sacred mountain of the south, near Laguna, New Mexico; the San Francisco Peaks, the sacred mountain of the west, near Flagstaff, Arizona; and Mount Hesperus, the sacred mountain of the north, near Durango, Colorado.

The land of the Navajos is extremely diverse in its physical makeup. Most of the land is sparse desert country (technically Great Basin desert scrub), grass-lands, and conifer forest, accented by red rock sand-stone canyons and other rock formations made famous in dozens of western movies. Scattered throughout the desert landscape are petran montane conifer forest and subalpine conifer forest, thick with pinon, juniper, and pine, and mountains reaching elevations of more than 9,000 feet. Among the larger of the mountains are the Chuskas, Lukachukais, and Tunichas. The Colorado River, and especially its major tributary, the San Juan River, form the northern border of the present Navajo Reservation. The diversity of the land lends itself to a surprising variety and abundance of wildlife. Navajo Country is home to a multitude of other mammals, birds, reptiles, amphibians, fish, and other life-forms.

Origins of the Navajos and Their Religious Traditions

The people we now know as the Navajos are, in reality, a product of the coming together of two very different cultures: the Southern Athabaskans, or Apacheans, and the Pueblos.

The most widely accepted anthropological version of early Navajo history states that the Southern Athabaskans, a hunting and gathering culture, migrated from the north into the southwest. These Athabaskans arrived in a number of separate bands, at different times, by different routes, and settled in different areas. In general, they diverged to become two separate groups, the Apaches—who further divided into various eastern and western subgroups—and the future Navajos. The exact date of the Navajo arrival into the Four Corners area is unclear, but it probably occurred prior to 1500 (Hester: 72). There is some evidence, however, to suggest an earlier date of arrival, perhaps as early as 1350 (see

Roessel: 31–34). The exact location of their arrival and early settlement was the upper San Juan River valley of southwestern New Mexico, specifically Blanco, Largo, Carrizo, and Gobernador Canyons and their surrounding drainages. Traditional Navajos know this area today as Dinétah, the "Holy Land."

The Southern Athabaskans lived in the Dinétah region for approximately two hundred years in relative isolation. During this period they came in contact with a number of other Native cultures, most notably the Pueblos of the Rio Grande River to the south, whom they often raided. In all probability, however, Southern Athabaskan culture remained relatively unchanged, though we assume that these people began to slowly adopt more of an agricultural and pastoral lifestyle. This included the raising of sheep and goats brought into the southwest by the Spanish and acquired from the Pueblos, whom the Spanish had conquered.

In 1680, the Pueblos launched a great revolt against the Spanish, driving the repressive European invaders out of the Rio Grande Valley. The Pueblos retained sole possession of their native homeland—and their culture—until the Spanish reconquest of the area in 1694. In the interim, hundreds, perhaps thousands, of Pueblos sought refuge among their Southern Athabaskan neighbors to the north. The resulting amalgamation of peoples and their cultures provided the genesis for the tribe we now know as the Navajo.

The Navajo people retained their Athabaskan language and thus an Athabaskan identity. In most other ways, however, the syncretism leaned heavily toward their Pueblo heritage. From the Pueblos the Navajos acquired agriculture and livestock, the art of weaving and perhaps silversmithing, and the addition of several clans or families. But nowhere is the cultural debt more prevalent than in the area of tribal religious beliefs and ceremonial practices. While the Navajos clung to many elements of the Athabaskan religion, including that which anthropologist Karl W. Luckert has called the Navajo hunter tradition, much that we now know as "traditional Navajo religion" is actually derived from Pueblo spirituality and practice. This is especially true in regard to origin or creation stories. In addition, many specific aspects of Navajo ceremonialism trace their origin to the Pueblos. Among these are the belief in certain deities and the use of masked dancers, sandpaintings, prayer sticks, and corn pollen.

In 1887, Washington Matthews, a United States. Army surgeon stationed at Fort Wingate, published the first important scholarly study of Navajo religion (see Halpern and McGreevy, 1997). In the years that followed, other anthropologists—most notably Father Berard Haile and Willard W. Hill, and later Gladys A. Reichard, Clyde Kluckhohn, Leland C. Wyman, Karl W. Luckert, Charlotte J. Frisbie, and James C. Faris—wrote extensively on this topic. What has emerged from their work is a portrait of a unique body of Navajo spiritual beliefs and practices, what I have referred to as "orthodox traditionalism" (Pavlik, 1995; 1997).

The Navajo creation stories form the foundation for orthodox traditionalism. These stories chronicle the Navajo journey from what might be termed the "other side of time" to the beginnings of recorded history. These stories are, in the truest sense, the moral and ethical blueprint for tribal existence. They tell the Navajo people who they are, their place in the world order, and their relationship to the Earth and all other living things. Foremost is the mandate that the Navajo live in harmony with themselves and everything around them. The Navajo refer to this state of balance as being *hozo*—a condition of "beauty" for the Navajo. It is based on the concept that everything in the universe—including humans themselves—is interconnected and interrelated in an orderly and delicate way that must be maintained. In effect, this might be viewed as being the natural law of the Navajo people. In sum, Navajo orthodoxy is not so much a religion as it is a value system and way of life.

There are three important things to keep in mind about the Navajo stories. The first is that orthodox traditional Navajos know these stories to be true and not merely myths or metaphors for western "truths." They are a factual rendering of a series of events that occurred before recorded time. They represent the sacred history of the Navajo people. To the western mind (and admittedly to many western-oriented Navajos) it is extremely difficult to imagine a time when humans, the Animal People—the furred, feathered, and scaled other nonhuman beings—walked the Earth together and shared a common language and experience. It is difficult for most of us to accept the miraculous events that occur in these stories, such as transformation (the act of, say, a bear transforming to become a human) or the idea of rebirth after death—a common occurrence with a trickster figure like Coyote. Such stories reflect a unique Navajo metaphysical view of time and space, an idea that modern physicists are just now beginning to accept as they delve deeper into the study of parallel universes and other similar realms. But traditional Navajos have always known and accepted such realities. As the late Cherokee scholar Robert K. Thomas once stated in a lecture: "Most Indians will tell you they *believe* these stories, a traditional Indian *knows* they are true."

I might add that the Navajo stories do not appear in a nice, orderly sequence of events. A main story line exists—Blessingway—from which branch off other stories that are often related to one another, are intertwined, or at least overlap. To understand these stories, one needs only to keep an open mind and accept the fact that all things are possible. Moreover, the stories are quite complex, one branching into another, and then another, and so on. In my opinion, the Navajo stories stand as the greatest epics of all time.

The second important point to remember is that there is no single version of the Navajo stories. Indeed, ten Navajos might very well provide ten versions of the same part of a story. In most cases these differences will be minor, and in some cases they might seem considerable. Navajos, like other Native people, do not argue over interpretations of spirituality, nor do they proselytize to others. Traditional Navajos accept the fact that there is no correct version of the stories and usually begin their own recitation by stating, "This was the way I was taught."

Two distinct traditions come together to form the Navajo creation stories and, subsequently, the foundation for Navajo tradition.

The first of these is the so-called Navajo hunter tradition as best explained by Karl W. Luckert. The stories of this tradition come from the Athabaskan origins of the modern Navajo—from the shamanic hunters whom anthropologists say originally migrated from the north, bringing with them their hunting gods, ideology, and rites. This was the time of what Luckert refers to as "pre-human flux," which he describes as

> *a term pertaining to a hunter's ideology, [one that] refers to man's primeval kinship with all creatures of the living world and to the essential continuity among them all. In prehuman mythological times all living beings existed in a state of flux—their external forms were interchangeable. This animate world includes all that grows and all that moves about in air and sky, on earth, below the earth, and in the sea; it includes even the gods and the everbearing earth in her totality. The thinking of archaic hunters about prehuman flux naturally tended to orient itself around the lives of animals which sustained and inspired their own lives. . . . Yet, regardless of the fascination for animal life among archaic hunters, the animals are regarded as "people" often alongside of trees, rocks, lakes, rivers, and celestial bodies. What differentiates one species of "people" from another is not something essential but is a matter of appearance only* (Luckert: 133).

The second tradition is derived from the Navajos' Pueblo origins. In brief, the Navajo origin stories deal with the people's emergence through four major underworlds—with numerous other minor underworlds—into the Fifth World, where they now live. Throughout these stories, the Navajos, beginning with First Man and First Woman, interact with other beings, including their deities, the Holy People. Among the most important of the Holy People are Sun, Talking God, Calling God, Black God, and Changing Woman (the most beloved of the deities) and Changing Woman's twin sons, Monster Slayer and Child Born of Water. The stories also include a variety of Animal People, anthropomorphic beings that in the beginning had the ability to speak and generally possessed varying degrees of supernatural power. In time these Animal People lost most of their anthropomorphic qualities to assume the forms and roles they possess today. Thus, Mountain Lion, for example, became the mountain lion that now inhabits the more remote areas of the Navajo Reservation today. It is important to note that traditional Navajos believe that the Animal People did not lose all of their supernatural powers. Bears, for example, perhaps the most powerful of the Animal People, still retain the ability to transform into other shapes, including that of human beings.

Most of Navajo religion and ceremonialism focuses on the curing of disease, illness, and injuries. Most Navajo ceremonies address various "etiological factors" that bring on these problems (Kluckhohn and Wyman). Very commonly these factors are animals or dangerous natural phenomena such as lightning or wind. The diseases or infections that are brought on by the Animal People are usually attributed to the initial transgressions of the victim. If a man offends a bear, for example, he is likely to contact "bear sickness." Other categories of illness brought on by animals include "coyote sickness" and "deer sickness." In addition, illness is often attributed to contact with the dead, the spirits of the dead, and witchcraft. The origin of all illnesses and the means to address them are found in the Navajo stories.

Sickness, disease, and injuries are treated in traditional ceremonies called sings, chants, or ways. Generally these ceremonies are named after some element of the story associated with them. Among them are the Enemyway, Shootingway, Mountainway, Beautyway, Nightway, Beadway, and Windway. Many of these ceremonies last nine days and nights and are focused on the healing of one or two individuals. Hundreds of people might attend these rituals as spectators and to support the patient.

Leland C. Wyman and Clyde Kluckhohn in their definitive classification of Navajo ceremonies list fifty-eight distinct rituals, not counting the various hunting rituals. Of these, Wyman and Kluckhohn thought nine to be extinct (Wyman and Kluckhohn: 36). I suspect that today the number of extinct ceremonies would be greater.

A Navajo who is in need of care due to some type of sickness or injury will first consult a diagnostician. The task of this individual, who is often a woman, is to diagnose the cause of the problem and decide what sing will be used to cure it. Diagnosticians employ several methods to determine the cause of the patient's troubles: stargazing, listening to the wind, or most commonly a procedure known as hand-trembling. In this last method, the diagnostician sings a prayer while extending her hands over the patient. In time her hands begin to move or tremble as the cause and cure for the problem reveals itself to her. At the end of the session, the diagnostician will inform the patient and his or her family as to the cause of the problem and the ceremony needed to correct it, and might even recommend the name of a practitioner who can perform the ceremony.

The earliest religious practitioners among the early Athabaskan hunters were probably shamans, individuals who acquired their powers divinely, perhaps by way of a vision quest, or perhaps given to them as a gift from the Animal People. In the case of hand-tremblers, their powers are said to be a gift from the Gila monster spirits; if you watch this lizard when it walks, its forefeet shake when it raises them from the ground (Wyman, 1936: 239).

A great deal of these practitioners' efforts probably focused on assuring success in the hunt. Later, after the amalgamation of the Athabaskans with the Pueblos, a different type of religious specialist emerged to administer Navajo ceremonies. These practitioners, called singers, chanters, or most commonly to non-Navajos, medicine men, were individuals who learned their trade by apprenticing under other recognized singers. Generally it takes several years to learn each new ceremony. Consequently, Navajo singers tend to be specialists. In administering the ceremony, the singer re-creates through song and prayer the mythological events that explain the illness. He also performs a number of activities that include giving medicine, creating sandpaintings, and evoking the spiritual powers from those sandpaintings. A sandpainting is a pictorial representation drawn with colored sand of the Holy People and other sacred images; its main purpose is to attract the deities so that they will help with the curing ceremony.

In its simplest form a Navajo ceremony might last only a day or two and will be held at the house of the patient. In its more complete and complex form, it requires nine days and nights. In such cases, most of the actual healing is done inside a traditional Navajo structure called a hogan. The final night of some ceremonies, such as the Nightway, Mountainway, Shootingway, and Beautyway, is a public event in which multiple groups of masked dancers known as *yeibichais* will perform, and hundreds of spectators will come to observe the proceedings.

The World War II and postwar economies served to dissolve what had been the relative isolation of the Navajo Reservation—and further erode Navajo traditional values and lifestyle. With the decline of traditionalism came the decline of tribal society. By the mid-1940s, anthropologists Clyde Kluckhohn and Dorothea Leighton were able to note that "instead of a patterned mosaic, Navaho culture is becoming an ugly patchwork of meaningless and totally unrelated pieces. Personal and social chaos are the by-products" (Kluckhohn and Leighton, 1946: 237).

Today, I estimate that only about 5 percent of the Navajo population might be classified as being orthodox traditionalists—people who follow the religious teachings and live their lives as prescribed by the Holy People. The largest number of Navajos—perhaps as much as 75 percent of the population—belong to the Native American Church (NAC). Another 20 percent of the tribe belong to one of the many Christian denominations, most commonly Catholicism and Mormonism (the Church of Jesus Christ of Latter-day Saints). "Mainstream" Christianity never made serious inroads among the Navajo people, and most of those who attend Christian church services also attend traditional ceremonies and especially meetings of the NAC. Religious syncretism is the norm among the Navajo people (Pavlik, 1992a; 1995; 1997; 1998; 2003).

The Native American Church is a pan-Indian religion that incorporates Native American philosophy with elements of Christianity and is characterized by its use of the psychedelic cactus peyote. The NAC established itself on the Navajo Reservation in the 1930s and continues to grow in popularity. Over time Navajo peyotists have increasingly added elements of orthodox traditionalism to the standard NAC rituals, serving to "Navajoize" the religion. Elsewhere I have referred to this as being the "New Traditionalism" of the Navajos (Pavlik, 1997; 2003). Ask most Navajos today if they are "traditional," and their reply will be an emphatic yes. But in reality they are traditional only in the Navajo version of the peyote religion. The New Traditionalism—focused around peyote meetings—is far less time intensive than orthodox traditionalism and allows its participants to engage in a tribal religion with a Navajo identity while maintaining a wage-based western lifestyle.

Over time the Navajo people, like other Americans, have largely lost their spiritual bond to the Earth. Fewer tribal members know the stories that connected them to the natural world and to their animal relations. One of the great challenges faced by the New Traditionalism will be to forge a spiritual way of life that can reclaim and build upon this foundation of knowledge. There are some encouraging signs that the Navajos are moving in this direction.

On November 1, 2003, the Navajo Tribal Council, by a vote of 45 in favor, 4 opposed, and with 1 abstention, amended Title 1 of the Navajo Nation Code to recognize the Fundamental Laws of the Navajo tribe. This included Article 5—the Natural Law of the people, which "declares and teaches" that

A. The four sacred elements of life, air, light/fire, water and earth/pollen in all of their forms must be respected, honored and protected for they sustain life; and

B. The six sacred mountains, Sisnaajini, Tsood-zil, Dook'o'oosliid, Dibé Nitsaa, Dzil Na'oodilii, Dzil Ch'ool'i'i, and all the attendant mountains must be respected, honored and protected for they, as leaders, are the foundation of the Navajo Nation; and

C. All creation, from Mother Earth and Father Sky to the animals, those who live in the water, those who fly and plant life have their own laws, and have rights and freedom to exist; and

D. The Diné have a sacred obligation and duty to respect, preserve and protect all that was provided for we are designated as the steward of these relatives through our use of the sacred gifts of language and thinking; and

E. Mother Earth and Father Sky is part of us as the Diné and the Diné is part of Mother Earth and Father Sky; the Diné must treat this sacred bond with love and respect without exerting dominance for we do not own our mother or father; and

F. The rights and freedoms of the people to the use of the sacred elements of life as mentioned above and to the use of the land, natural resources, sacred sites and other living beings must be accomplished through the proper protocol of respect and offering and these practices must be protected and preserved for they are the foundation of our spiritual ceremonies and the Diné life way; and

G. It is the duty and responsibility of the Diné to protect and preserve the beauty of the natural world for future generations (Royster and Blumm: 7–8).

These Fundamental Laws represent the heart and soul of Navajo orthodox traditional beliefs, and in adopting them as the foundation for all Navajo law, the members of the Navajo Tribal Council—most of whom were also members of the NAC—were issuing a powerful statement as to the importance—indeed, the centrality—that traditional values and beliefs will continue to play in the future of the Navajo people. I might add that the Navajo Nation is the only Indian tribe to have taken such action.

The Navajo and the Animal People

Native Americans, including the Navajos, were not "close" to nature, nor did they "love" nature as we tend to oversimplify—*but rather they were an integral part of the natural world.*

No scholar has done more to explain the relationship of Native Americans to the natural world than Vine Deloria Jr. In *Power and Place: Indian Education in America* (coauthored with Daniel R. Wildcat), Deloria explained how two basic concepts—power and place—offer a window into understanding the metaphysical world of Native Americans. Deloria defines "power" as being the "living energy that inhabits and/or composes the universe," while "place" refers to the "relationship of things to each other." Together these two combine to create the very essence of traditional Native Americans lifeways.

Deloria's power is a spiritual power. The universe—everything and every entity—is alive with this spiritual power: humans, animals, plants, water, air, and the very Earth itself are spiritually alive. Included in this Native understanding of a sacred universe is the knowledge that beings also exist who are wholly spiritual in nature. Deloria refers to these supernaturals collectively as "energetic entities."

The Navajos have long known that the universe is spiritually alive. *Everything* is a living, breathing, spiritual entity. Every mountain and river, for example, possesses a spiritual essence, and every mountain and river is assigned a sexual identity based on the stories or the emotional qualities it exhibits. The Navajos also know that there are wholly spiritual beings that reside at these places and protect them. The Navajos refer to these energetic entities as the *Yeis*, or the Holy People.

Deloria's use of the term *place* refers first to the physical aspects of the universe. Native people are intimately tied to the landscape. This is land that they have lived on since time immemorial, and they relate to it in a way that no other people can. Every physical location, for example, is connected to their creation stories. This is certainly true for the Navajos, for whom every event in their creation stories is place-based. Consequently, certain locations are deemed to be sacred in terms of meaning and power.

But Deloria's concept of place encompasses far more than simply the physical aspects of the sacred universe—it also emphasizes the reality and importance of *relationships*. Since all entities—and the land itself—are spiritually alive, all relationships must be of a *personal* nature and must be approached in that manner. Deloria elaborates this point by saying:

> The personal nature of the universe demands that each and every entity in it seek and sustain personal relationships. . . . The broader Indian idea of relationship, in a universe that is very personal and particular, suggests that all relationships have a moral content. For that reason, Indian knowledge of the universe was never separated from other sacred knowledge about ultimate spiritual relationships. (Deloria and Wildcat: 23)

Deloria stresses that "the spiritual aspect about the world taught the people that *relationships must not be left incomplete*" (my emphasis). This implies that relationships must be *reciprocal* in nature. He goes on to say: "There are many stories about how the world came to be, and the common themes running through them are the completion of relationships and the determination of how the world should function" (ibid.).

Deloria also noted that it is important that relationships are *appropriate*:

> *The corresponding question faced by American Indians when contemplating action is whether or not the proposed action is appropriate. Appropriateness includes the moral dimension of respect for the part of nature that will be used or affected in our action. Thus, killing an animal or catching a fish involved paying respect to the species and the individual animal or fish that such actions have disturbed. Harvesting plants also involved paying respect to the plants. These actions were necessary because of recognition that the universe is built upon constructive and cooperative relationships that had to be maintained. Thus ceremonies . . . celebrated and completed relationships properly or ensured their continuance for future generations. (Ibid.: 24)*

The idea of maintaining a personal reciprocal and appropriate relationship with the Earth and all other living things was not lost on the Navajo—indeed it formed the very foundation of the Navajo concept of *hozo*: the knowledge that a balance, a beauty, existed in the world that could be upset by the thoughtless or reckless actions of humans.

Perhaps the best explanation as to the Navajos' early knowledge, understanding, and relationship to the natural world can be found in an unpublished—and consequently relatively unknown and unread—manuscript written by Washington Matthews in 1884 entitled "Natural Naturalists." (This important paper has fortunately been reproduced by Katherine Spencer Halpern and Susan Brown McGreevy Halpern.)

The Navajo relationship to the Animal People is a case in point and can perhaps be best understood by a comparison with Judeo-Christian belief. In the Judeo-Christian tradition, a supreme God created man in his own image. It was only afterward that God created animals. This concept provides mankind with preeminence and an elevated, almost godly, stature that set the table for all future relationships with the animals. The Book of Genesis 1:26 goes on to state, "Let him [man] have dominion over the fishes of the sea, and the birds of the air, and the beasts of the earth." Later, "First Man"—Adam—was assigned the task of naming all of the animals—an act that also cemented his control and dominance over them. In sum, Judeo-Christian theology tells us that all other life on Earth was placed there for mankind's use and pleasure.

In contrast, the Navajo creation stories do not tell of a separate act of creation for humans. A number of the Animal People, including the Insect People, were there with mankind at the beginning in the First World. One version of the Navajo stories has it that Coyote preceded humans. No significance is attached to the order of appearance or to the physical form of the being.

Humans are not acknowledged to have any particular position of superiority or importance in the

Navajo creation stories. They are simply one being—the "Five-fingered People"—that live among many. In contrast to the Judeo-Christian tradition, animals do not exist solely for the exploitation of humankind. While Navajos and other Native Americans hunted and killed animals as a source of food and for other reasons, they did not kill for sport or recreation, they did so out of necessity—a life for a life—and with the greatest respect and appreciation for the life they had taken.

Thus the traditional relationship between the Navajos and the Animal People was based on the following tribal knowledge:

- Animals, like humans, are products of a common divine creation.

- Animals are different from humans only in outward appearance.

- Animals are related to humans and in some cases are viewed as kin.

- Animals are bound to humans in a network of reciprocal and appropriate relationships.

- Animals possess a purpose independent of the needs and desires of humans.

- Animals are equal to humans in terms of their right to life and pursuit of purpose.

- Animals possess individual personalities.

- Animals (individual species) are inherently neither good nor bad, but like humans are capable of good or bad actions.

- Animals possess a wide range of emotions and feelings.

- Animals possess knowledge, intelligence, and the ability to reason.

- Animals purposefully pass down their knowledge—their cultures—to their young.

- Animals possess their own language and sometimes choose to communicate with humans.

- Animals possess spirits and/or souls and the promise of an afterlife.

- Animals possess and can demonstrate individual spiritual power.

- Animals willingly and of their own volition offer themselves or their knowledge as gifts to humans.

Of course, there is room for disagreement with certain items on this list. But my interpretation of the Navajo stories, based on my reviews of early anthropological literature and especially on the time I have spent listening to what traditional people have to say, leads me to believe that all of these points contribute to a philosophical foundational understanding of how the Navajos once viewed and related to the Animal People. This, in the purest sense, is Navajo traditional ecological knowledge that we can all learn from.

References

Deloria, Vine, Jr. and Daniel R. Wildcat. 2001. *Power and Place: Indian Education in America.* Golden, CO: Fulcrum Publishing.

Halpern, Katherine Spencer and Susan Brown McGreevy, eds. 1997. *Washington Matthews: Studies of Navajo Culture, 1880–1894.* Albuquerque: University of New Mexico Press.

Hester, James J. 1962. *Early Navajo Migrations and Acculturation in the Southwest.* Museum of New Mexico Papers in Anthropology, no. 6. Santa Fe: Museum of New Mexico Press.

Kluckhohn, Clyde and Dorothea Leighton. 1946. *The Navaho*. Cambridge, MA: Harvard University Press.

Kluckhohn, Clyde and Leland C. Wyman. 1940. "An Introduction to Navajo Chant Practice," *Memoirs of the American Anthropological Association*, Supplement 53: 1–204.

Luckert, Karl W. 1975. *The Navajo Hunter Tradition.* Tucson: University of Arizona Press.

Matthews, Washington. 1884. "Natural Naturalists," in *Washington Matthews: Studies of Navajo Culture, 1880–1894,* edited by Katherine Spencer Halpern and Susan Brown McGreevy. Albuquerque: University of New Mexico Press, 1997.

Pavlik, Steve. 1992a. "Of Saints and Lamanites: An Analysis of Navajo Mormonism," *Wicazo Sa Review*, 8(1): 21–30.

Pavlik, Steve. 1992b. "The U.S. Supreme Court Decision on Peyote in Employment Division v. Smith: A Case Study in the Suppression of Native American Religious Freedom," *Wicazo Sa Review*, 8(2): 30–39.

Pavlik, Steve. 1995. "Navajo Orthodox Traditionalism." Paper presented at the Navajo Studies Conference, Farmington, New Mexico, March 12.

Pavlik, Steve. 1997. "Navajo Christianity: Historical Origins and Modern Trends," *Wicazo Sa Review,* 12(2): 43–58.

Pavlik, Steve. 1998. "The Role of Christianity and Church in Contemporary Navajo Society," in *A Good Cherokee, A Good Anthropologist: Papers in Honor of Robert K. Thomas*, edited by Steve Pavlik. Los Angeles: UCLA American Indian Studies Center: 189–200.

Pavlik, Steve. 2003. "Robert K. Thomas and the Taproots of Navajo Peoplehood." Paper presented at the Robert K. Thomas Symposium, Vancouver, British Columbia, Canada, July 23.

Roessel, Robert A. 1983. *Dinétah: Navajo History, Volume III.* Chinle, AZ: Navajo Curriculum Center.

Royster, Judith V. and Michael C. Blumm. 2008. *Native American Natural Resources Law: Cases and Materials.* Durham, NC: Carolina Academic Press.

Wyman, Leland C. "Navaho Diagnosticians" (AA, 38, 1936, 236-46)

Wyman, Leland C. and Clyde Kluckhohn. 1938. "Navajo Classification of Their Song Ceremonials," *Memoirs of the American Anthropological Association*, 50: 3–38.

 # Chapter One

The Powerful Mountain People

This chapter was originally presented as a paper at the Western Social Science Association Conference held in Reno, Nevada, April 19, 1996. An edited version was published as 'The Role of Bears and Bear Ceremonialism in Navajo Orthodox Traditional Lifeway" in The Social Science Journal, *Volume 34, Issue 4, 1997.*

The high mountain trail was wide and well worn by generations of humans and animals, both wild and domestic. Ahead of me a few feet walked Will Tsosie. From time to time, Will would stop to point out a particular plant growing along the trail and explain how the Navajos traditionally used this plant. We were making no particular effort to be quiet, which surprised me considering the nature of our quest that morning on the mountain: we were hunting for bear.

The genesis of this trip had come the evening before, when Will and I sat in my living room in Chinle drinking coffee and talking about the Navajo traditional relationship to the natural world. As usual, much of our conversation dealt with Navajo religion and ceremonialism and, on that particular evening, a topic that I was especially interested in, the Mountainway—a Navajo healing ceremony that focused on illnesses brought on by bears. At some point in our discussion, I mentioned the fact that despite the considerable amount of time I had spent hiking and hunting the mountains of Navajo Country, I had never seen a bear. Will was surprised. "Really, you haven't seen a bear? We'll go up to Yellow Gate tomorrow morning and I'll show you a bear."

And so here we were. An hour earlier we had passed through the yellow gate from which this area of the Lukachukai Mountains received its name. Soon after that we crossed a pasture where Will's aunt and uncle kept their sheep in the summer, to a point where a trail began that climbed higher up into the mountains. Almost immediately upon reaching the trail, we began to see bear sign. The unmistakable tracks, raspberry and serviceberry bushes smashed down as if by small tanks, rocks turned over in the quest for the tasty insect life that hid beneath, and scat—bear droppings so saturated with berries that one could seemingly scoop them up and put them right into a pie for baking. Everywhere I looked I saw evidence of bear.

And then we saw one. We had rounded a slight bend and found ourselves face-to-face—and I do mean *face-to-face*—with a very large black bear standing right in the middle of the trail in front of us. The bear, which was actually brown rather than black in color, looked up at us with an alert, yet somewhat disinterested, look. I would guess that no more than ten feet separated us. This sudden encounter brought all three of us to an immediate halt. I remember that my initial thought was how "ratty" the bear looked. Strands of dead, shaggy hair hung like drapes from its body. Still, he—perhaps it was a *she*—was obviously in good physical condition, a beautiful, if somewhat disheveled, animal in the prime of its life. For what seemed like minutes but was in fact only seconds, men and bear stared at each other. Then the spell was broken by the sound of Will's voice. I don't recall the exact words he said, but the gist of it was a clear message to the bear to let us humans pass by. Will said these few words as if he was speaking to another person—which indeed in the Navajo way he was. He said them politely, yet firmly. The bear blinked once or twice and then seemed to understand the message. He slowly ambled a few feet off the trail into the bushes, where he began to contentedly munch away at the succulent berries. We passed by.

Will and I continued up the trail to a point where we could turn and watch the bear foraging below us. For a few minutes we watched this powerful animal, who never once gave us a second look. Obviously we were not that interesting to him. For my part, I could not take my eyes off of him. He was beautiful; he was awesome. I had never been that close to a wild bear before. When we had first blundered into him I had been *feet* away. Another step or two and I could have reached out and touched him. I would guess that he weighed about two hundred pounds—and all muscle. Had he chosen to attack us, there would have been nothing we could do about it. But he chose not to, and I am sure that the thought never crossed his mind. We were no threat to him, and he knew it. I had felt no fear, not even any nervousness. Perhaps it had all happened too quickly. More likely, however, this was due to the calmness with which Will handled the situation. He had treated the bear not as a wild animal, but rather as a fellow being that could be talked to and reasoned with. The bear had responded accordingly.

In time we resumed our hike. About a mile farther up the trail, we found our second bear. Incredibly, this encounter mirrored exactly the first. In fact, this second bear could have been an identical twin to the first. Again, he—or she—blocked our way only feet in front of us. Again, Will talked to the bear, asking him to allow us to pass, and again the bear complied with his request. This time I was not surprised.

Eventually Will and I reached the top of the mountain, where we found a shady spot beneath a large ageless pinon pine. Here we spent the next hour or so eating our lunch as we looked out across the Defiance Plateau. We talked of Navajo things. We talked of Navajo religion and ceremonies, and we talked of men and bears. We saw no other bears that day. We did not have to. The day had far exceeded my wildest expectations. I had been given a rare glimpse into another world. I have since thought a lot about that day, of Will's communicating with the bears. I know now that it was not a trick, novelty, or simply an act of bravado. It was a vestige of another time and perhaps another place. Traditional Navajos have long been known for their ability to communicate with bears (see, for example, McPherson: 88–89). This was the way that Will's ancestors—and perhaps even my own—had *normally* dealt with life-forms that were different from our own. And, sadly, it is a way that is quickly passing from this Earth.

The Bears of Navajo Country

Navajos use the generic name *shash* to refer to all bears. They also commonly refer to bears are as being the "Mountain People," a term applied to all animals that reside in the mountainous regions of the Navajo Reservation but most regularly used to denote bears specifically. Sacred names—names used ceremonially to refer to bear—include "Reared in the Mountains," "Fine Young Chief," and "That Which Lives in the Den" (Franciscan Fathers, 1910). Historically, two species of bears, the grizzly and the black bear, inhabited Navajo Country.

The grizzly bear *(Ursus arctos)* possesses a number of names in the Navajo language that translate to white bear, speckled bear, silvertip bear, long back bear, frosted-faced bear, and tracker bear (Franciscan Fathers). This last name reflected the Navajo belief that the grizzly tracked down and hunted man (Pavlik, 1992). The grizzly, which can weigh more than 600 pounds, is now extirpated in the American Southwest, having been killed off mostly by ranchers and government hunters. By 1923, grizzlies had been eliminated from New Mexico and Utah, and by 1935, the last of the great bears had been killed in Arizona (Housholder; Brown). The last grizzly in Colorado was believed to have been killed in 1951. Incredibly, however, a female grizzly materialized from the shadows of extinction in 1979 only to be killed by a bow hunter it had attacked and severely mauled. The killing of the bear proved to be very controversial, with many people believing that the hunter must have provoked the attack, quite possibly by shooting the bear with his bow. The true details of this event will never be known. It happened along the Navajo River in the San Juan Mountains of southwest Colorado, land historically traveled by the Navajos. The San Juans are also a mountain range that figures predominantly in a number of the Navajo mythological stories involving bears, including grizzlies. A few individuals, myself included, cling to the hope that grizzlies may still exist within the sanctuary of these rugged mountains (Brown; see also Bass; Peterson).

On the Navajo Reservation, grizzlies historically inhabited the Chuska and Lukachukai Mountains. One particularly notorious outlaw grizzly operating out of the Chuskas destroyed an estimated $5,000 worth of sheep and goats from 1905 until his death at the hands of a professional hunter in 1911. The hunter received $180 in reward money for killing this bear (Housholder). In all probability the grizzly was exterminated from the Navajo Reservation sometime in the 1920s. It is interesting to note that when C. Hart Merriam, biologist and research associate for the Smithsonian Institution, published his then-definitive taxonomy of grizzly and brown bears in 1918, he included an *Ursus texensis Navaho* as one of his eighty-six recognizable species of grizzly bears. This classification of the "Navajo grizzly" was based on one badly damaged skull of a bear killed in the Chuska Mountains in 1856 (Merriam). Although biologists have long since discredited the Merriam classification and today recognize only one species of grizzly—with an open number of subspecies—the Navajo name will forever be linked historically with the great bear.

The second bear that continues to inhabit Navajo Country is the black bear *(Ursus americanus)*. This animal is the dominant being among the Mountain People. It is estimated there may be as many as three hundred black bears inhabiting the forested and mountainous regions of the Navajo Reservation (McCoy). Full-grown male black bears average 250 to 350 pounds, females 120 to 180 pounds. As their name indicates, most black bears are black in color, although on the Navajo Reservation most are brown, blond, or cinnamon (O'Conner).[1]

The relationship between the Navajo and bears is a long one, dating from when the Athabascans first moved into the Four Corners region. This is evidenced by the existence of a magnificent bear track etched into the sandstone in Gobernador Canyon in Dinétah. It is believed that this petroglyph was made sometime between 1696 and 1775 (Schaafsma: 14, figure 6).

Bear Sickness and Other Bear Beliefs

Bears play a major role in the Navajo stories. In Sandoval's version of the origin story, told to Aileen O'Bryan, Bear appears in the Third World as one of the four "chiefs," along with Big Snake, Mountain Lion, and Otter, who advised First Man and the other Animal People (O'Bryan: 6). Bear or bears serve as the guardians and protectors of Sun and Changing Woman, and later Changing Woman assigns the bear to be one of the special companions or "pets" to the people—the others being Mountain Lion, Weasel, and Porcupine—to protect them on their travels (Reichard: 384). In addition, bears form a special kinship with the *Kiyaa'aanii* clan, who once wore bear-fur caps given to them by the Bear People (Haile, 1981: 170). At one point in the origin story, the four original Navajo clans are attacked by an enemy—the "Arrow People" (probably the Ute Indians)—and initially it is only Bear who fights to protect them. Before doing so he sings ten "bear songs," including the following:

> *My hogan,*
> *I being a whirlwind,*
> *My hogan,*
> *I being a gray bear,*
> *Lightning strikes from my hogan,*
> *There is danger from my hogan,*
> *All are afraid of my hogan,*
> *I am of long life of whom they are afraid,*
> *hihinyi hi'*
> *I blow my breath out.*
>
> *They are afraid of my black face,*
> *I am a whirlwind,*
> *They are afraid of me.*
> *I am a gray bear,*
> *They are afraid of my black face,*
> *It lightens from my black face,*
> *They are afraid of the danger issuing from my black face,*
> *I am long life, they are afraid. (Goddard, 1933: 171)*

After Bear's initial attack, all of the clan's animal protectors joined together to destroy the enemy of the Navajos in a horrible massacre. When the killing was completed, the pets were sent into the mountains away from humans to be the Animal People we know today because they presumably had tasted human blood and could not be trusted. The bear was sent away to Black Mountain, and it is for that reason Navajos say that bears are mean there. But in appreciation for protecting them from their enemies, members of the *Kiyaa'aanii* clan will not kill or harm a bear (ibid.: 179; Haile, 1981: 172).

At least two Monster Bears also play an important role in the Navajo stories. The origin of these beasts could be wholly mythical or perhaps even derived from the grizzly bear that once inhabited Navajo Country. The first of these bears, Tracking Bear, was one of the monsters hunted down by Monster Slayer with an arrow of zigzag lightning given to him by his father, the Sun (Haile, 1938: 125–127). The second of these Monster Bears is Changing Bear Maiden. Initially a beautiful young girl with twelve brothers who were great hunters, she was taught the art of transformation by her husband, Coyote. When her brothers killed her husband, she became a fierce bear that tracked down each and killed all of them except for the youngest, who was finally able to take her life. He did so by shooting his arrows into her heart and lungs, which she had hidden. Afterwards he cut out her sexual organs and threw them into a tree, where they became the pitch that is found on cedar and pinon trees. He cut off her breasts and threw them into a tree, where they became pinon nuts (O'Bryan: 44–48; Tsosie).

Bears are considered to be the most powerful of the Animal People and even in contemporary times are known to still possess considerable supernatural power—including the ability to transform into the shape of an inanimate object, like a tree stump or a boulder, or into another animal or even a human. Bears can also cause illness—or as it is commonly called, bear sickness. Killing or offending a bear, eating its meat, coming in physical contact with a bear or its body parts (especially the head and hide), or the mere acts of handling an object such as a stone or piece of wood touched by a bear, drinking at a bear's watering place, stepping on bear tracks, or crossing its path—all can lead to bear sickness. Even the breath of a bear coming from a distance can do harm, as can dreaming about bears or speaking the bear's name aloud. Most bear sickness falls into two general categories: swollen, painful arms, legs, and other extremities; and mental illness (Wyman). Several years ago, I attended a Mountainway, the major ceremony used to deal with bear sickness, for a woman in her late sixties who was experiencing what Western physicians would describe as a severe case of arthritis. Her grandson explained the true cause of her illness in the following manner:

> When grandmother was three years old she wandered off and became lost. She was gone for three days. Several times they found her tracks which were always accompanied by the tracks of a bear. When she was finally found she told them she had stayed with an old woman and that they had done many things together including butchering a sheep. Since that time she has always felt poorly (Pavlik, 1992).

On another occasion, I had the opportunity to sit in on a ceremony conducted for a young woman who was experiencing emotional problems, which were manifested, among other ways, in her hearing voices that she responded to by taking off her clothes and running off in the middle of the night to roam in the woods. The family attributed her problems to the girl having petted a bear while visiting a zoo as a young child. In the words of one family member, "The Mountain People have taken her mind. So now she wants to run with the bears" (Pavlik, 1992). Other similar cases have been documented (see Morgan).

Because of fear associated with the powers of the bear, Navajos make every effort to avoid the animal. If one is met, it is prayed to as a "Holy being" and not molested (Hill). Seldom are bears hunted—quite possibly because of the close resemblance of a skinned bear to a human body hunted, an obvious sign of close kinship, and almost never is its flesh eaten except for ceremonial reasons. Sometimes a bear may be hunted and killed if its body parts are needed for ceremonial use. Bear paws, for example, are used to make the medicine bag or *jish* used by medicine men who practice the Mountainway ceremony. Bear claws are also used in conjunction with this ceremony, as well as for wristlets worn by patients during the "blackening" portion of several ceremonies. Bear claws are also historically attached to wristlets worn by warriors to give them power (Frisbie, 1987; Hill.)

When Navajos find it necessary to hunt and kill a bear, they do so ritualistically and in a manner that demonstrates great respect for the animal. In brief, the hunter, often a medicine man, finds the den of a bear, explains to it why it must be killed, then offers prayers and songs to bring it out of its den. He then kills the bear with a special club made of pine. The carcass of the bear is handled with great reverence and prepared in the following way:

> When the bear was killed pollen was sprinkled on the hide wherever an incision was to be made when skinning it. The first cut was made from the breast up to the throat; then a cut was made from the breast toward the tail. Next, incisions were made on the inside of the right front, left front, right hind, and left hind quarters, in that order. The animal was then skinned. . . . The head was never skinned. If the paws were to be used as medicine bags in the Mountain Way chant, these were skinned separately. Throughout the process the skinner and his assistants uttered the call of the Talking God (Hill: 157).

After skinning the bear, the Navajo hunters would ritualistically deposit the bones and hide of the animal. Various accounts exist regarding this procedure. Commonly these body parts were returned to the bear's den or placed nearby with the bear's head facing toward the entrance of the den. In one account, the bear's bones were reassembled in their original positions, and precious stones or beads representing the organs were placed among them. The hide was then placed on top of the bones and the whole covered with spruce boughs (Hill).

It is my opinion that most Navajo beliefs regarding bears, and certainly most elements of bear ceremonialism, are a product of the tribe's Athabascan origins.

While the Navajos share a body of bear beliefs and practices with the Pueblos, their similarities to both the Northern Athabaskans of Western Canada and Alaska and especially to the other Southern Athabaskans—the Apaches—are more direct and obvious. This is especially true in regard to preparation for a bear hunt and the treatment of the bear's carcass and hide after the kill is made (Rockwell). One major difference, however, needs to be noted. Northern Athabascans are active bear hunters who regularly consume bear meat as an important part of their diet (Nelson, 1976, 1983; Clark). Navajos, in contrast, believe that killing a bear should be done only in very extreme circumstances. Furthermore, Navajos believe that eating bear meat is an act akin to cannibalism and can make an individual lose his mind or cause other severe mental and physical problems. Consequently, Navajos usually ate bear meat only under extreme conditions of starvation (Hill; Rockwell). This reluctance to hunt, kill, and consume bears, along with a near-pathological fear of the spiritual power of bears, are characteristics shared with, and possibly adopted from, the Pueblos (Rockwell; Parsons). Other Southern Athabascans, most notably the Western Apaches of the White Mountain and San Carlos reservations, as well as the Jicarilla, Chiricahua, and Mescalero Apaches, also share similar beliefs (Goodwin; Opler, Morris, 1941, 1943). Only the Lipan Apaches—a tribe heavily influenced by Plains Indian culture—formerly hunted bears and ate their flesh. They also exhibited no fear of the animal's supernatural power (Opler, 1943).

Occasionally Navajos will kill a bear that has taken livestock. In an early narrative, Left Handed, Son of Old

Man Hat described such a bear killing in a manner that some might think of as being particularly violent, brutal, and a paradox to the way bears are generally viewed and treated by the Navajos (Dyk: 282–284). This episode seems to reflect the Navajo concept that this bear was an individual "being" that had willfully and purposefully chosen to kill livestock and would very likely do it again. In such a case, this individual bear was viewed—and treated—like any human enemy. This attitude stands in sharp contrast to the later preemptive and scorched-earth predator control campaigns introduced by western society.

In historic times, bears have been known to come to the aid of Navajos in need. Tezbah Mitchell once related a story in which one of her grandmothers, who had escaped from captivity at Bosque Redondo Reservation, received help from what might have been a grizzly bear or a large brown-phased black bear:

> After running away from Fort Sumner she reached some big mountains where she saw a red (brown) bear. It appeared friendly. They stood looking at each other for a while. Then, because the bear acted like he was motioning her to follow him, she did so. This big animal was her guide and protector for three days and nights as they traveled together, he was always some distance ahead of her. Sometimes the bear would stop, climb a tree and eat something. It seemed to be a sign for her; so she would sit down and eat a bit of food she had gathered.
>
> One time, while resting and eating, a big black bear appeared and came toward her, advancing slowly, showing his long white teeth. In an instant, the brown bear attacked and killed the black bear by chewing its throat.

*The following day, about noon, the bear stopped under a
tree and ate berries from the bushes. After a while he walked
away a short distance, turned and looked at my grandmother. He stood there making motions with his head as if
to say he was leaving, which he did. My grandmother told
me that she used to talk to the bear during their journey
together and that it seemed to understand what she was
saying. (Roessel: 252)*

Navajo Bear Ceremonialism[2]

Navajo religion, and indeed the totality of the existence
of the Navajo people, is based upon the philosophical
premise that a balance and harmony exist and must be
maintained in one's personal life as well as the environment one lives in. Physical and emotional problems are
viewed as being products of a disruption of that balance and harmony. Such disruptions are usually caused
by man's transgressions against some element of the
natural world. Bears, the most powerful of the Mountain People, are thus often linked as a source of many
illnesses and diseases. When this happens, prayers, and
in some cases a ceremony, must be offered to pacify the
bear or correct the transgression that has brought on
the problem. These prayers and ceremonies are usually
prescribed by a diagnostician, often a crystal gazer or
hand-trembler, and are then performed by a practitioner
commonly known as a medicine man or singer. The origins of the problem and the procedure to correct it are
found in the Navajo stories of creation. Thus, the sacred
body of knowledge regarding bears, bear sickness, and
bear ceremonialism exists in Navajo mythology.

Ceremonies that focus on bears range from a simple litany of prayers given by a few orthodox traditionalists to honor the harvesting of pinon nuts (a food product that in Navajo mythology comes directly from the bear), to much more complex events such as the Shock Rite, which is used to test whether a ceremony being performed is the correct one (Farmer). The following brief description of a Shock Rite illustrates the power attributed to bears:

> The patient is seated on a specially prepared sandpainting, usually one of the House of the Bear and Snake, or Bear's Sitting Place, which has been surrounded with spruce branches. At a signal from the singer, a man costumed to represent a bear leaps out from a dark corner of the dwelling and confronts the patient. If the patient faints or otherwise reacts to the sight of the "bear," then he or she is revived and it is believed that the correct ceremonial is being performed. (Ibid.: 111)

The most important Navajo ceremony used to cure bear sickness is the Mountain Top-Way, or simply the Mountain Chant or Mountainway. This ceremony usually lasts nine days and cannot be performed before the first killing frost in the fall. The seasonal restriction allows for it to be held at a time when rattlesnakes and bears are hibernating and cannot be offended by hearing their names spoken. The Mountainway has three "branches" or variations: the Male, Female, and Cub branches. The variation used depends on the nature and source of the illness. The final night of the Mountainway climaxes with a spectacular event commonly called the Fire Dance (see Haile, 1946). This performance, which is also known as the Corral Dance or

Dark Circle of Branches Dance, has been likened to a great vaudeville show and attracts hundreds of spectators (Wyman). Teams of dancers perform around a large blazing fire surrounded by a corral made of cedar or pinon boughs with an entrance left open in the east. The dance teams perform according to the prescription of the various ceremonials they represent—most commonly Shootingway, Beautyway, Nightway, Windway, and of course, the Mountainway. The Mountainway is also well known for its "specialty acts," the most anticipated of which is a visit from a bear impersonator, or as I once heard it referred to at a ceremony I attended, "the animal" (Pavlik, 1992). The bear impersonator, who is covered with pine and spruce branches to represent hair, walks around the fire within the corral on his hands and knees, representing the movement and sounds of a bear. I have witnessed this on numerous occasions, and it is always an exciting moment when the bear impersonator enters the arbor. The "bear" then ends his appearance by presenting the patient with medicine, thus demonstrating the power of the bear to heal as well as cause sickness. In earlier times it is said that actual bears were trained for this part of the ceremony (Newcomb: 108).[3]

It is interesting to note that a similar ceremony, the Holiness Rite, exists among the Jicarilla Apaches. This ceremony has also been referred to as the "fiesta, the grizzly dance," or simply, the bear dance (Goddard, 1911). It is possible that the Navajo Mountainway is derived from the Jicarilla Holiness Rite, since the Navajos and the Jicarillas were among the more northerly of the Southern Athabascans and were closer neighbors before the former tribe migrated more to the west (Wyman). The two ceremonies share a similar origin mythology and exhibit close correspondence in ritual behavior (Ibid.). The Holiness Rite is performed within an evergreen corral and employs the use of sandpaintings and a bear impersonator dressed in spruce boughs (see Opler, 1943; see also Haile, 1932). In contrast, the popular bear dance of the neighboring Ute tribe, a non-Athabascan people, is largely social in nature and shares almost no similarities with either the Mountainway or the Holiness Rite (Opler, Marvin, 1941).

The Mountainway is a rare, perhaps even vanishing, ceremony, mainly because of a scarcity of Mountainway singers. There may be more Nightway singers today than ever in the tribe's history, so many that some have complained they are not being called upon enough, this despite the fact that James C. Faris reported in 1988 that he knew of at least seven Nightway ceremonies that were in various states of presentation at a single time (Faris: 81; 237). In contrast, there are to the best of my knowledge only three practicing Mountainway singers. The most popular of these is called upon almost every week to do a ceremony. Several factors appear to account for this discrepancy. While the Nightway, a major nine-day-and-night ceremony, is an extremely elaborate and difficult ceremony to learn, the Mountainway is much harder and requires an even greater commitment to master. Also, Mountainway medicine bundles are extremely difficult to assemble. Certainly many potential Mountainway singers are also discouraged from apprenticing for this ceremony due to fear of bear sickness.

A Closing Story and Some Final Thoughts

The Navajo Nation Fair, held during the first week of every September, is a much anticipated event in Navajo Country. One of the most popular exhibits has always been a collection of wildlife provided by the New Mexico Department of Game and Fish.

Prior to the 1963 fair, a simple telephone call kicked off a series of interesting events. In this conversation, a New Mexico Game and Fish official and a fair organizer discussed what animals should be put on display for the upcoming fair. Reportedly, the tribal official said something to the effect that "the tribe wants a bear." The Game and Fish officer interpreted this to mean that the tribe actually wanted a bear. Consequently, the New Mexico Department of Game and Fish brought a full-grown black bear to the fair. When workers went to take down the exhibit tent after the fair was over, they were shocked to find the caged bear still there. A hurried phone call to Game and Fish confirmed the misunderstanding: the bear had been left behind as a "gift" to the Navajo Nation. After discussing the matter further, tribal officials decided to keep the bear, whom they called Yogi.

Yogi was housed at the Navajo Tribal Museum under the care of its director, Martin Link, and for the next several years, the bear was hauled out to be exhibited at the annual fair, where he proved to be a popular attraction. During the 1966 fair, fate struck again. Link was sitting in his office when someone came running in saying that a woman had fainted near the bear exhibit. Link hurried to the scene, where he found a young Navajo woman lying unconscious on the ground. As Link leaned over the woman to help revive her, he was startled to see splatters of blood dripping down on the woman's blouse. Looking up, he saw an elderly Navajo woman standing over him, her hand wrapped in a blood-soaked handkerchief. The older woman had reached into Yogi's cage to place corn pollen on his tongue as a blessing, and the bear had responded by biting off her finger! The younger woman, her daughter, had fainted when she saw the blood. To avoid a lawsuit, the tribe agreed to the woman's only demand: they made a truck payment for her. The tribe also decided that it would be wise to build Yogi a more secure and permanent enclosure, and thus the Navajo Nation Zoological Park was created. Link volunteered to act as its first director (Link). In the years that followed, the tribal zoo has always maintained bears on exhibit, including another bear named Yogi that was born at the facility and was a descendant of his namesake. A former and longtime director of the Navajo Nation Zoological Park, Lolene Hathaway, states that during her tenure, which ended in 1996, it was not uncommon for traditional people to come in and pray to (or for?) the bear and to leave offerings (Hathaway).

But bears are not always granted reverence and respect by the Navajo people. Each year a number of bears, no one knows how many, are killed by tribal members who feel that they are protecting their livestock and crops. Most of these killings are unjustified. I once had the opportunity to examine the remains of two bears shot by a Navajo landowner who believed that they had killed two of his cattle. My investigation convinced me that the cattle had been struck by lightning and that the bears later came along to scavenge on their remains. While some livestock deprivation by bears undoubtedly takes place, most attacks on sheep, goats, and cattle are carried out by coyotes or, more likely, feral dogs. In addition, I believe that the majority of livestock losses are caused by illness and accidents; bears later seen feeding on the carcasses are then blamed for losses.

With the passing of each generation, traditional knowledge of the natural world, and consequently respect for bears and the role they play in Navajo tribal worldview, is progressively being lost. In the 1960s, the Navajo Nation Department of Fish and Game attempted to implement a tribal bear hunting season. This hunt was short lived, however, as traditional people came together to protest. In 1994, Navajo Fish and Game again opened a hunting season on bears, this time with the expectation that most permits would be sold to white hunters. License sales in the first two years totaled only three. It is revealing, however, that no one from the tribe stepped forward to protest this hunt, an event that in some minds might be likened to arranging a contract killing on a fellow kin member. This attitude of indifference toward the tribally sanctioned bear hunts reflects a change of attitude due to the loss of traditional culture and values over the past several decades.

Another major concern is the loss of bear habitat. The Navajo population continues to grow dramatically, and this growth most certainly will lead to addition-al encroachment of people and livestock into areas inhabited by bears. In addition, tribal logging practices have come under attack by Navajo environmentalists as being overly destructive to mountain habitat. If such claims are true, critical bear habitat, not to mention me-dicinal plant life vital to the continuation of ceremonies such as the Mountainway, are in danger of being lost forever.

The summer of 1996 was a particularly bad one for bears and their relationship with humans in Arizo-na. A severe drought, combined with the irresponsible actions of campers and some residents of the state's mountainous regions, resulted in a high number of bear-human conflicts, including several serious inju-ries to people and a number of bears being destroyed. It is important to note that each summer thousands of Navajos move into the mountains to pasture their herds of sheep, goats, and other livestock. These people cook and sleep outdoors and make no particular effort to maintain a "clean camp" in terms of the precautions taken by experienced campers. Despite this situation, there has never been a reported bear attack on the Na-vajo Reservation. One longtime Navajo Game and Fish biologist attributes this peaceful coexistence to the fact that the Navajo bear population—an unhunted popula-tion—is in his estimation an older population and thus experienced in dealing with humans (McCoy). In addi-tion, traditional knowledge and cultural beliefs result in humans also maintaining a distance between them-selves and bears. It appears that the Navajos and the Mountain People have been able to peacefully coexist because they share a timeless state of mutual understanding and respect.

Notes

1. The best source of information on the natural history of black bears is *The Great American Bear* by Jeff Fair and Lynn Rogers (1990). The best source of information on the natural history and management of black bears in Arizona is my report "*Ursus* in a Sky Island Range: The Ecology, History, and Management of Black Bears in the Huachuca Mountains of Southeastern Arizona" (2006), available at www.wildlandsnetwork.org.

2. Bear ceremonialism is one of the world's oldest forms of religious practice. Among the Native people of North America, bear ceremonialism reveals its richest and most varied expression. The best general overview of cultural bear beliefs and practices can be found in Paul Shepard and Barry Sander's *The Sacred Paw* (1985). Native American beliefs and practices are best reviewed in A. Irving Hallowell's classic "Bear Ceremonialism in the Northern Hemisphere" (in *American Anthropologist* 28:1, 1926) and in David Rockwell's *Giving Voice to Bear* (1991).

3. It is not within the scope of this chapter to provide further description of the Mountainway ceremony. Readers are advised to refer to the sources listed in the references below, especially Matthews (1887), Wyman (1975), and Haile (1946).

References

Bass, Rick. 1995. *The Lost Grizzlies.* Boston: Houghton Mifflin Company.

Brown, David E. 1985. *The Grizzly in the Southwest.* Norman: University of Oklahoma Press.

Clark, Annette F. 1970. "Kuyukon Athabascan Ceremonialism," *Western Canadian Journal of Anthropology,* 2(1): 80–83.

Dyk, Walter, ed. 1938. *Son of Old Man Hat: A Navaho Autobiography.* Lincoln: University of Nebraska Press.

Fair, Jeff and Lynn Rogers. 1990. *The Great American Bear.* Minocqua, WI: NorthWord Press.

Faris, James C. 1990. Nightway: *A History and a History of Documentation of a Navajo Ceremonial.* Albuquerque: University of New Mexico Press.

Farmer, Malcolm. 1982. "Bear Ceremonialism among the Navajos and Other Apacheans," in *Papers in Honor of Leland C. Wyman*, edited by David M. Brugge and Charlotte J. Frisbie: 110–114. *Museum of New Mexico Papers in Anthropology,* 17. Santa Fe: Museum of New Mexico Press.

Franciscan Fathers. 1910. *An Ethnologic Dictionary of the Navajo Language.* St. Michaels, AZ: St. Michaels Press.

Frisbie, Charlotte J. 1987. *Navajo Medicine Bundles or Jish: Acquisition, Transmission, and Disposition in the Past and Present.* Albuquerque: University of New Mexico Press.

Frisbie, Charlotte J. 1992. "Temporal Change in Navajo Religion: 1868–1990," *Journal of the Southwest*, 34(4): 457–514.

Goddard, Pliny E. 1911. "Jicarilla Apache Texts," *Anthropological Papers of the American Museum of Natural History*, XXIV(I). New York.

Goddard, Pliny E. 1933. *Navajo Texts*. Washington, DC: American Museum of Natural History Anthropological Papers, 34(1).

Goodwin, Grenville. 1938. "White Mountain Apache Religion," *American Anthropologist*, 40(1): 24–37.

Haile, Father Berard. 1932. "Beardance: A Ceremony of the Jicarilla Apache," Manuscript, University of Arizona Special Collections.

Haile, Father Berard. 1938. *Origin Legend of the Navaho Enemy Way*. New Haven, CT: Yale University Press.

Haile, Father Berard. 1946. *The Navajo Fire Dance.* St. Michaels, AZ: St. Michaels Press.

Haile, Father Berard. 1981. *Upward Moving and Emergence Way*. Lincoln: University of Nebraska Press.

Hallowell, A. Irving. 1926. "Bear Ceremonialism in the Northern Hemisphere," *American Anthropologist,* 28(1): 1–175.

Hathaway, Lolene. 2006. Personal conversation. February 23.

Hill, Willard W. 1938. *The Agricultural and Hunting Methods of the Navaho Indians*. New Haven, CT: Yale University Press.

Housholder, Bob. 1966. *The Grizzly Bear in Arizona*. Privately printed manuscript.

Link, Martin. 2006. Personal conversation. January 10.

Matthews, Washington. 1887. "The Mountain Chant: A Navajo Ceremony," *Annual Report of the Bureau of American Ethnology*. Washington, DC: 379–467.

Matthews, Washington. 1897/1994. *Navaho Legends*. Salt Lake City: University of Utah Press.

McCoy, K. 1996. Personal conversation. July 10.

McPherson, Robert S., ed. 2000. *The Journey of Navajo Oshley*. Logan: Utah State University Press.

Merriam, C. Hart. 1918. "Review of the Grizzly and Big Brown Bears of North America," *North American Fauna*, 4: 1–136.

Morgan, William. 1936. *Human-Wolves among the Navajo*. New Haven, CT: Yale University Publications in Anthropology, No. 11.

Nelson, Richard K. 1976. *Hunters of the Northern Forest*. Chicago: University of Chicago Press.

Nelson, Richard K. 1983. *Make Prayers to the Raven: A Kuyukon View of the Northern Forest*. Chicago: University of Chicago Press.

Newcomb, Franc J. 1964. *Hosteen Klah: Navaho Medicine Man and Sand Painter.* Norman: University of Oklahoma Press.

O'Bryan, Aileen. 1956/1993. *Navajo Indian Myths.* New York: Dover Publications.

O'Conner, Jack. 1945. *Hunting in the Southwest.* New York: Alfred A. Knopf.

Opler, Marvin H. 1941. "A Colorado Ute Indian Bear Dance," *Southwestern Lore,* 7(2): 21–30.

Opler, Morris E. 1941. *An Apache Life-Way: The Economic, Social, and Religious Institutions of the Chiricahua Indians.* Chicago: University of Chicago Press.

Opler, Morris E. 1943. "The Character and Derivation of the Jicarilla Apache Holiness Rite," *University of New Mexico Bulletin,* No. 390.

Parsons, Elsie Clews. 1939/1996. *Pueblo Indian Religion.* 2 volumes. Chicago: University of Chicago Press.

Pavlik, Steve. 1992. Field notes.

Pavlik, Steve. 1993. "Navajo Christianity: Historical Origins and Modern Trends." Paper presented at the Robert K. Thomas Symposium, Vancouver, British Columbia, July 19.

Pavlik, Steve. 1995. "Navajo Orthodox Traditionalism." Paper presented at the Navajo Studies Conference, Farmington, New Mexico, March 12.

Pavlik, Steve. 1997a. "Navajo Christianity: Historical Origins and Modern Trends," *Wicazo Sa Review*, 12(2): 43–58.

Pavlik. Steve. 1997b. "The Role of Bears and Bear Ceremonialism in Navajo Orthodox Traditional Lifeway," *The Social Science Journal*, 34(4): 475–484.

Pavlik, Steve. 2006. "*Ursus* in a Sky Island Range: The Ecology, History, and Management of Black Bears in the Huachuca Mountains of Southeastern Arizona." www.wildlandsproject.org.

Peterson, David. 1995. *Ghost Grizzlies*. New York: Henry Holt & Company.

Reichard, Gladys A. 1950. *Navaho Religion: A Study in Symbolism.* New York: Bollingen Foundation.

Rockwell, David. 1991. *Giving Voice to Bear: North American Indian Myths, Rituals, and Images of the Bear.* Niwot, CO: Roberts Rinehart Publishers.

Roessel, Ruth. 1973. *Navajo Stories of the Long Walk Period*. Tsaile, AZ: Navajo Community College Press.

Schaafsma, Polly. 1966. *Early Navaho Rock Paintings and Carvings*. Santa Fe, NM: Museum of Navaho Ceremonial Art.

Shepard, Paul and Barry S. Sanders. 1985. *The Sacred Paw: The Bear in Nature, Myth, and Literature*. New York: Viking Press.

Spencer, Katherine. 1957. *Mythology and Values: An Analysis of Navajo Chantway Myths*. Philadelphia: American Folklore Society.

Tsosie, Will. 1992. Personal conversation. November 11.

Wyman, Leland. 1975. *The Mountainway of the Navajo*. Tucson: University of Arizona Press.

 # Chapter Two

Will Big Trotter Reclaim His Place?

The chapter was originally presented as a paper at the Eleventh Navajo Studies Conference held in Window Rock, Arizona, on October 23, 1998. An edited version was published as "Will Big Trotter Reclaim His Place? The Role of the Wolf in Navajo Tradition" in American Indian Culture and Research Journal, Volume 24, Number 4, 2000. It was also reprinted in the anthology El Lobo: Readings on the Mexican Gray Wolf, edited by Tom Lynch, University of Utah Press, 2005.

The Wolf in the Southwest and Navajo Country

Sometime shortly after his arrival in the Southwest in 1917, a US Forest Service biologist named Aldo Leopold participated in the killing of a wolf somewhere in the White Mountains—a range that stretches across the borderlands of south-central Arizona and New Mexico. Leopold and a number of companions were eating lunch on a high rimrock position overlooking a river when they spotted a female wolf and her six grown pups playing in an open area below. Immediately, the men pulled out their rifles and "with more excitement than accuracy" began blasting away at the wolf family. When the rifles were empty and the shooting stopped, only the female wolf was down and one pup was seen dragging its leg into a rockslide. Leopold, who would go on to become perhaps the most famous conservationist in American history, described the death of this wolf—and his personal transformation—in one of the most eloquent and quoted passages in the literature of wildlife conservation:

> We reached the old wolf in time to watch a fierce green fire dying in her eyes. I realized then, and have known ever since, that there was something new to me in those eyes—something known only to her and to the mountain. I was young then, and full of trigger-itch; I thought that because fewer wolves meant more deer, that no wolves would mean hunter's paradise. But after seeing the green fire die, I sensed that neither the wolf nor the mountain agreed with such a view. (Leopold: 130)

The gray wolf, *Canis lupus*[1], had long been part of the Southwest American landscape—and an integral part of Navajo origin stories and culture. The Leopold incident took place during the heyday of the war of extermination against the wolf. With the arrival of cattle ranchers and sheepherders in the 1880s, and the subsequent destruction of the native herbivore species on which the wolves preyed, wolves were perceived as a serious threat to the livestock industry. Consequently, a program of wolf extermination was soon initiated by the Predatory Animal and Rodent Control (PARC) branch of the US Biological Survey, predecessor to the US Fish and Wildlife Service. Using firearms, steel traps, poisons, and denning—digging wolf pups out of their dens and clubbing them to death—the professional "wolfers" of PARC were relentless in their efforts to eradicate the wolf (see Robinson). By 1925, the wolf ceased to be a major predator in the Southwest, with all resident animals eliminated except for a few holdouts on isolated pockets of land such as the San Carlos, White Mountain, and Jicarilla Apache reservations and on the Navajo Reservation. By the 1940s, the wolf was all but extirpated in the Southwest, with the last wolves killed in Arizona and New Mexico in the early 1970s. Although documentation is scarce, it is believed that wolves were once relatively abundant on the Defiance Plateau and in the Lukachukai and Chuska mountains of the Navajo Reservation (Brown: 24; see also Bailey: 310). In all probability the last wolf on the Navajo Reservation was killed before 1950.

In 1973, the United States Congress passed the Endangered Species Act (ESA). This law directed the Secretary of the Interior to develop and implement a recovery plan for species and subspecies of wildlife in danger of human-caused extinction. The act also mandated the reintroduction of endangered species when feasible. In 1976, the Mexican wolf, *Canis lupus baileyi,* or the lobo as it was once commonly called, was listed as an endangered species under the ESA. Two years later, the entire gray wolf species in North America south of Canada was listed. The listing of the entire species served to initiate efforts to reintroduce wolves to the West.

In 1996, wolves captured in Canada were released in Yellowstone National Park in Wyoming and in Montana and central Idaho. The success of this reintroduction—especially in Yellowstone—became one of America's great conservation stories and encouraged federal wildlife officials to develop and implement a recovery plan to reintroduce Mexican wolves to the Southwest. The last remaining Mexican wolves were live-trapped in Mexico and, together with animals already in various zoos, formed the nucleus of a captive breeding population of about one hundred. In the spring of 1998, the first Mexican wolves were released in the White Mountains of Arizona—the site of Aldo Leopold's encounter with a dying wolf almost eighty years earlier. The plan was to continue to reintroduce family groups of wolves until the recovery goal of one hundred wolves was sustained through reproduction within the wild population.

Although the return of the wolves has been highly controversial, public opinion has always been overwhelmingly in support of reintroduction. Environmental groups view wolf reintroduction as the cornerstone of their efforts to promote biodiversity and restore balance to the natural world. However, livestock ranchers, hunting organizations, and a number of other special interest groups see no place in the modern world for wolves and have posed stiff opposition to reintroduction.[2] Regardless of one's position, wolves have certainly reentered the minds, hearts, and lives of the American public.

One indication of the resurgence of interest in wolves is the proliferation of books and articles written about the animal. A visit to any decent-sized bookstore usually reveals an impressive collection of wolf-related publications. Most of these books include some reference, and often even one or more chapters, regarding wolves and American Indians.

Writers, especially environmental writers, tend to emphasize the positive relationship between wolves and this country's Native American inhabitants. In general, the literature reflects the fact that most American Indian tribes have always held the wolf in the highest regard. For many tribes—the Cheyenne, Sioux, Pawnee, and Nez Perce, to name a few—the wolf is an important figure in their origin stories, usually portrayed as a powerful being possessing admirable qualities such as courage, strength, wisdom, family devotion, and the ability to work cooperatively. Many tribes have wolf clans, and some tribes have warrior and hunting societies that associate themselves with the wolf and draw power from this animal. An extensive list could be compiled of Native American warriors, hunters, spiritual leaders, and diplomats who adopted or were given wolf-related names of honor.

One tribe supposedly stands in sharp contrast to others regarding views and attitudes toward the wolf: the Navajo. In writing about the relationship of the Navajos to the wolf, most writers, including Barry H. Lopez and Robert H. Busch, unfortunately focus on the question of witchcraft and its role in shaping the relationship of the wolf to the Navajos. In reality the wolf, *Ma'iitsoh* or Big Trotter as he is known to the Navajos, was an important and almost totally positive figure in tribal tradition.

At least four books have been published in recent years specifically on the Mexican wolf: David E. Brown's *The Wolf in the Southwest: The Making of an Endangered Species* is the standard work on this subspecies and provides basic background on the animal's natural history and on man's efforts to eradicate the animal. Brown, however, does not address the topic of the wolf's relationship to the Native people of the South-west. James C. Burbank's *Vanishing Lobo: The Mexican Wolf in the Southwest* does focus more on the nature of the wolf-human relationship beyond government exter-mination efforts and includes excellent chapters on the role played by the wolf in Pueblo and Navajo cultures. The talented nature writer Rick Bass has written *The New Wolves: The Return of the Mexican Wolf to the Amer-ican Southwest.* As the subtitle suggests, this book docu-ments the early efforts to reintroduce the Mexican wolf to its historic Blue Range of the White Mountains. But again, no mention is made about the role of the wolf in Southwest Native American cultures and lifeways. More recently, Tom Lynch has edited an anthology entitled *El Lobo: Readings on the Mexican Wolf*, which includes an earlier version of this chapter.

The Divine Wolf of the Navajos

As noted earlier, what we now recognize as traditional Navajo beliefs are a syncretism of the hunter-gatherer Athabascan or Apacheans with the largely agricultur-al-based Pueblos. While most religious and ceremoni-al beliefs, including their emergence stories, actually are derived from the Pueblo side of their heritage, the traditional role of Wolf in the Navajo stories originates mostly from the Athabascan hunter tradition.

In the Navajo emergence story, the Earth was first inhabited by Holy People, beings of supernatural power, and some Animal People, who preceded and then coex-isted with humans. Anthropologist Gladys A. Reichard provided the following summary:

The Holy People might well be considered those who in mythological times were able to help man in cases where he could not help himself. In those days snakes, birds and other animals could speak and behave like men, and to human powers, they added supernatural powers which made them dangerous. Nowadays they no longer speak, but their powers remain for good or evil to man, depending upon how he receives them and upon the side with which they allied themselves in ancient times. (Reichard, 1939/1977: 16)

Wolf, the deity, and wolf, the animal, fall into such categorization. In the beginning he existed as an anthropomorphic figure, a being possessed of considerable supernatural power. Today we see him only in his animal form retaining only a remnant of the power he once held. However, those powers are still considerable. Consequently, wolves (along with bears and coyotes) are thought to be among the so-called dangerous animals in terms of their potential to harm humans. The danger they present is largely in terms of the sickness they can bring to people who have offended them in some way.

In Father Berard Haile's version of the Upward Moving and Emergence Way story, as told to him by Gishin Biye', the Red Underworld is the home of Wolf, who lives in a white house in the east. In one of his first appearances in the narrative, Wolf attacks the house of First Man, whose guardians, Wildcat and Puma, catch the arrows Wolf shoots at them. First Man then uses those arrows to kill sixteen Wolf People. In return for First Man restoring life to their slain kin, the Wolf People create four songs for each member restored, a total of sixty-four songs, which they give to First Man. Haile notes that this story explains the presence of wolf songs in Navajo ceremonials (Haile, 1981: 11–12).

In another emergence story, again recorded by Haile from Gishin Biye', a separation of sexes occurred when Wolf, chief of the east, finds his wife to be irresponsible and disrespectful. Because of this he leads the other male beings to the opposite side of a great river to live away from the female beings. In time, however, the two sexes find they need each other. It is Wolf who calls a meeting of the chiefs and proposes reconciliation. This series of events suggests that Wolf is held in the highest esteem and is considered the leader of the other chiefs, who are quick to accept his proposals (ibid.: 39–43, 93–94).

Wolf is also the first to raise the alarm over the omens that ultimately foretell a great flood brought on by Coyote stealing Water Monster's baby. As the floodwater rises, Wolf, along with Mountain Lion and Bear, dig a hole through the roof of the underworld so they can escape into the upperworld (ibid.: 111, 116–117. See also Franciscan Fathers: 351). Upon entering the new world, Wolf continues his role as chief (Haile, 1981: 128).

The other side of Wolf's character is his impatience and short temper. In another emergence story, Wolf becomes angry over the introduction of foods he sees as being inferior, including certain plants and salt. In his anger he offends Salt Woman. This story explains why people today take offense at different things (ibid.: 144).

Another origin story, as recorded by Washington Matthews, deserves mention because it draws a comparison between Wolf and his cousin Coyote. In this story, Coyote visits Wolf, who buries two arrows with wooden heads in the hot ashes beside his fire, then pulls them out to reveal two fine pieces of meat that he serves his guest. Later, Wolf visits Coyote, who tries to impress him by attempting the same magical act. However, when Coyote pulls the arrows out of the ashes, he has only burnt wood to show for his efforts (Matthews: 87–88). Clearly Wolf and Coyote do not share the same character and abilities.

Wolf's most prominent role in the Navajo mythology can be found in the stories associated with the Beadway ceremony and related Eagle Way ritual. In the version of the Beadway story as told by Miguelito to Gladys Reichard, the hero, Scavenger or Holy Boy, wanders off and is buried under a pile of rocks. The Eagles, who have befriended Scavenger, call upon the hunters—Wolf, Mountain Lion, Lynx, and Bobcat—to rescue him. Although the hunters fail in their attempt, Badger eventually recovers his bones. A ceremony is held to bring him back to life using four feathers from different birds: Bald Eagle, Blue Hawk, Yellow Hawk, and Magpie. These feathers are transformed, respectively, into Wolf, Mountain Lion, Beaver, and Otter. When the transformation is complete, Scavenger is restored to life. It is for this reason that the skins of these four animals are used in the Beadway ceremony (Reichard, 1950: 32).

Wolf appears several other times in the Beadway story. At one point, in Haile's version, Wolf is chosen as the meal sprinkler and, traveling supernaturally on sun-rays, is sent to spread the word of an impending Beadway ceremony (Haile, 1943: 90). In Reichard's version, Wolf is portrayed as traveling to perform a Beadway himself. In both versions Wolf encounters his friend and fellow hunter Mountain Lion, who is on a similar mission. Since neither wants to miss the other's sing, they agree that Mountain Lion should postpone his ceremony for one night. To bind this agreement, the two great hunters exchange quivers. A sandpainting used in Beadway depicts this event, showing Wolf wearing a quiver made of mountain lion skin.

Another sandpainting from Beadway shows the Wolf People joining the Mountain Lion People in a Fire Dance performance. Yet another Beadway sandpainting shows both the Wolf People and the Mountain Lion People dancing while wearing packs of corn on their backs—corn secured by the Hunters through use of their magical powers to plant, cultivate, and harvest the crop, all within minutes, before performing their dance (Reichard, 1939/1977: 34–35, plate VII).

Wolf also plays an important role in a life-restoring origin story associated with the Flintway ceremony. In this story, White Thunder destroys the hero, Holy Young Man. Wolf is one of the deities summoned to help restore him. Wolf, because he did not devour the hero's flesh at the time of his death, is asked to regulate the Flintway method of administering liquid medicine. An accompanying Wolf song is also sung. One such song imitates the growl of Wolf and mentions him four times in which he represents both himself and other animals whose fur and body parts are used in the Flintway ceremony. Dark Wolf represents the bear, White Wolf represents the wolf itself, Yellow Wolf represents the mountain lion, and Glittering Wolf represents all three collectively, the wildcat, or possibly otter (Haile, 1943: 53–54). The wolf, along with the mountain lion, is one of the key animals whose death blood, tallow, marrow, and menstrual flux are utilized in Flintway.

In looking at the role played by Wolf in the emergence story, and subsequent stories leading up to various ceremonies, it is clear he is a figure of considerable power and prestige. He is highly respected by the other Holy People for his wisdom and powers and is looked to for advice and often given important assignments upon which the welfare of the people depends. Consequently, Wolf must certainly be ranked as one of the leading Animal People. Most importantly, Wolf appears throughout Navajo mythology as a divine personage who, on the whole, is a positive and beneficial figure to the Navajo people.

The Wolf and the Navajo Hunter Tradition

Of his many attributes and abilities, Wolf is always recognized and respected for his skills as a hunter. It is not surprising then that in the stories of the Navajo hunter tradition, Wolf plays a major role. Indeed, the Navajo use the word *naatl'eetsoh*—which literally refers to wolves—for all hunters and predators, including man (Luckert, 1975: 169 note 4).

As noted earlier, the origin of these hunter stories traces back to the Athabascan period of Navajo prehistory.

Karl W. Luckert, whose work I draw from extensively, credits this period with providing the foundation for Navajo hunting stories, especially regarding the role of animal elders and hunter tutelaries. Later contact with the Pueblos and the consequent incorporation of an emergence mythology served to elaborate and enrich the Navajo hunter tradition. This view complements the anthropological assertion that the Navajo did not arrive at many of the geographical places mentioned in their hunter stories until the late 1700s (Luckert, 1975: 11–13).

In the Deer Hunting Way, as told by Claus Chee Sonny to Luckert, the deer gods themselves provided the divine hunters, Wolf, Mountain Lion, Tiger (Jaguar), Bobcat, and Cat (Lynx?), the necessary knowledge to hunt them. In time, men appeared and soon acquired this knowledge to pass down through the generations (ibid.: 18). Presumably, the deer gods taught man how to hunt them, but man also acquired specific knowledge of hunting from the divine predators.

In the second version of the Navajo hunter tradition, as recorded by Luckert from Billie Blackhorse, a hierarchy of gods presides over animals: Black God, who ranks highest; Talking God; and Calling God. Since these gods presumably preside over the hunt, they are theoretically the leaders of the *naatl'eetsoh* as well. Blackhorse gave Luckert the impression that these three gods were regarded no differently than other *naatl'eetsoh*. Consequently, Luckert feels that all *naatl'eetsoh* should be called gods. However, it should be noted that the animal gods predate Black God,

Talking God, and Calling God. Since Wolf bestowed his mythical name on all hunters of both animal and human form, he was in the truest sense the highest ranking of the Navajo hunter deities (ibid.: 172–175).

The Navajos traditionally distinguished between two types of hunting: ritual and nonritual. The wolf itself, whose body parts are needed for certain ceremonies, was killed nonritually. Only deer, antelope, bear, and eagles were hunted ritually (Hill, 1938: 97). Perhaps a dozen specific hunting rituals or "ways" existed. These animals were apparently singled out for ritualistic hunting due to their importance in Navajo tradition and lifeway and certainly because of the degree of power they possessed. For example, deer were very powerful and could cause deer sickness called *ajilee* (Luckert, 1978: 30). For these ritual hunts, the hunter was obligated to follow certain procedures that regulated all aspects of the hunt, from preparation and planning through breaking camp when the hunt was over. Only by strictly observing ritualistic procedures could the hunter honor the game he hunted, ensure his success—and future success—in the hunt, immunize himself against *ajilee*, and cleanse himself of the guilt associated with taking a life. Most of these procedures were used to hunt deer, the most important of the game animals (see Elmore).

The Wolfway hunt began with the participants retiring to a sweathouse. In doing so, they not only purified themselves, but also, through prayer and the recitation of songs, entered the mythical world of preemergence and the animal gods that gave birth to the hunter tradition. Hill states:

*The most outstanding feature of the ritual hunt was the
complete reversal of the psychology of the participants.
Through the hunt they found release from ordinary restrictions. In everyday life around the hogan the hunters were
normal individuals of the group. They shunned speaking of
death, blood, or killing. Their hunting songs could not be
sung because of their danger to women, children and sheep.
However, as soon as the party left on a hunting trip the individual behavior underwent a complete change. The hunters
did everything possible to emulate the animal in whose
Way they were hunting: eating from branches, sleeping like
animals, and using animal cries to call other members of the
party. Topics that dealt with blood and death, which under
ordinary circumstances were avoided, were now spoken of
with the utmost freedom. The hunters were charged to keep
their minds on killing and things pertaining to death. (Hill,
1938: 98)*

In summary, the hunters emerged from the sweathouse transformed into the predator whose power they
sought. Those who hunted in the Wolfway did not simply
imitate they wolf, they assumed the wolf identity. During
the hunt they referred to each other as *naatl'eetsoh*. They
thought, behaved, and even communicated as wolves.
In the story behind the Wolfway ritual, Wolf gave permission to the human hunters to use his voice. If a hunter
howled like a wolf four times to the north, he could fend
off bad weather. Also, hunters used the howl of the wolf
to signal each other. Indeed, it was the only form of com-
munication permissible while on the hunt. One hunter
familiar with the hunter tradition stated that

*the Wolf's voice may be used in hunting, to signal one
another if more than one person are out hunting together.*

The Wolf gave that. Today those people who know about this make use of it in their hunting. You never talk to another hunter in your own voice. You always imitate the voice of the wolf. If you recognize the importance of this in hunting, you will observe it. If you do not, then you may see deer all around you, but you will never hit one (Luckert, 1975: 51).

When a hunter killed a deer, he used the call of the wolf to attract the attention of his fellow hunting partners. Reportedly, this tradition traced its origin to an earlier story in which the wolf, after running down a deer, gave a call to signal others of his success. "This was to invite everyone to come and eat of his meat, crows, coyotes, etc." (Hill, 1938: 109). It is interesting to note that among Chiricahua Apaches, who had their own "wolfway" of hunting, howling was also used to communicate after a kill was made (Opler: 320). In addition, both Navajo and Chiricahua warriors used the howl of the wolf to communicate with each other in times of war (Hill, 1936: 36; Opler: 347).

In most ways, other than those aspects already discussed, the Wolfway did not differ significantly from other hunting ways. However, one element that deserves mention are the songs associated with this hunting ritual. It is thought that at an earlier time, the Wolfway had a long litany of songs attached to it. Unfortunately, they no longer exist. Nevertheless, the following wolf identification is found in a Stalking Way song and might originally have been a Wolfway song:

He goes out hunting

Big Wolf am I

With black bow he goes out hunting

With tail feathered arrow he goes out hunting

The big male game through its shoulder that I may shoot

Its death it obeys me. (Hill, 1938: 136)

The Wolfway hunt ended as it began, with a purifying sweat. Luckert notes that hunting involves the "dirty business of killing." It was for this reason that the concluding sweat allowed the hunter to cleanse himself of the death—to shed his wolfish identity and transform himself back into a man. With the hunt over and the transformation completed, Blessingway songs were sung to bring closure to it all (Luckert, 1975: 142–146).

The transformation from human to wolf in the Navajo hunter tradition illustrates that the Navajo, like other Native American tribes, recognized that a thin line existed between humanity and the rest of the animal world. The Navajo hunter changing himself into a wolf to acquire the hunting abilities of that animal represents the act of transformation in a positive and beneficial light. There was, however, a darker side of transformation that manifested itself in a far more negative form, that of the skinwalker.

The Wolf and the Skinwalker Tradition

In 1987, I was an administrator at a high school on the Navajo Reservation. One morning our attendance secretary walked into my office to show me the following note from a parent excusing her son for missing school:

To Whom It May Concern;

Please excuse my son Wilson [pseudonym] from being absent on Thursday and Friday, the 6th and 7th. He was very ill and we took him to a medicine man. The medicine man told us that a Skinwalker had witchcrafted him, so we took him to another medicine man so he would be OK.

Mary Yazzie [pseudonym]

This note provides testimony to the Navajos' strong belief in witchcraft and its most popular manifestation: the skinwalker, a human witch who dons the skin of an animal and goes out into the night to wreak havoc, destruction, and even death on its human victims. Clyde Kluckhohn, who has written the definitive study on Navajo witchcraft, notes that skinwalkers take the shape of many animals: bear, mountain lion, fox, owl, or crow, but most commonly a coyote or a wolf (Kluckhohn: 25–28). The Navajo word for *skinwalker* is *yenaldlooshi,* a term that translates to "it walks on all four feet." Kluckhohn states that he found this word, as well as the Navajo word for *wolf,* to be the common colloquial term for *witch* (ibid.: 26). However, Will Tsosie, a Navajo orthodox traditionalist and scholar, states that the word *yenaldlooshi* would be used for any form of were-animal and would not necessarily mean a wolf. If a person said she saw a *yenaldlooshi,* a typical Navajo response, according to Tsosie, might be, "What kind did you see?" (Tsosie). Navajos generally believe that witches are initiated by others of their kind, commonly relatives, in secretive rites usually held in caves. After putting on the skin of one of the aforementioned creatures, these were-animals then set out to do their evil deeds. They are said to frequent cemeteries, where they dig up the dead, sometimes for the purpose of performing sexual acts with the corpses. In addition to necrophilia, skinwalkers engage in incest and cannibalism. Most commonly, the skinwalker climbs on top of a Navajo hogan at night and drops powder made from the ground bones of dead children down the smoke hole. This powder causes its victims misfortune, illness, and death.

The Navajos continue to pass down the skinwalker tradition through the generations by way of the oral tradition (see Brady). When I taught on the reservation, all of my students knew skinwalker stories, and many professed to have seen the creatures themselves. It is also a phenomenon that is well known to the general public, in large part due to popular fiction writers, and especially the late Tony Hillerman, who wrote a best-selling murder mystery entitled *Skinwalker*. Unfortunately, some environmental writers have also chosen to write of wolves and skinwalkers and have singled out the relationship of wolves to the *yenaldlooshi* and witchcraft as their primary focus regarding the role of the wolf in Navajo culture. Two such examples deserve mention.

In his classic work *Of Wolves and Men*, Barry H. Lopez dedicated three chapters to documenting the close, special, and often sacred relationship that existed between Native Americans and the wolf. The Nunamiut, Naskapi, Pawnee, Cheyenne, Hidatsa, Nuxalk, Sioux, Arapaho, Cherokee, Nez Perce, Arikara, Crow, Ahtna, Kwakiutl, Blackfoot, Nuu-chah-nulth, Quillayute, and

Makah are all tribes Lopez discusses or mentions for their positive attitude toward the wolf. Only the Navajos are specifically singled out as exceptions. Lopez writes: "Other tribes, notably the Navajo, feared wolves as human witches in wolves' clothing. The Navajo word for wolf, *Mai-coh,* is a synonym for witch" (Lopez: 123).

Another writer, Robert H. Busch, in his otherwise excellent *The Wolf Almanac,* states: "Almost unique in North American Indian wolf mythology is the Navajo werewolf myth. The Navajo word for wolf, *mai-coh*, means witch" (Busch: 99).[3]

Both the Lopez and Busch books are important contributions to the literature on wolves and are especially welcome due to their inclusion of Native American wolf beliefs. These two books, along with L. David Mech's *The Wolf: The Ecology and Behavior of an Endangered Species*, are probably the most popular and widely read works on wolves. It is unfortunate that the information they provide on the Navajo-wolf relationship is so scant and misleading. Moreover, the distinction they give for *mai-coh*, or more correctly, *ma'iitsho*, is inaccurate and also misleading.

The Navajo name for coyote is *ma'ii,* and the wolf is called *ma'iitsoh*, or simply "large coyote." The origin of this word is probably *ma'i*, an Apachean term for "animal." For example, in the Chiricahua Apache language, the word for *coyote* is *mbai* and the wolf is called *mbai'tso*. That this Athabascan or Apachean term extends to all animals can be seen in the Chiricahua word for *lizard*, *mba'ishoi* (Luckert, 1975: 7). None of these words in themselves have anything to do with witches.

Aileen O'Bryan states that in one version of the Navajo creation stories, First Man and First Woman named the Wolf *ma'iitsoh* (O'Bryan: 33–34). According to this version, Wolf had stolen something and, although a chief, would from that time be called *ma'iitsoh*, the "big wanderer" because he now had to "travel far and wide over the face of the earth." O'Bryan offers no explanation as to the exact origin of the term but, again, no inference is made about werewolves or witchcraft.

The verbal concept of the wolf as Big Trotter comes from the mythical name for Wolf as used in ceremonies: *naatl'eetsoh*. For this reason *naatl'eetsoh* is usually considered the ceremonial or sacred name for the wolf. This term brings together the words *nadleeh*, which means "to become or revert to," and *tl'eeh*, which translates to "trots." *Naatl'eetsoh* thus translates to "big one who becomes a trotter," "big one who trots," or simply "big trotter" (Franciscan Fathers: 140–141, 175). Again, there is no inference of werewolves or witchcraft in the term.

Interestingly, Gladys A. Reichard, in her classic study *Navaho Religion: A Study in Symbolism*, does make such a connection. In describing the ceremonial use of words, she writes:

> The special terms of one chant may differ from those of another; all are not necessarily understood by every singer. In one chant the names of characters may be in lay terms; in another, they may be completely or partly changed. For instance, the ordinary name for "wolf" is a "large coyote," but ceremonially he may be called "large-one-who-trots-like-a-person," doubtless a reference to the werewolf [my emphasis]. (Reichard, 1950: 268)

I have seen no other reference to wolves being ceremonially referred to as "large-one-who-trots-*like-a-person*." I have heard Will Tsosie refer to wolves as being "the ones who trot people." Perhaps Reichard heard something similar and misinterpreted it. Perhaps she simply heard what her Quaker background conditioned her to hear. To anyone who has ever seen the long-legged, mile-eating gait of a wolf, the term "trot" comes quickly to mind. I am confident that the Navajo, who were keen observers of the natural world and tended to relate what they witnessed in a highly descriptive manner, were simply describing and naming the wolf as they saw him. In the Navajo language he was *ma'iitsoh,* big coyote. In the Navajo ceremonies he was *naatl'eetsoh*, the big trotting animal-god.

How then did the wolf become associated with witchcraft? What is the origin of the Navajo werewolf tradition? Unfortunately, no scholar has adequately addressed these questions.

The belief in witches and witchcraft is almost universal throughout world cultures and was certainly common among many Indian tribes. In Navajo culture, witchcraft goes back to the earliest times. The most commonly accepted belief is that Navajo witchcraft traces back to the emergence stories and, specifically, to First Man and First Woman (Kluckhohn: 25). Another view is that witchcraft originated with Coyote (O'Bryan: 3). The association between Coyote and witchcraft might also explain what I believe to be the much later association of the wolf with witchcraft. Wolf and Coyote were traditionally viewed as being two very different deities, especially in regard to their character and the way they used their powers. This diametric view of Wolf and Coyote carried over to their animal counterparts. However, this distinction became blurred in later times when Navajo life turned toward livestock and farming and away from hunting and its traditions. As a consequence of this move, the wolf came under attack, both physically and in thought. In time, almost all traditional knowledge of the animal was lost. At that point, the wolf, now extinct in Navajo Country, was remembered and viewed simply as the "big coyote."

The Athabascans who entered the Southwest undoubtedly brought with them their own set of witchcraft beliefs. Moreover, as hunters who ritually transformed themselves into predators, they knew that a fine line existed between humanity and the rest of the natural animal world. It is exactly for this reason—namely, that this fine line needed to be maintained—that I believe the Navajo concept of were-animals, and specifically werewolves, does not trace its origin to the Athabascan hunter tradition. Evidence for this view can be seen in that other Southern Athabascans, various Apache tribes, possess strong beliefs in witchcraft but have no werewolf tradition. For example, the Western Apaches, who are closest to the Navajo in terms of shared traits, including similarities in witchcraft beliefs, have no werewolf tradition (Basso: 34).

Luckert believes that what he calls the "defamation" of the divine predators, such as Wolf, began when the Athabascan hunting culture came into contact and subsequent conflict with the agricultural-based

Pueblos. Luckert notes that "all hunter gods eventually suffer defamation if their human protégés cease to be hunters and if they learn to answer to different types of gods" (Luckert, 1979: 10). After the Athabascan-Pueblo merger, and the subsequent transformation into the people we now know as the Navajo, a new worldview emerged. An accompanying religious and ceremonial system, one that was more a product of an agricultural rather than hunting way of life, emerged. I do not believe, however, that this alone explains the defamation of certain Navajo animal gods, especially the wolf. Nor does it explain the association of the wolf to witchcraft. The Pueblos, like most tribes, tend to view animals rather favorably. Wolf, in particular, played an important and positive role in many Pueblo stories. He was the Beast God of the East, playing the roles of warrior, guardian, and healer. Most Pueblos also had hunting societies whose members drew their powers through association with the wolf (Tyler: 154–175; Parsons, 1939: 187). Since hunting societies remained strong well into the 1900s, it can be assumed that the Pueblos with whom the Navajo made contact three and four centuries earlier had little direct influence in the defaming of the divine predators of the Athabascans. Indeed, the knowledge of the Pueblo hunters may have enriched, at least initially, the stories and rituals associated with the Navajo hunter tradition.

Pueblo mythology contains many witch-related stories. Animal transformation—which may or may not be associated with witchcraft—usually involves Coyote and is a central theme in many of the tribal stories. It is interesting to note that among some Pueblo groups, witchcraft is believed to have begun with Coyote, which is similar to a version of Navajo witchcraft origin mentioned earlier. For example, in one Tewa tale, Coyote married Yellow Corn Girl and taught her how to transform herself into a wolf by jumping through a hoop. Before this mythical event took place, the Tewa say that there were no witches (Parsons, 1927: 1226–1227). Other Pueblo stories credit witches with transforming into animals and prowling cemeteries to rob graves of their possessions and corpses (Parsons, 1939: 106, 136). This concept is very similar to Navajo skinwalker beliefs.

In summary, it seems highly probable that the Navajo skinwalker tradition came, at least in part, from Pueblo origins. But what about wolf defamation? The most likely source for this seems to be the elements of Christianity that were passed down from the Pueblos to the Navajo.

Parsons states that while the precontact Pueblos undoubtedly possessed their own "black magic," such traditional Native beliefs and practices, including wearing animal skins and taking on powers associated with these animals, were certainly "enriched by Spanish witchcraft theory" (Parsons, 1939: 128). Spanish witchcraft beliefs, founded on the Christian tradition, included animal transformation. Moreover, Christianity, in contrast to Native American religious traditions, has long associated particular animals (snakes, bats, owls, lions, and wolves) with evil. Schaafsma reports finding Spanish crosses carved on boulders in the West Mesa area north of Albuquerque, New Mexico, in association with Tewa rock art images of mountain lions and snakes (Schaafsma: 149). This, along with written doc-umentation, reveals a Spanish attempt to exorcise, or at least neutralize, what they perceived to be demonic symbols. Without doubt the Spanish transferred their fear (and defamation) of certain animals to the Pueblos. This attitude might have then been passed from the Pueblos to the Navajos.

Will Tsosie sees a later, more direct, connection between Christianity and Navajo beliefs toward animals like the wolf. Since the Navajo wore animal skins as hunting disguises and for personal adornment well into the twentieth century with no apparent negative associ-ations, he believes it is more likely that wolf defamation and the skinwalker tradition is a twentieth-century re-sponse to Christian missionary activity among his peo-ple (Tsosie). Elsewhere I have written about the history, development, and impact of Christianity on the Navajo people (Pavlik, 1997). Without question, much of the early missionary efforts were made by various Protes-tant denominations that sought to discredit, condemn, and suppress traditional culture and religion. In doing so, they also contributed to the defaming of animals like the wolf. Moreover, the new Christian-influenced traditionalism that has emerged, and the contempo-rary lifestyle of most Navajos, is far removed from the knowledge and values promoted by the emergence stories and by the Navajo hunter tradition.

The Future of Wolves in Navajo Country

A 1908 survey conducted in the Chuska Mountains of the Navajo Reservation noted that "wolf tracks were

found common in the trails over the tops of the mountains where most of the cattle and great numbers of
Navajo sheep ranged during the summer. They were
evidently thriving here unmolested by the Indians and
with an abundance of food" (Bailey: 310). However,
this situation soon changed as efforts were made to
exterminate predators on tribal lands. It is difficult to
document this event because most written records
have been lost to time. The pattern, however, seems to
generally follow what had been taking place throughout the American West. Market hunting, carried out to
satisfy the needs of border towns along the Santa Fe
Railroad, reduced the deer population to less than one
hundred on the entire reservation. With the deer gone,
predators were forced to kill and eat Navajo livestock,
especially sheep. As both the human and livestock populations grew, conflicts with predators increased. Predators became a perceived threat to Navajo livelihood.
It was a threat that had to be eliminated. Professional
hunters from PARC, with the support of the Navajo
tribe, initiated a serious predator control program on
the reservation. This soon resulted in the extermination of wolves and grizzly bears. Black bears, mountain
lions, and coyotes were also hunted relentlessly.

The purposeful destruction of predators was not
without its price. The coyote was hunted because of its
predatory raids against sheep and because of its association with witchcraft. Luckert noted that so many
coyotes were killed in the Black Mesa area in the 1940s
that an epidemic of "coyote illness" broke out in the
area, a problem serious enough to create an increased
demand for medicine men to perform the Coyoteway

healing ceremony. Luckert's Navajo consultant explained the situation:

> When a Coyote person is shot and left to die, his last spasms and twitchings, as they suddenly cease in the animal person, leap onto the killer. This happens most easily if somehow in the process of killing the hunter has eye contact with his victim—Coyote continues to recognize and to haunt the offender. But this can also happen through physical contact with the dead animal's body or even with the decayed remains of a Coyote person. And in this regard no shepherd who strolls through the sagebrush pastures can be sure of his personal immunity. Killing a Coyote person means offending him. The symptoms of the animal's suffering which are thrown onto the offender continue as a sort of a nervous malfunction, as a shaking of the head, hands, or of the entire body. (Luckert, 1979: 8–9)

Coyote sickness and wolf sickness (the two are actually the same) can be remedied through the same Coyoteway ceremony. This illness is not caused by the animal but by the transgressions of man, when man shows disrespect toward one of the Animal People. In a sense, it is an example of defamation coming full cycle back to the offender.

In Navajo traditional thought, no animal is inherently good or bad. Like man, the other beings with which we share the Earth—including the wolf—generally go about their lives in a manner ordained by the Creator and other Holy People. Over time, however, and for whatever reasons, Navajo attitudes toward the natural world and particularly toward some animals have changed. Once the howl of a wolf or the call of an owl was interpreted as a message from a more powerful but benevolent being. With the loss of knowledge and change in attitude, these same howls and calls came to be interpreted as omens of evil, sounds to be feared.

The howl of wolves can still be heard echoing in the red rock canyons of Navajo Country. The source of this sound, however, is not the beautiful Chuska or Luka-chukai mountains, but the confines of the Navajo Nation Zoological Park in Window Rock. For the past ten years, the tribal zoo has been home to Mexican wolves, the most endangered of the gray wolf species. These animals are the descendants of two of the last wild Mexican wolves known to have existed in the Southwest: a male live-trapped near Tumacacori, Arizona, in 1959 and a female captured in Sonora, Mexico, two years later. Together this breeding pair served as the nucleus of what is known as the Ghost Ranch lineage. Initially, some questions existed regarding the genetic purity of this bloodline (Steinhart: 202–206, 209–210). However, subsequent DNA testing verified the bloodline's status, and today the Ghost Ranch descendants are one of only three DNA-certified genetically pure lines of Mexican wolves in existence. In all, there are only about 180 Mexican wolves on earth. With the exception of the animals that have been reintroduced in the White Mountains, there are no other Mexican wolves left in the wild, either in Mexico or the United States.

The Navajo Nation Zoological Park is one of only thirty zoological parks in the world that has Mexican wolves. More importantly, it is one of only a handful of zoos approved as a breeding facility for the reintroduction program. Over the years, the Navajo Nation zoo, like other zoos throughout the world, has been criticized for keeping wild animals locked in cages. Some tribal members have expressed their concern that zoos are not consistent with Navajo cultural values. On December 26, 1998, two Navajo deities, or Holy People, reportedly visited a family in the remote community of Rocky Ridge. Included in their message to the Navajo people was a denouncement of the imprisonment of sacred animals in the zoo. Some tribal officials called for the immediate release of all zoo animals back into the wild. Zoo supporters countered that to do so would mean certain death for the animals. In the end, Navajo Nation president Kelsey Begaye, in part due to the large number of letters sent to him by Navajo children, elected to keep the facility open (Donovan, 1999a, 1999b; Robbins. See also Pavlik, 2000b, 2000c).

It is not a purpose of this book to debate the merits or cultural appropriateness of zoos. However, it is clear that the future of the Mexican wolf lies in the hands of captive breeding populations like those held at the Navajo Nation Zoological Park. For this reason, I hope that the Navajo tribal government and its people support the efforts under way to restore the Mexican wolf to its historic Southwest habitat. Wolf has long been an integral and positive part of Navajo tradition and life. The Navajo are poorer without him. While the day will probably never come when wolves can again roam freely through the Navajo mountains, it is important that their spiritual presence and powers remain for the Navajo people to draw upon.

Will Tsosie best summarized the importance of the wolf to the Navajo, and indeed to all of us, when he stated to me:

Wolves are the most misunderstood creature in the Navajo world. People fear what they do not know. It is sad to think that we have the capability to destroy an entire species of fellow beings—the "ones who trot people." We, as humans, are perhaps not that far behind. Maybe this is a prelude of what is to come. Maybe we are orchestrating our own demise. (Tsosie)

The foundation of Navajo culture has been the maintenance of harmony with all life. But the Navajos' harmony with the wolf has been destroyed. Support of the Mexican wolf program provides the Navajo people with an opportunity to correct the defamation of the past and, in doing so, restore the harmony that once existed. Only when this is done will Big Trotter reclaim his rightful place in the minds and the hearts of the Navajo people.

Notes

1. Originally there were twenty-four recognized subspecies of the gray wolf, *Canis lupus*, inhabiting North America. The subspecies that once inhabited what is today the Navajo Reservation, *C. l. youngi,* is now extinct. Considering the historic range of the early Navajo people, tribal members undoubtedly encountered at least two other subspecies, *C. l. mogollonensis*—also extinct—and *C. l. baileyi,* the Mexican wolf, which is the focus of much of this chapter.

2. Three Apache tribes, the White Mountain, San Carlos, and Mescalero, also officially opposed reintroduction of the Mexican wolf. For additional information on the Mexican Wolf Reintroduction Program and Apache attitudes toward wolves and the reintroduction program, see Steve Pavlik, "San Carlos and White Mountain Apache Attitudes toward the Reintroduction of the Wolf to Its Historic Range in the American Southwest," *Wicazo Sa Review*, 14(1): 129–145.

3. The language used by Lopez and Busch is strikingly similar in content and wording. It is interesting, however, that in Lopez's book *mai-coh* is a synonym for wolf, whereas in Busch's publication *mai-coh* is said to mean wolf, especially since it appears from his bibliography that Busch's source for his Navajo werewolf comment must be Lopez. In turn, Lopez cites two sources for his Navajo werewolf information: William Morgan's anthropological publication *Human Wolves among the Navajo* (1936)—perhaps the single most important though largely anecdotal work on the subject—and a special edition of *El Palacio* (1974) dealing with Southwest witchcraft that includes an uncredited article on Navajo witchcraft. However, neither of these sources use the term *mai-coh* for wolf. This word seems to be first used by Kluckhohn (1944) in his *Navaho Witchcraft*. I can only assume that Lopez also used this work but did not include it in his bibliography.

References

Bailey, Vernon. 1931. *Mammals of New Mexico.* Washington, DC: US Department of Agriculture, Bureau of Biological Survey.

Bass, Rick. 1998. *The New Wolves: The Return of the Mexican Wolf to the American Southwest*. New York: The Lyons Press.

Basso, Keith. 1969. *Western Apache Witchcraft.* Tucson: University of Arizona Anthropological Papers, No. 15.

Brady, Margaret K. 1984. *Some Kind of Power: Navajo Children's Skinwalker Narratives*. Salt Lake City: University of Utah Press.

Brown, David E., ed. 1983. *The Wolf in the Southwest: The Making of an Endangered Species.* Tucson: University of Arizona Press.

Burbank, James C. 1990. *Vanishing Lobo: The Mexican Wolf and the Southwest*. Boulder, CO: Johnson Publishing Company.

Busch, Robert H. 1995. *The Wolf Almanac*. New York: The Lyons Press.

Donovan, Bill. 1999a. "Navajos May Close Zoo," *Arizona Republic*. January 8.

Donovan, Bill. 1999b. "Navajos Weigh Options to Keep Tribal Zoo Open," *Arizona Republic*. February 1.

Elmore, Francis H. 1953. "The Deer and His Importance to the Navajo," *El Palacio,* 60: 371–384.

Franciscan Fathers. 1910. *An Ethnologic Dictionary of the Navajo Language*. St. Michaels, AZ: St. Michaels Press.

Haile, Father Berard. 1943. *Origin Legend of the Navaho Flintway*. Chicago: University of Chicago Press.

Haile, Father Berard. 1981. *The Upward Moving and Emergence Way*. Lincoln: University of Nebraska Press.

Hill, Willard W. 1936. Navaho Warfare. New Haven, CT: Yale University Publications in Anthropology, No. 5.

Hill, Willard W. 1938. *The Agricultural and Hunting Methods of the Navaho Indians*. New Haven, CT: Yale University Publications in Anthropology, No. 18.

Hillerman, Tony. 1986. *Skinwalkers*. New York: Harper & Row.

Kluckhohn, Clyde. 1944. *Navaho Witchcraft*. Boston: Beacon Press.

Leopold, Aldo. 1949. *A Sand County Almanac*. New York: Oxford University Press.

Lopez, Barry H. 1978. *Of Wolves and Men*. New York: Charles Scribner's Sons.

Luckert, Karl W. 1975. *The Navajo Hunter Tradition*. Tucson: University of Arizona Press.

Luckert, Karl W. 1978. *A Navajo Bringing Home Ceremony: The Claus Chee Sonny Version of the Deerway Ajilee*. Flagstaff: Northern Arizona University Press.

Luckert, Karl W. 1979. *Coyoteway: A Navajo Holyway Healing Ceremonial*. Tucson: University of Arizona Press.

Lynch, Tom, ed. 2005. *El Lobo: Readings on the Mexican Wolf*. Salt Lake City: University of Utah Press.

Matthews, Washington. 1887/1994. *Navaho Legends*. Salt Lake City: University of Utah Press.

Mech, L. David. 1970. *The Wolf: The Ecology and Behavior of an Endangered Species*. Minneapolis: University of Minnesota Press.

Morgan, William. 1936. *Human-Wolves among the Navajo*. New Haven, CT: Yale University Publications in Anthropology, No. 11.

Murray, John A., ed. 1993. *Out among the Wolves: Contemporary Writings on the Wolf*. Anchorage: Alaska Northwest Books.

O'Bryan, Aileen. 1956. *The Diné: Origin Myths of the Navaho Indians*. Washington, DC: Bureau of American Ethnology Bulletin No. 163.

Opler, Morris E. 1941. *An Apache Life-Way: The Economic, Social, and Religious Institutions of the Chiricahua Indians*. Chicago: University of Chicago Press.

Parsons, Elsie Clews. 1927. "Witchcraft among the Pueblos: Indian or Spanish?" *Man*, 27: 106–112.

Parsons, Elsie Clews. 1939. *Pueblo Indian Religion, Volume I*. Lincoln: University of Nebraska Press.

Pavlik, Steve. 1997. "Navajo Christianity: Historical Origins and Modern Trends," *Wicazo Sa Review,* 12(2): 43–58.

Pavlik, Steve. 1998. "The Role of Christianity and Church in Contemporary Navajo Society," in *A Good Cherokee, A Good Anthropologist: Papers in Honor of Robert K. Thomas,* edited by Steve Pavlik. Los Angeles: UCLA American Indian Studies Center: 189–200.

Pavlik, Steve. 1999. "San Carlos and White Mountain Apache Attitudes toward the Reintroduction of the Mexican Wolf to Its Historic Range in the Southwest," *Wicazo Sa Review*, 14(1): 129–145.

Pavlik, Steve. 2000a. "Will Big Trotter Reclaim His Place? The Role of the Wolf in Navajo Tradition," *American Indian Culture and Research Journal*, 24(4): 107–125.

Pavlik, Steve. 2000b. "The Navajo Nation Zoological Park Controversy: Cultural Implications for Wildlife Rehabilitators," in *22nd Annual International Wildlife Rehabilitation Council Conference Proceedings*, edited by Mary D. Reynolds. Suisun City, CA: 160–168.

Pavlik, Steve. 2000c. "It's All Happening at the (Navajo) Zoo: Divine Visitations, Sacred Animals, and Tribal Politics," Paper presented at the 42nd Western Social Science Association Conference, San Diego, California, April 28.

Reichard, Gladys A. 1939/1977. *Navajo Medicine Man Sandpaintings*. New York: Dover Publications.

Reichard, Gladys A. 1950. *Navaho Religion: A Study in Symbolism*. New York: Bollingen Foundation.

Robbins, Catherine. 1999. "Tradition Clashes with Some Needs to Endanger Zoo," *Gallup Independent*. March 30: 2.

Robinson, Michael J. 2005. *Predatory Bureaucracy: The Extermination of Wolves and the Transformation of the West*. Boulder: University Press of Colorado.

Schaafsma, Polly. 1992. *Rock Art in New Mexico*. Santa Fe: Museum of New Mexico Press.

Steinhart, Peter. 1995. *The Company of Wolves*. New York: Alfred A. Knopf.

Tsosie, Will. 1999. Personal conversation. July 30; September 26.

Tyler, Hamilton. 1975. *Pueblo Animals and Myths*. Norman: University of Oklahoma Press.

 # Chapter Three

The Defamation of Slim Trotter

This chapter was originally presented as a paper at the Western Social Science Association Conference held in Albuquerque, New Mexico, April 10–13, 2002.

Without question, Coyote is the most enigmatic, controversial, mystifying, and versatile figure in the Navajo stories. On one hand he is a hero, creator, warrior, hunter, provider, teacher, healer, lover, and most sacred of the Holy People. On the other hand he is a villain, destroyer, coward, beggar, thief, trickster, buffoon, seducer, and the worst of characters. In other words, he is much like you and me. His earthly counterpart, the coyote, shares many of these traits. Coyote the God and coyote the animal are bundles of contradictions that have long fascinated mankind, including the Navajos.

The coyote, *Canis latrans*—the "barking dog"—is found throughout Navajo Country. It is numerous and widespread in its distribution across the landscape. The word *coyote* is a derived from an Aztec term, *coyotl.* Navajos know the coyote as *ma'ii.* The origin of this term comes from the more generic Athabaskan word *mai'*, which means "animal." The coyote is also quite commonly called Slim or Little Trotter by traditional Navajos, as well as the First Angry or First Scolder, or "the

Roamer." The sacred or ceremonial name for Coyote translates to "the fine young chief howling in the dawn beyond the east."

In the Beginning, There Was Coyote

As one might expect in dealing with a figure as nebulous as Coyote, more than one story exists to account for his beginnings.

In Navajo cosmogony, as related to Father Berard Haile by Gishin Biye' in 1908, there existed twelve underworlds, with the present realm being the thirteenth world. In the first three worlds there existed only Insect People. It is the Fourth World to which the Navajos traced their origin. This world was inhabited by First Man and First Woman, a second First Man and First Woman, First Made and Second Made, First Boy and First Girl, and First Scolder or Coyote. Thus, in this version Coyote was there at the very beginning of Navajo existence as one of the first Holy People (Haile, 1981: 5–6).

In another version of the origin story (this one provided to Aileen O'Bryan by Sandoval), First Man, First Woman, and "Great Coyote Who Was Formed in the Water" were the initial beings present in the First World. This Coyote, who was a male, said that he had been "hatched from an egg" and that he "knew all that was under water and all that was in the skies. Soon they were joined by another being that "had the form of a man, but he wore a hairy coat, lined with white fur, that fell to his knees and was belted at the waist." This being identified himself as *Atse'hashke'*, First Angry or Coyote.

He said to the three: "You believe that you were the first persons. You are mistaken. I was living when you were formed" (O'Bryan: 3).

This is also the version that Will Tsosie was taught, though he said he knew nothing of the "Underwater Coyote" coming from an egg. Will stated that this Coyote was the ancestor of all earthbound coyotes, while the second Coyote, First Angry, which Will referred to as being "Forever Coyote," went on to live in the realm of the Holy People. He went on to state that each of these Coyotes transformed into two additional Coyotes, then again into four, then again into eight, and finally into sixteen Coyotes each, for a total of the thirty-two different Coyotes that he says appear throughout the Navajo stories. I must admit, as I listened to Will's explanation of the ancestry of each Coyote and the relationship that each had to the others, I felt a little like Lou Costello trying to grasp Abbott's account of "Who's on First?" (Tsosie, 2001).

Another version of the origin of the earthbound coyote, this one told to Washington Matthews, also deserves mention. According to this account, one day in the Fourth World, the sky stooped down and the Earth rose to meet it. For a moment the two bodies came in contact, at which time from the Earth sprang the first Coyote and Badger. Coyote rose first and for this reason is said to be the "elder brother" of the badger. While Coyote "skulked among the people," Badger entered into a hole in the ground at the Place of Emergence that led to the lower world. Since that time both the coyote and the badger are said to be "children of the sky" (Matthews: 71).

Whatever Coyote's origin might be, his role in early Navajo mythology is primarily that of a companion and servant to First Man. Often he goes out on journeys on behalf of First Man to see and hear things that he then reports back on. It is for this reason that some Navajos call the coyote God's Dog. At other times he acts on his own as a free agent. From the beginning he is bold and inquisitive. Others resent him for this quality, but it is obvious that First Man relies on him for information and perhaps advice. As the people enter each new world during the emergence myth, Coyote is the first to investigate and report back.

In the first ceremonial hogan created by First Man, Coyote situated himself at the doorway to the East and was the first to address those assembled (Haile, 1981: 21).

Early in the emergence myth, Coyote demonstrated his stubbornness and power. He became angry because the people were calling him roamer and scolder, so just as the people were preparing to move to the next world, he tied down the light in the four directions so that all was dark. Only after he was given sacrifices of white bead, turquoise, abalone, and red-white stone did he untie the light and make the world holy again (ibid.: 27).

When First Man called a meeting and displayed various precious stones for the purpose of creating the Sun, Moon, Dawn, Earth, Sky, Twilight, Darkness, the sacred mountains, and the genitalia of men and women, only Coyote knew what each stone was for. Not surprisingly, he obnoxiously flaunted this knowledge before the others who had gathered (ibid.: 36–37).

At this same meeting it was Coyote who said that the same people should not always inhabit the Earth, that there should be birth. First Man agreed and began the process of procreation (ibid.: 38).

With birth came other Coyotes, including Coyote-from-the-folded-dawn. It was this Coyote who first sang the four songs that were the beginning of the Male Shooting Chant (ibid.: 85).

Coyote's most important underworld exploit, however, came with his theft of Water Monster's baby and the resulting flood that forced the people into the present world. For many days, the people had heard the cry of a mysterious baby coming from the river. Coyote, of course, went to investigate. Looking into the river, he saw a baby, which he took out and hid under his arm, near his heart. In time he rolled the baby into a small ball and kept it hidden under his arm. The baby belonged to Water Monster, who, in her anger, caused the river to rise. Days went by, and the river continued to rise. The people became frightened at the rising water. First Man created mountains for the people to climb to safety, but the water continued to rise. Then the Gourd Children planted a reed for the people to climb, but still the water continued to rise. The people began to search for a cause of their troubles. Only Coyote seemed indifferent to their plight, so they knew that somehow he was to blame. The people confronted Coyote, who at first pled his innocence. Thereafter, thieves always protest their innocence. At this point the people had climbed their eighth joint of reed with the water still rising. There they encountered a hard, glossy roof that they attempted to claw through. Again the people accused Coyote, and this time they searched his body, eventually finding the small ball that was Water Monster's baby. First Man took the baby and, with jewels as an offering, placed the baby back into the water. Immediately the water ceased its rise.

The people then continued their effort to break through the roof. Eventually they were successful and were able to enter into the present-day world (ibid.: 112–122).

Coyote continued his important role as creator, though often inadvertently, in the new world. Black God assumed the responsibility of placing the various stars in their heavenly positions. In this manner his created the Big Snake and Bear constellations, as well as Ursa Major, Canis Major, Cassiopeia, and Orion to name a few. He also created the Milky Way. At this point he stopped to rest. Coyote snatched his star bag and blew its contents across the sky. Consequently, there are many stars without names. One star was left in the star bag. This one Coyote took out and placed in the southern skies. "This will be my star," he proclaimed. Thereafter it was known as the "No-month" or "Coyote's Star" (ibid.: 128–129).

Coyote is also credited with being the deity who decided the nature of birth as well as that mankind should experience death. In doing so, Coyote proclaimed:

It can not remain always the same. Some will die, some too should come to life. There should be births. As there is time for plants and animals to die and revive, so should it be

with men and women. . . . Let them give birth and increase!
If there be no births, you must continuously create things
again. Let humans get old, let them die. But let women also
beget children. (Ibid.: 132)

Coyote then from his own body furnished the pubic hairs for both man and woman.

The question of Coyote's name also came up again in the new world. First Man determined that Coyote should be called *ma'ii*, the Roamer. But Coyote protested, saying that he was not a roamer. First Man then said that he should be called First Scolder. But again Coyote protested, saying that he never got angry. Finally First Man said that he would be called White-coyote-howling-in-the-dawn. Coyote was pleased with this name, although he continued to also be known by the two names he rejected (ibid.: 133).

In addition to his role in the Navajo stories, Coyote is the focal character of a second, entirely separate, body of oral tradition, the Coyote Stories.

Coyote Stories are designed to stand alone. They are not really part of the creation stories, nor are they necessarily related to any other story. They are stories told and retold by the older generation to the younger generation during the winter, usually at night around a camp or hogan fire. The stories center around the humorous misadventures of Trotting Coyote, a mythological character who always falls short of his ambitions and expectations. In these stories, Trotting Coyote attempts to cheat, trick, or destroy his fellow Animal People. In the end, however, his intentions are reversed and it is he who pays the price. While these stories are meant to be an entertaining diversion on long, cold winter nights, they also serve a more serious purpose, that of perpetuating tribal norms and values. They are a teaching tool for the purpose of instructing children as to the finer points of being a good Navajo.

The exact origins of the Coyote Stories remain somewhat clouded. Will Tsosie believes that they date back to a time that precedes the origin stories. He bases his belief on the fact that the vast majority of these stories involve Coyote's dealings with other Animal People rather than with humans (Tsosie, 2001). If Tsosie is correct, and I believe that he is, then in all likelihood these stories go back to the Athabaskan hunters and quite possibly began as Raven Stories rather than Coyote Stories. Northern Athabaskans still tell Raven Stories, and many of these are similar to the Navajo Coyote Stories. When the Southern Athabaskans arrived in the Southwest, Coyote, in time, came to replace Raven as the main namesake character of these stories. Further evidence to support Tsosie's theory is found in the fact that there is a close correlation between Navajo Coyote Stories and those told by other Southern Athabaskan tribes such as the Jicarilla, Lipan, White Mountain, and Chiricahua Apaches. Indeed, the stories are often nearly identical (see Hill and Hill). On the other hand, little correspondence exists between the Southern Athabaskan Coyote Stories and those of the Hopi (see Malotki and Lomatuway'ma).

Whatever their origin, it is the Coyote Stories that give rise to Coyote's reputation as the Navajo "trickster."

These stories have been published in a number of other volumes that are readily accessible to the interested reader (see Roessel and Platero; see also Haile, 1984).

Coyote the Hunter

Not long ago, I was hiking with my good friend Tony Salandro in the White Mountains of eastern Arizona. The trail we were hiking would take us to the 11,420-foot peak known as Mount Baldy, a most sacred place for the White Mountain Apaches. We had gone only about a mile when the trail entered a long, narrow meadow. With Mount Baldy itself easily seen in front of us, it was a peaceful and beautiful piece of country.

Suddenly the peace was shattered by a strange sound, a loud plaintive "eeeh" made at intervals of several seconds. Moreover, the sound was getting louder, coming closer. To our left was a small stream that ran parallel to the trail, and at first I thought the sound was the scream of an osprey or some other bird of prey. Then in front of us, perhaps two hundred yards away, I saw the source of the sound, an elk calf, coming toward us and literally running for its life. It was a big calf, perhaps two hundred pounds, but still showing the spots that marked it as a yearling. Soon the cause of its flight also came into view: a pair of coyotes in close pursuit. They were perhaps one hundred feet behind the calf. Their pace was measured and deliberate—the pace of hunters who were merely waiting for their prey to tire before coming in to make the final kill. The terrified elk calf passed by us no more than five feet away, all the time continuing its pitiful cry. I could have reached out and touched it. I was certainly close enough to look into its eyes and see what I can only describe as a look of sheer terror, the look of a creature facing an imminent and horrific death. It ran by us, continuing down the canyon. Meanwhile, the coyotes slowed down a little as they approached us. I heard my voice utter a feeble "Hey!" as they neared us—a single word that I regretted the moment it left my lips. The coyotes swerved and circled around us, undoubtedly to resume their pursuit farther down the canyon. I had probably succeeded only in buying the elk calf a little more time, a postponement of the inevitable. The calf, cut out from the herd and separated from the protection of its mother, was doomed. Most certainly it would die later that day, or perhaps that evening. I thought about my role in the drama. Why had I intervened? Why had I interfered in the natural order of things? The coyotes were undoubtedly a pair. Quite possibly they had a litter of pups hidden away in a den somewhere. If so, these pups had as much right to life as did the elk calf. In order for one to live, another has to die. I knew that, yet I had acted emotionally, not rationally. Moreover, I knew that if a similar circumstance ever again presented itself, I would probably respond in the same way.

Predators illicit powerful feelings from deep within us. On the one hand we are drawn to their power and beauty. On the other hand we are repulsed by what we perceive to be their savagery. Only now are we beginning to understand and appreciate the great dance of life and death that exists between predator and prey. Native people, however, have long understood it. Native people universally admired the great carnivores. They saw in these animals the traits that they themselves hoped to possess: leadership, courage, and wisdom. They associated with and emulated these animal hunters. They elevated them to positions of hunter and warrior gods, and sought to draw power from them. And while they appreciated and gave credit to the hunted, it was to the predator that the early Native people felt the closest kinship to. The Navajos were no exception.

The Athabaskan hunters who migrated into the Southwest probably had little or no knowledge of the coyote. These people, however, possessed a long familiarity with the coyote's larger cousin, the wolf. One can only guess that when the first of these Apachean hunters laid eyes on his first coyote, he probably wasn't too impressed. Wolves are large impressive carnivores that eat large impressive herbivores, animals like musk ox, moose, caribou, elk, and deer. Coyotes are scarcely half the size and generally (the young elk I had seen being something of an exception) feed mostly on small lagomorphs and rodents, animals like hares, rabbits, rats, mice, and the like, not to mention a large assortment of fruits, nuts, berries, and grasses. And yes, coyotes spend much of their time scavenging for carrion.

In the Navajo hunter tradition there exists a pantheon of animal hunting gods: Wolf, Mountain Lion, Spotted Lion, Wildcat, and Big Snake. These are the "divine" or "master" predators, the ones who themselves were taught how to hunt by the Deer People and who in turn taught the Navajos how to hunt. Of these predator deities, Wolf, Mountain Lion, and Big Snake possess special ways of hunting that have been taught to mankind.

Coyote is notably absent from the list of hunting gods. But while he may be absent, he is not forgotten. Instead he finds his way into the hunting tradition as a braggart and an impostor. At one point, he busts into a meeting of the hunter gods, proclaiming "I am the master of all game" and telling the hunters "Although you Holy-people are quite numerous, not one of you has any sense." The gods ignore this act of indiscretion. On another occasion, Coyote boasts to the hunting gods, "Do they [the game] come around here when you are hunting? It is to me alone that you should be praying and to me alone that you should be singing." Coyote then proceeds to interfere with the hunt, succeeding only in foolishly chasing the game away, an act for which the other hunters curse him (Luckert, 1975: 105, 115).

Karl W. Luckert notes, "Wherever in Navajo hunter myths Coyote appears, he shows up in an unfavorable light." He suggests that to the early Athabaskan hunters from the north, who were accustomed to the stately wolf, Coyote must have appeared "ridiculous." He adds that upon Coyote, the Athabaskans "heaped scorn, ridicule, and off-color jokes" (ibid.: 170–171). Luckert does, however, hold out some hope that at one time in the distant past Coyote might have been considered a hunting deity. He believes that early Athabaskan hunters might have tried to imitate Coyote's trickery in the hunt. He also notes that in one version of the Coyoteway ceremony, Coyote appears in several sandpaintings that might have been part of a lost hunting rite (Luckert, 1979: 10, 230–233). Still, the evidence that he offers is less than compelling.

So, in the Navajo hunter tradition, Coyote is left out in the cold as a hunter, but still he at least *appears* in the hunter stories, whereas other predatory animals, such as the foxes and the weasels, do not seem to have any association with the hunt. How did this come to be? And what exactly is the nature of Coyote in the hunting stories?

In all probability, the Athabaskan hunters did not encounter Coyote until they arrived in the Southwest. To these people, Wolf was the dominant hunting god, and so he remains until this day, with other hunting deities, most notably Mountain Lion and Big Snake, being added as time went by.

In the meantime, among the Pueblos—many of whom possessed hunting societies and with whom the Athabaskans would merge—Coyote appears to have fared no better. In no Pueblo except for Zuni does Coyote appear among the hunting deities. Although Coyote is an incredibly important figure in Pueblo mythology and life, he is not a hunter. In Zuni, the lone exception to this rule, the hunting society is referred to as the *Suskikwe*, the Coyote people. Zuni also have a coyote kachina that is a hunting kachina (Tyler: 188; Parsons, 1939/1996: 159–183). This lack of respect for Coyote's hunting abilities among the Pueblos, and subsequently the Navajos, is difficult to explain. Obviously Coyote is a hunter, a rather good one in fact. So why isn't he given any credit?

Quite possibly Coyote's reputation as a trickster and buffoon simply overpower whatever other activities he engages in. If this is true, then Coyote in a rather curious way does play an important role in the Navajo hunter tradition, as he does in Navajo life in general. By demonstrating how not to hunt, Coyote reinforces the Navajo hunter tradition. Luckert hints at this when he writes:

> But Coyote is not the real exemplary Navajo trickster who functions on the hunter's side as mediator of game; rather he is a defamed trickster—an incurable villain and bungler. His tricks generally boomerang on him. In this negative sense, surprisingly, Coyote has become the exemplary model of a sort. A hunter without success can find comfort in the fact that since immemorable times Coyote has proven a greater failure than he—and he still roams. (Luckert, 1975: 171)

The Evil Coyote

Let me state at the onset that I do not like to use or even consider the word *evil* when discussing traditional Navajo views toward any animal. To begin with, I am not sure that the Navajos even had a concept of evil until missionaries and anthropologists entered into their world. The dictionary defines evil—the origin of which is the Old English word *yfel*—as being: "Morally reprehensible: sinful, wicked, arising from actual or imputed bad character or conduct" (*Merriam Webster's Collegiate Dictionary,* 1994: 402).

Certainly the Navajos had the concept of good and bad, and more to the point they believed that things could be *very* good and *very* bad, but the term *evil*, at least in my mind, has decidedly *Christian*—or sinful—implication. It is difficult, however, to determine exactly where and how the term *evil* entered into the Navajo vernacular. Did an early "informant," one already familiar with the language of Christianity, first use this word? Or, as I suspect, did an early anthropologist *interpret* one of his or her informants to infer *evil* when he was in fact describing something that was *very bad*? Will Tsosie believes that in all probability early Navajos explained very complex concepts in very simplified language to anthropologists—as one would explain things to a child (Tsosie, 2001). In any event, it is a moot issue. The term is used in every book describing Navajo tradition, and I will share the guilt by continuing to use it here.

The one person most responsible for popularizing the myth of Coyote as an evil being was the anthropologist Gladys A. Reichard. In her classic book *Navaho Religion: A Study in Symbolism*, she associates Coyote with the concept of evil no less than eight times. The following comment is typical of her view toward Coyote:

> *In Coyote many aspects of evil power are embodied—he is active, with unlimited ability to interfere with people's affairs; his potentiality for turning up unexpectedly is enormous. He has a life principle that may be laid aside, so that any injury done to the body affects his life only temporarily and he may even recover from apparent death. He possesses an incredible fund of evil knowledge which man must match and, as he may appear in any form, he is the werewolf of Navaho witchcraft. (Reichard: 105)*

Some of what she states here might very well be true. But I would argue that Coyote's "incredible fund of evil knowledge" is no greater than, say, that of First Man and First Woman. I also believe that Reichard greatly overstates Coyote's role as a "werewolf." My main complaint with her analysis, however, is that she is guilty of presenting only one side of Coyote. She is implying that Coyote is *wholly* a bad or evil being—and nothing could be further from the truth.

Navajos have long recognized that no animal—or person, for that matter—is wholly good or evil. All beings, be they god, Animal Person, or human, possesses both a good and dark side. Consequently, Reichard's analogy flies in the face of one of the basic tenets of Navajo philosophy. Moreover, she makes the same connection of evil to other animals, most notably the snake and wolf. Seldom does she present the good, and often not even the neutral, of these animals. In sum, it seems Reichard—whose own religious background was strongly Quaker—has an obsession with some animals being evil. This is certainly unfortunate in that I believe that many young Navajos who do not have access to traditionally knowledgeable elders read her books (and those of other anthropologists who simply follow her example) and accept what I consider a distorted view of tribal beliefs.

Navajos believe that witches might wear the skins of various animals—including coyotes, wolves, bears, owls, foxes, and crows—to assume the guise of the famous skinwalker (see Kluckhohn: 26). But why is the coyote, more than any other animal, associated with evil? I believe the reason is Coyote's primacy in the Navajo stories. Navajos logically assume that all things have an origin and that the best place for any origin is at the beginning. The First World was inhabited by Insect People, who were evil. Then, in the Second World, there appeared First Man, First Woman, and the two Coyotes, all of whom were also evil and practiced witchcraft. Later beings that appeared in subsequent worlds were not initially evil. Consequently, evil itself begins with the Insect People, First Man and First Woman, and the two Coyotes.

Pueblo mythology contains many witch-related stories. Animal transformations, which may or may not be associated with witchcraft, usually involve Coyote and are central themes in Pueblo stories. It is interesting to note that among some Pueblos (as with the Navajos), witchcraft is believed to have originated with Coyote. For example, in one Tewa tale Coyote married Yellow Corn Girl and taught her how to transform herself into another coyote (or perhaps wolf) by jumping through a hoop. Before this mythical event took place, the Tewa say that there were no witches (Parsons, 1927: 1226–1227). Considering that Athabaskans had no Coyote tradition—only a wolf tradition—prior to their arrival in the Southwest, could the Navajo Coyote-witchcraft origin story be the product of Pueblo tradition? In addition, as I have argued elsewhere, might the Pueblos have taken their own witchcraft beliefs from Christianity? (see Pavlik, 2000: 118–119).

Christianity has a long tradition of viewing certain animals as aligning themselves with the devil and witchcraft. Elsie Clews Parsons states that while the precontact Pueblos undoubtedly possessed their own "black magic," such traditional Native beliefs and practices, including wearing animal skins and taking on powers associated with these animals, were certainly "enriched by Spanish witchcraft theory" (Parsons, 1927:

128). Spanish witchcraft beliefs, founded on the Christian tradition, included animal transformation. Without a doubt the Spanish (and later Christian missionaries) transferred their fear—and defamation—of certain animals to the Pueblos. Might this be the ultimate source of Navajo beliefs regarding Coyote and witchcraft? Might later Christian missionary work among the Navajos have brought about a direct transfer of negative attitudes? Certainly these are questions that deserve future research.

Coyote, more so than any of the other Animal People, does indeed engage in activity that is morally reprehensible. His lustful appetite for sex, for example, is legendary. It should be noted, however, that many of his acts that first appear to be bad are in fact necessary for the long-term survival of the people. In other words, the end justifies the means. The role that Coyote plays in determining there should be death and in the theft of Water Monster's baby—which forced the people to enter into the present world—are examples of such actions. Any final analysis of Coyote as an *evil* entity must take such factors into account.

I also think that Coyote has been the victim of, for the lack of a better term, popular culture. In 1949, a popular booklet entitled *Know the Navajo* was published by Sandy Hassell. This booklet was widely distributed and popular enough to go through at least sixteen printings, the last being in 1972. So it is safe to say that thousands of people read this book. The book is composed of hundreds of small paragraphs, each describing the Navajos and every conceivable aspect of their culture. It is also riddled with inaccuracies and misinformation. In regard to the coyote, one paragraph reads, "A bad Navajo may become a coyote, owl, or crow when he dies. He believes the Devil often uses the coyote for a steed." A caricature drawing next to this statement shows the Devil—complete with horns, tail, and trident—riding on the back of a speeding coyote (Hassell: 38–39).

Finally, the writings of some popular authors, such as the late Tony Hillerman, have promoted a negative view of Coyote. While Hillerman was a talented writer who generally conducted thorough research for his novels, he also tended to provide only the negative side of Coyote (see, for example, Hillerman's *Skinwalkers*, 1986).

In the final analysis, many people, including many young Navajos, have gained their knowledge of "traditional" tribal beliefs from various popular—and often inaccurate—sources.

Coyote Leads the People Home

A final Coyote story needs to be told. It is a historical story, but not one found in any mainstream history book. It might be the most important Coyote story of them all. It is the story of how Coyote saved the Navajo tribe.

Without question, the darkest period in Navajo history began with their defeat by Colonel Christopher "Kit" Carson in 1863. Shortly afterward, they were marched on the tragic Long Walk—a more than three-hundred-mile-long trek to Fort Sumner on the forty-square-mile Bosque Redondo Reservation along the Pecos River in southern New Mexico. More than two thousand died en route; another four thousand would die under wretched conditions during their Bosque Redondo captivity. The soil was unfit for agriculture, and droughts and insect infestation killed what few crops could be grown. Political corruption, mismanagement, and governmental red tape resulted in supplies arriving late or not at all. Navajos died almost daily from disease and starvation. Comanche Indians and New Mexicans continued to raid the reservation for livestock and Navajo children for the slave trade. By 1868, the United States government finally admitted that its "experiment" with the Navajos had proved to be a disastrous failure. The decision was made to close the Bosque Redondo. Two "peace commissioners"—General William T. Sherman and Colonel Samuel F. Tappen—were dispatched to New Mexico to negotiate a final treaty with the tribe. For the lead government representative Sherman, the solution to the Navajo problem was an obvious one: send the tribe to Indian Territory in Oklahoma.

Shortly before the arrival of Sherman and Tappen, the Navajos gathered and selected their own four headmen to serve as negotiators, including famous leader Barboncito. But the Navajos knew they were dealing from a position of weakness and needed help. Consequently, they sought spiritual power to offset the military and political power of the United States. In seeking this power they turned to Coyote and a ceremony known as *Ma'ii Bizee'nast'a*—translated in English to mean "Put Bead in Coyote's Mouth."

The story of this ceremony comes from tribal oral tradition. In *Navajo Stories of the Long Walk Period* collected by Ruth Roessel, no fewer than six different elders recounted how this ceremony was performed to give "coyote power" to the headmen who would be negotiating with the government agents. The fact that so many people knew of it indicates that this ceremony was most certainly performed and was considered to be important enough to pass down through the generations.

The accounts given of this ceremony vary in detail. In one version Barboncito conducted the ceremony; in another version a medicine man named Lamb Cap performed it. A young female coyote (in one version, two coyotes—one male, one female) was captured and a white shell bead was tied to its tongue. The coyote was then placed within a tight circle of men. Slowly the men stepped back, creating openings through which the coyote could escape. The coyote headed west—in the direction of the Navajo homeland. This was a sign that the Navajos should fight to go home. The coyote also bestowed upon the four selected headmen its manipulative powers of persuasion (see Roessel, 1973: 136, 178, 212, 238, 244, and 270). Blessed with "coyote power," the headmen were able to accomplish the impossible—convince a steadfast Sherman not to send them to Oklahoma—but rather to allow them to return to their beloved Navajo Country.

This ceremony no longer exists. Will Tsosie is familiar with the story and believes that the ceremony was undoubtedly a ritual that traced its descent back to the tribe's shamanic Athabaskan roots. He also believes that quite possibly this was the only time this ceremony was conducted (Tsosie, 2009).

The Future of Coyote in Navajo Country

I was hiking the beautiful red rock canyons behind Many Farms, out on one of my weekend excursions, looking for wildlife, for Anasazi ruins, looking quite frankly for anything that I might come across. Stopping under the shade of a pinon tree to rest, I took a drink from my water bottle and then pulled out my binoculars. I was sitting on a rock ledge overlooking a small canyon that ran along one of the countless dirt roads that weave their way through this awesome country. Eventually I trained my field glasses on a pair of ravens who were performing aerial maneuvers along the canyon's walls. Watching ravens is one of my favorite things to do. Ravens, at least to my way of thinking, are among the most beautiful and fascinating creatures in nature. Their glistening black bodies and raucous, irreverent behavior never ceases to intrigue me. I can, and often do, watch them for hours. I was thoroughly enjoying this latest round of entertainment when something else caught my attention, something white that stood out against the brown background. I focused my sight on this location and could now see that there was a lot of white in the wash along the road, but I could not make out exactly what it was. With my interest piqued, I headed down to determine what it was that had caught my attention.

When I arrived at the site, I discovered that what I had been looking at were bones—a lot of bones. A closer examination revealed them to be the remains of coyotes, somewhere between fifteen and twenty carcasses in various states of decomposition. As a hunter I am familiar with death, but I found this sight repulsive. For a brief moment, I thought about searching through the pile of bodies and retrieving a good skull for my collection, but then I decided against it. There was something very forbidding about this place of death, and I felt uncomfortable. I took a few photographs, then beat a hasty retreat back to my truck. All thoughts of ravens had vanished.

Unfortunately, the discovery I made is not unusual. In 1998, forty-one coyote carcasses were found dumped in a wash near Window Rock. Tribal officials investigating the incident believed that these animals were killed— mostly by Navajo hunters—as part of one of the "contest predator hunts" commonly held on the reservation (Donovan: 1). Such slaughters of coyotes on the Navajo Reservation date back at least sixty years. Luckert reported that so many coyotes were killed in the Black Mesa area in the 1940s that an epidemic of "coyote sickness" broke out for which there was an insufficient amount of singers to perform the Coyoteway ceremony (Luckert, 1979: 8–9). Luckert's Navajo consultant offered the following view as to how Coyote sickness occurs:

> When a Coyote person is shot and left to die, his last spasms and twitchings, as they suddenly cease in the animal person, leap onto the killer. This happens most easily if somehow in the process of killing the hunter has eye-contact with his victim—Coyote continues to recognize and haunt the

offender. But this can also happen through physical contact with the animal's dead body or even the decayed remains of a Coyote person. And in this regard no shepherd who strolls through the sagebrush pastures can be sure of his personal immunity. Killing a Coyote person means offending him. The symptoms of the animal's suffering which are thrown onto the offender continue as sort of a nervous malfunction, as a shaking of the head, hands, or of the entire body. (Ibid.)

In sum, Coyote sickness is not caused by the animal itself, but rather by the transgressions of man. It occurs when man shows disrespect toward the coyote.

Throughout the United States there is a war of extermination against coyotes—and other animals considered to be a threat to livestock and agriculture. Moreover, this war is federally sanctioned and publicly financed. The United States Department of Agriculture's Wildlife Services program—formerly and more honestly called Animal Damage Control—"serves" wildlife by killing more than three million animals each year at the cost of over thirty million taxpayer dollars. In the year 2000, for example, Wildlife Services killed 174 wolves, 447 black bears, 1 grizzly bear, 598 mountain lions, 2,666 bobcats, 9,010 foxes, and numerous other smaller predators and "pests." But the principal target of this government agency is coyotes. Every year for at least the past twenty years, Wildlife Services average death toll of coyotes has been about 90,000.

About a third of these coyotes were killed by aerial gunning. The rest were killed by M-44s (better known as "coyote getters"), ejectors that shoot a toxic load of cyanide into the mouth of the animal; trapping; and "denning"—digging puppies out their dens, then usually clubbing them to death.

In addition to the Wildlife Services program, the Navajo Nation operates its own predator control program with a full-time agent, a Navajo, assigned the task of killing animals—again mostly coyotes—that pose a threat to Navajo livestock. In the summer of 2001, I visited their headquarters and was shown a shed that contained perhaps two hundred number 3 steel traps that were stamped "Property of the Navajo Nation." I am unsure how extensive the tribe's predator control program is.

The fact is that coyotes are under constant siege wherever they are found, including the Navajo Reservation. Sheep remain an integral part of Navajo life and identity, and many Navajo sheepherders, as well as recreational hunters, follow the time-honored western tradition of "shoot on sight" when it comes to the coyote. But it wasn't always that way. In 1931, biologist Vernon Bailey reported that the Navajos seldom killed coyotes "because of their belief that the coyote man was one of their mighty ancestors" (Bailey: 319). While Bailey's knowledge of Navajo deities might have left something to be desired, he was a first-rate wildlife biologist who would have been familiar with any tribal effort to control the coyote population.

Karl W. Luckert believes that Coyote—and consequently the coyote—has experienced the same "defamation" as did Wolf and the other divine hunters. According to Luckert's hypothesis, certain Athabaskan hunter-gods began to decline in importance shortly after contact with the more agricultural Pueblo Indians. To again quote Luckert, "All hunter gods eventually suffer defamation if their human proteges cease to be hunters and if they learn to answer to different types of gods" (Luckert, 1979: 9–10). After the Athabaskan-Pueblo merger, and the subsequent transformation into the people we now know as the Navajo, a new worldview emerged. An accompanying religious and ceremonial system, one that was more a product of an agricultural rather than a hunting way of life, emerged.

Again, I agree in principle with much of the Luckert hypothesis. But again, as in the case of Wolf, I believe that the reasons behind the defamation of Coyote are far more varied and complex. Specifically, I think the following factors have combined to defame Coyote:

- The adoption of several of the more negative Pueblo beliefs about Coyote—including the notion that Coyote was the initiator of witchcraft.

- The advent of a pastoral lifestyle and the resulting coyote depredation on Navajo sheep—and the encouragement by the federal government to "control" predators.

- The acceptance of Christianity and its accompanying belief that certain animals are evil.

- The replacement of traditional teachings (passed on by the oral tradition) of elders with the often inaccurate or misinformed traditional teachings perpetuated (passed on by the written tradition) by anthropologists and popular writers.

So what is the future of Coyote—and his earthly descendant, the coyote—in Navajo Country? For coyote the animal, the future is bright. He is a survivor. Despite the best efforts of mankind to destroy him, he continues to expand his range, and I suspect that he will do the same thing on the Navajo Reservation.

Sadly, however, I think that Coyote, the famed Slim Trotter of Navajo tradition, will continue to be defamed and continue to decline in importance and respect. Contemporary Navajo society seems to have no place for Coyote. But who knows? After all, Coyote remains a trickster second to none. In story after story he has defied death to arise again, stronger than ever. In the end, Coyote just might have one more trick up his sleeve.

References

Bailey, Vernon. 1931. *Mammals of New Mexico.* Washington, DC: US Department of Agriculture, Bureau of Biological Survey.

Cooper, Guy H. 1987. "Coyote in Navajo Religion and Cosmology," *The Canadian Journal of Native Studies*, VII(2): 181–193.

Donovan, Bill. 1998. *Navajo Times.* December 12.

Haile, Father Berard. 1981. *The Upward Moving and Emergence Way.* Lincoln: University of Nebraska Press.

Haile, Father Berard. 1984. *Navajo Coyote Tales.* Lincoln: University of Nebraska Press.

Hassell, Sandy. 1949/1972. *Know the Navajos*. Estes Park, CO: Vic Walker.

Hill, Willard W. and Dorothy W. Hill. 1945. "Navaho Coyote Tales and Their Position in the Southern Athapaskan Group," *Journal of American Folklore*, 58: 317–343.

Hillerman, Tony. 1986. *Skinwalkers*. New York: Harper & Row.

Kluckhohn, Clyde. 1944. *Navaho Witchcraft*. Boston: Beacon Press.

Luckert, Karl W. 1975. *The Navajo Hunter Tradition.* Tucson: University of Arizona Press.

Luckert, Karl W. 1979. *Coyoteway: A Navajo Holyway Healing Ceremonial.* Tucson: University of Arizona Press.

Malotki, Ekkehart and Michael Lomatuway'ma. 1994. *Hopi Coyote Tales: Istutuwutsi.* Lincoln: University of Nebraska Press.

Matthews, Washington. 1897/1994. *Navaho Legends.* Salt Lake City: University of Utah Press.

O'Bryan, Aileen. 1956. *The Diné: Origin Myths of the Navaho Indians*. Washington, DC: Bureau of American Ethnology Bulletin No. 163.

Parsons, Elsie Clews. 1927. "Witchcraft among the Pueblos: Indian or Spanish?" *Man*, 27: 106–112.

Parsons, Elsie Clews. 1939/1996. *Pueblo Indian Religion*. 2 volumes. Lincoln: University of Nebraska Press.

Pavlik, Steve. 2000. "Will Big Trotter Reclaim His Place? The Role of the Wolf in Navajo Tradition," *American Indian Culture and Research Journal*, 24(4): 107–125.

Reichard, Gladys A. 1950. *Navaho Religion: A Study of Symbolism*. New York: Bollingen Foundation.

Roessel, Robert A., Jr. and Dillon Platero. 1974. *Coyote Stories of the Navajo People*. Phoenix, AZ: Navajo Curriculum Center Press.

Roessel, Ruth. 1973. *Navajo Stories of the Long Walk Period*. Tsaile, AZ: Navajo Community College Press.

Selinger, Bernard. 2007. "The Navajo, Psychosis, Lacan, and Derrida," *Texas Studies in Literature and Language*. 49(1): 64–100.

Tsosie, Will. 2001. Personal conversation. October 19.

Tsosie, Will. 2009. Personal conversation. August 16.

Tyler, Hamilton A. 1975. *Pueblo Animals and Myths*. Norman: University of Oklahoma Press.

Wheelwright, Mary C. and David P. McAllester. 1956/1988. *The Myth and Prayers of the Great Star Chant and the Myth of the Coyote Chant.* Tsaile, AZ: Navajo Community College Press.

 Chapter Four
The One Who Walks Silently

This chapter was originally presented as a paper at the Western Social Science Association Conference held in Albuquerque, New Mexico, 1997. An adaptation of the paper was published as "The Sacred Cat: The Role of the Mountain Lion in Navajo Mythology and Traditional Lifeway" in Listening to Cougar, *edited by Marc Bekoff and Cara Blessley Lowe, University of Oklahoma Press, 2007.*

I was breathing rather heavily as I reached the top of the road, where it passed through a yellow gate. For the two-mile hike from where I had parked my truck, I has been slipping and sliding in first mud and then, as I gained altitude, snow. Beyond the gate stretched the sheep pastures and land belonging to the family of my good friend Will Tsosie. Initially that had been my destination; now I wasn't so sure. In the summer I had seen several black bears in this area. Spring was breaking and I was eager to find any sign of the animals having emerged from hibernation. I hoped I might even find the smaller footprints of cubs born to a mother during her winter's sleep. But the bitter cold and several inches of fresh snow on the ground told me that any self-respecting bear would still be snug asleep in its den. I had made the climb for nothing.

Another road—or at least what was once a road—
veered to the right and into a canyon. For no apparent
reason, I decided to take it. I had walked only a short
distance when I saw a set of tracks emerging from
a smaller side canyon onto the road I was now on. I
knelt to get a better look, and my heart stopped in
midbeat as I realized what I was looking at. The round,
four-toed, fist-sized, clawless prints were unmistakable:
they belonged to a mountain lion. Moreover, they were
fresh, very fresh. It had snowed lightly the night before,
perhaps even that morning, and these tracks had been
made after the snow.

Anxiously I looked around, clutching my hiking
stick a little tighter. I reminded myself that lions don't
attack people. Well, at least they don't usually attack
people. Earlier that year, mountain lions had killed two
hikers in California. After the shock at finding the tracks
wore off, I began to savor the experience. It was hum-
bling to think that this lion was very nearby, perhaps
even watching me at that very moment.

I followed the tracks a hundred or so yards down the
road until they veered again to disappear into the darkness of another side canyon. Here I stopped. Reaching
into my backpack, I brought out my small buckskin bag
of corn pollen. I sprinkled a little onto the tracks and offered a prayer to the great cat. I prayed for its continued
safety and well-being, and I thanked the Holy People
who had granted me this special encounter.

Origins of a Deity

The mountain lion is a cat of many names. Western scientists call it *Puma concolor*, the cat of one color. To the early white settlers in the eastern United States, it was known as the catamount, panther, or painter. In the mountains, mesas, and desert lands of the West, the names cougar or puma are most commonly used, the latter derived from Quechua, an Inca language, and meaning "powerful animal." Every American Indian tribe probably knew the mountain lion—the animal once possessed the largest range of any North American mammal with the exception of humans—and had its own name for the great cat. The Navajo word for mountain lion is *nashduitso*. When its name is invoked in a ceremony, it is called *nishduikhizh dzilkhae natani*. In addition, a number of more colloquial names are used to describe the animal in the Navajo language. One of these translates to "The one who walks silently among the rocks." Most Navajos I have talked to, however, know this animal as the cougar. For the purpose of this book, I will use both the names mountain lion and cougar.

Mountain lions have long been an integral part of the Native American experience, especially in the Southwest. This reality is perhaps best illustrated by the many rock art images of the animal left behind by the prehistoric people who first inhabited the continent. For the Anasazi, the prehistoric ancestors of the Navajos, rock art images of the cougar became a common motif after AD 1300. Important sites that have numerous realistically portrayed mountain lion petroglyphs and pictographs include Bandelier National Monument and the Petrified Forest (see Rohn, Ferguson, and Ferguson; see also McCreery and Malotki). Often the Anasazi depicted the mountain lion ritualistically, wearing ceremonial items such as feathers, rainbows, and shamanic hats (Schaafsma: 17). The imagery of the mountain lion as an anthropomorphic being, perhaps as a deity possessing supernatural power, reached its highest measure of expression along the Pecos River in Texas at a site named, appropriately, Panther Cave (see Jones, 1994; 1995; see also Zintgraff and Turpin).

It was from the Anasazi that the historic Pueblo tribes acquired an especially rich mountain lion tradition. Without question this tradition was then passed down from the Pueblos to the Navajos.

In regard to the Navajos, Mountain Lion appears early in the creation stories. In the Upward Moving and Emergence Way myth as told to Father Berard Haile by Gishin Biye', Mountain Lion originates in the Red World. This world, also known as the Seventh World, was the home of the Cat People, a collection of anthropomorphic beings that also included Wildcat and Puma (Jaguar). In this story, Mountain Lion is assigned by Changing Woman to be the protector, provider, or "pet" of one of the four original clans, the *Kiyaa'aanii* or Towering House People. At one point in the story the four clans went on a journey upon which they were attacked by an enemy Haile identifies as being the Ute Indians. In describing this encounter, Haile wrote:

> *In a bound Mountain Lion was through the smoke hole, swept around the enemy, and tore them to pieces or bit off*

their arms as he circled them four times. After that he re-
turned to his former place without a word. (Haile, 1981: 172)

Following their attack upon the Ute Indians, Mountain Lion and the other "pets," presumably because they had now tasted human blood, became so mean that they were dismissed by the clans into the mountains, where they now reside. Because of the service Mountain Lion rendered to the people, however, certain clans will not harm cougars and traditional members of the *Kiyaa'aanii* clan keep cougar pelts for protection. The special relationship between the mountain lion and the *Kiyaa'aanii* provides a background, perhaps even the origin, for subsequent beliefs held by the Navajo regarding the mountain lion. It is probably no accident that the *Kiyaa'aanii* clan traces its origins to an outlier settlement of the prehistoric Anasazi of Chaco Canyon, ancestors of the Pueblos and, ultimately, of the Navajos. Polly Schaafsma notes that mountain lions are a relatively common rock art motif throughout the Chaco Canyon region (Schaafsma: 13–17.) This rock art, classified as belonging to the Pueblo II and III of the prehistoric tribe's development, provides a direct connection to the historic Pueblos, people who possessed a particularly rich body of mythological beliefs regarding the mountain lion (see Tyler: 211–269). This Pueblo connection can also be found elsewhere. In the Navajo stories, Mountain Lion, Big Snake, Otter, and Bear are considered to be the Chiefs of the Four Directions. Mountain Lion serves as the Guardian of the North (O'Bryan: 6), the same position assigned to him in the mythologies of almost every Pueblo tribe, including the Zuni (Gunnerson: 231–232; Cushing: 25–26).

Mountain Lion also appears as a protector in a number of the Navajo stories—a role he plays almost universally among the Pueblo tribes as well (Gunnerson: 234–235). In the Navajo Blessingway story, the Hero twins, Monster Slayer and Child Born of Water, undertake a journey to find their father, the Sun. Upon reaching his house, they find Mountain Lion, along with Bear, Big Snake, Thunder, and Wind, serving as guardians to the house of the Sun. To gain safe entrance, the Twins have to speak Mountain Lion's sacred name, "He who is speckled over with earth," before he allows them to pass through (Wyman, 1970a: 538, 540).

In his role as protector to the house of the Sun, Mountain Lion is also mentioned in the Shootingway ceremony and consequently appears in sandpaintings used in this ritual. In one such sandpainting made in 1940 by Sam Tilden, Mountain Lion is portrayed realistically as opposed to anthropomorphically and appears alongside a black bear—another protector of the house of the Sun—as a "paired guardian" on the sandpainting (Wyman, 1970b: 44, plate 24; 74).

The most prominent role played by the mountain lion in Navajo mythology is in the origin stories behind the Beadway and Eagle Way ceremonies. The origins of these ceremonies share a common beginning before branching off into different legends.

In the version of the Beadway as told by Miguelito to Gladys A. Reichard, the hero, Scavenger or Holy Boy, is taken by the Pueblos, who then try to trick him into capturing young eagles for them. They lower him into an eagle's nest, but upon the advice of Talking God and the Wind, Scavenger refuses to throw the young eagles down to his captors. In anger the Pueblos leave Scavenger in the nest to die, but in gratitude for sparing their young, the eagles rescue and befriend him. Each time the eagles go out to hunt, however, Scavenger gets into mischief. At one point he wanders off and is buried under a pile of rocks—a trap set for him by the black-tailed sparrows. The eagles appeal to the Hunters, of which Mountain Lion is considered "chief," for help. It is the Lion People who discover Scavenger under the rocks. Mountain Lion tries to dig the boy out, but succeeds only in wearing off his claws. Wolf, Lynx, and Bobcat also fail at their attempts to rescue Scavenger. Finally Badger reaches him, but only to find his bones. A ceremony is then held to bring him back to life. Four feathers from different birds—Bald Eagle, Blue Hawk, Magpie, and the Yellow Hawk—are placed around the skeleton. The Bald Eagle, Blue Hawk, and Magpie feathers then transform respectively into a wolf, beaver, and otter. The Yellow Hawk feathers turn into a mountain lion. When the transformation is complete, Scavenger is restored to life. It is for this reason that the skins of these four animals are still used in the Beadway ceremony (Reichard: 32).

Mountain Lion makes several more appearances in the Beadway legend. At one point in the story, he is traveling to Black Mountain to perform a Beadway Chant at a Fire Dance. Along the way, he encounters his friend Wolf, who is on a similar journey. Since neither wants to miss the other's sing, they agree that Mountain Lion should postpone his for one night. To bind the agreement, the two great hunters—who often appear together in Navajo mythology—exchange quivers. A sandpainting used in the Beadway ceremony depicts this event, showing Mountain Lion carrying Wolf's white quiver made of wolf skin, and Wolf with a yellow quiver made of mountain lion skin. A third hunter, Spotted Lion, whom Reichard identifies as being the anthropomorphic version of the "Mexican jaguar," appears twice in this sandpainting entitled *Exchange of the Quivers.* These Jaguars are carrying quivers made of lynx and wolverine skin. Rainbow Goddess also appears in this sandpainting (Reichard: 33, plate V).

Another version of this sandpainting is also used that, in addition to depicting Mountain Lion and Wolf as the central characters, includes double images of Spotted Lion, Bobcat, Lynx, and Badger (Reichard: 33–34, plate VI). A third sandpainting shows the Mountain Lion People joining the Wolf People in a Fire Dance performance. In this sandpainting, both sets of dancers are shown wearing packs of corn on their backs. This corn is secured through the use of their magical powers to plant, cultivate, and harvest the crop only minutes before performing the dance—an interesting agricultural twist to Animal People better known for being great hunters. In this sandpainting, Mountain Lion and Wolf are again joined by their fellow hunters Spotted Lion, Bobcat, Lynx, and Badger (Reichard: 34–35, plate VII).

Mountain Lion also plays an important role in the legend of the Eagle Way Chant, which, as noted earlier, shares a common origin with and is thus closely related to Beadway. In this story, the hero, Monster Slayer, meets White Shell Girl and Turquoise Girl, daughters of

Changing Woman, near Mount Taylor. He informs them of a place where a mountain lion has killed a deer. "If you go there," he tells them, "you can see what deer looks like and even obtain pieces of skin." They do so, cutting off a piece of the hide—sacred buckskin—which they scrape to make a sack in which to carry seed (Newcomb: 52). Later in the same legend, Monster Slayer encounters Mountain Lion, who is camped with his fellow hunters Wolf, Spotted Lion, Lynx, White Weasel, Yellow Weasel, and Rattlesnake. Monster Slayer offers to watch their camp while they hunt. The hunt, which lasts four days, proves unsuccessful. Each day Mountain Lion sees what he thinks is a deer. Climbing to a place above it, he jumps on his intended prey, only to find it to be a log. Scratched and skinned from his failed efforts, Mountain Lion and the other hunters who have met with similar failure blame Monster Slayer, who they believe must have broken some law or taboo. When Monster Slayer falls ill, perhaps witched by the hunters, Mountain Lion, who possesses "mixed medicine," and the others refuse to help him (ibid.: 66–69).

In another Navajo myth, this one the origin of the Red Antway ceremony, Mountain Lion and Wolf are attacked by Lightning after they have killed a game animal belonging to that deity. Lightning begins his assault by shattering a tree under which the two hunters are butchering their game. Angered, Mountain Lion holds up a magical whisker toward the sky. He then sings and prays until Lightning falls to the ground before them. Mountain Lion then blows at the Black Cloud of Lightning, thus allowing the Sun to shine through. "I thought I was the only destroyer," Lightning says to Mountain

Lion, "but you're more powerful." In honor of Mountain Lion, Lightning gives a song and prayer to the Ant People (Wheelwright: 7–8; see also Wyman, 1965: 99).

The Mountain Lion Way of Hunting

Navajos traditionally distinguished between two types of hunting: ritual and nonritual. Deer, antelope, bear, and eagles were ritually hunted, with the hunting under direction of a "singer" or medicine man who instructed the hunters as to their conduct and directed the ritualistic aspects of the hunt. Accordingly, a number of traditional hunting ways existed, each with its own mythology and procedures. One of the most important of these ways was the Mountain Lion Way, or Tiptoe Way. This method was also called the Deerway because it was primarily directed at hunting that particular game animal.

In addition to a special set of songs, this way of hunting was distinguished from others, such as the Wolfway, Big Snake Way, and Talking God Way, in that certain specific procedures were followed. Among the most important of these was that the hunter always kept an arrow on his bowstring ready to shoot and would walk continually on tiptoe against the wind and along game trails where deer would most likely be hiding. By hunting in this manner, it was believed that the hunter took on the qualities possessed by the mountain lion, the greatest of all deer hunters. The departure date for the hunt was always set an odd number of days away. Cornmeal and meat were taken as supplies. If luck was with the hunters, the hunt usually lasted about ten days. If game was scarce, the hunt might continue for as long as a month (Hill: 117–118).

Other rituals and restrictions pertained to proper conduct while on the hunt, especially in regard to the prescribed method of skinning, butchering, and disposing of various body parts of the game animal after it had been killed. Such ritual was observed in order to demonstrate to the game animal that the hunter was respectful and deserving of the life he sought to take. This was important because it was believed that after death, a deer would return "home" and report on its treatment. Any transgression might result in sickness, accident, or perhaps even death to the hunter. At the very least, future hunting success would be jeopardized. As one Navajo source told anthropologist Willard W. Hill, "If a hunter observed all ritual the game allowed itself to be killed. No game would want to be killed by a man who is careless" (ibid.: 98). This comment well reflects the special relationship that existed traditionally between all living things, including creatures such as the deer and the predators—animal or man—who hunted them.

According to one version of the Navajo hunting tradition as told by Claus Chee Sonny to Karl Luckert, it was the deer gods who originally taught the hunting ways to the "divine predators" before the creation of man—foremost of whom was Mountain Lion (Luckert: 18). In relating his version of the hunter tradition, Claus Chee Sonny at one point in his narrative allowed the Deer People to speak for themselves: "He [Mountain Lion] takes the power away from us so that we become weak and cannot run very fast. If lion hunts us in this manner, he can carry one of us to his home every day" (ibid.: 40).

The Navajo belief that it was the Deer People themselves who taught the divine predators—and thus indirectly humans—how to hunt is revealing. It shows them offering their lives not only for the benefit of predator and human survival, but perhaps also because they knew it was necessary to control their own population.

Special songs are another characteristic of the Mountain Lion Way of hunting. The purpose of these songs was to honor the game being hunted, ensure good fortune, and draw upon the powers of the mountain lion. Unfortunately, no songs or prayers have been recorded in connection with the Mountain Lion Way. The cougar, however, is referred to in one of the Stalking Way songs, and quite possibly a song like this once belonged to the Mountain Lion Way of Hunting (ibid.: 171–172).

He goes out hunting

The Mountain lion am I

With the mahogany bow he goes out hunting

With the yellow tail feathered arrow he goes out hunting

The finest of female game through the shoulder that I may shoot

Its death it obeys me. (Hill: 136)

In addition to the songs and prayers, hunters also traditionally acquired power and good fortune through the use of mountain lion fetishes. The one Navajo mountain lion fetish I have had the opportunity to examine appears identical to one shown as figure number 6, plate IV in Frank Cushing's book *Zuni Fetishes* (Cushing: 24). This Navajo fetish, two inches in length, is carved of an unidentified stone and can be distinguished as a mountain lion by the long tail laid across its back from the rump nearly to the shoulders. The ears carved on this fetish are rounded, and the eyes seem disproportionately large. Most Pueblo tribes carved and used mountain lion hunting fetishes and considered them living entities. Often these fetishes were fed the blood of slain game animals or offered corn pollen (Gunnerson: 240–242).

The Mountain Lion in Navajo Material Culture

As noted earlier, Navajos traditionally distinguished between ritual and nonritual hunting, with the pursuit of the cougar falling into the latter category. When W. W. Hill asked one of his Navajo sources how mountain lions were hunted, he was told, "Oh, we do not hunt Mountain lions, we merely kill them. We hunt deer, but not Mountain lions." From the Navajo point of view, there was no such thing as hunting mountain lions because there was no ceremony involved in their killing. In contrast, deer, antelope, eagles, and bears were "hunted" with a complex set of rituals surrounding the hunt and the taking of the animal's life (Hill: 97).

Certainly, mountain lions were killed occasionally, often with the use of dogs to help track and tree the cat. Mountain lions were seldom hunted alone, since they were viewed as being dangerous. The first hunter to reach the slain mountain lion had the right to claim its skin (Hill: 168).

Navajos sometimes ate the meat of the mountain lion. One of Hill's sources claimed, "It has a different flavor," and said that the females were considered to be especially good food.

Cougars were most commonly killed for their skins. These skins were used for a multitude of purposes, mainly ceremonial (Hill: 168). Since mountain lions are few in number in Navajo Country, and consequently are seldom encountered, few contemporary Navajo hunters have ever killed a cougar. Historically, most mountain lion skins were, and still are, acquired through trade. The Ute Indians often provided the Navajos with cougar skins. Today, non-Indian traders provide these pelts (Kluckhohn, Hill, and Kluckhohn: 186). In 1996 and 1997, I visited and interviewed a number of traders who provided mountain lion skins to the Navajos, and I found that a complete skin with the necessary claws still attached brought around three hundred to four hundred dollars.

The relatively high price of mountain lion skins reflects the fact that they remain highly prized and sought by traditional Navajos, who associate them with wealth. My own principle Navajo collaborator, Will Tsosie, once stated that "he who possesses the pelt of a cougar is considered wealthy. Only the wealthy have cougar pelts" (Tsosie). This concept traces back to the origin stories. In the "wealth songs" of Blessingway, mountain lions are frequently mentioned, including a reference to the house of the Sun, who is very wealthy, being "covered from wall to wall with Mountain lion skins." Tsosie added that these songs are known by only a few people and are jealously guarded. His father, for example, performs Blessingways but never uses his "special" wealth songs in the presence of anyone other than close family members (ibid.).

The most common use of mountain lion skin is for the production of hunting and war equipment, especially the quivers used to hold bows and arrows. The use of mountain lion skin for quivers is almost universal among Southern Athabaskans and indeed among tribes throughout North America. The rationale for this is undoubtedly the desire to transfer the characteristics of the cougar—stealth, speed, power, and courage—to the human hunter or warrior. The exact origin of the tradition is unknown. Stuart J. Baldwin suggests that the use of cougar skin quivers in the Southwest originated with the Athabaskans and was quickly adopted by the Pueblos (Baldwin: 2, 9–10). I believe, however, that a reverse scenario is more plausible.

In Navajo tradition, the people were taught to make quivers by the Twins, Monster Slayer and Child Born of Water (Kluckhohn, Hill, and Kluckhohn: 49). In the origin stories, a number of deities, including the elder twin, Monster Slayer, possessed quivers made of mountain lion skin. A photograph of the great Navajo leader Manuelito shows him with a mountain lion quiver. Dangling from this quiver is the long and unmistakable tail of a cougar (Wardwell: 3:22). Although Navajos made quivers from a variety of animals, including deer, otter, antelope, wildcat, and badger, mountain lion was highly preferred (see ibid.: 46–49).

Mountain lion quivers consisted of two pouches sewn or lashed together to create the arrow pouch or quiver proper, and the bow case. Both pouches were usually made from a large cougar skin. After the cougar skin was dressed, it was folded along the back and various sections marked for cutting. The hide was then laid out flat and cut along a pattern. Any remaining pieces of hide was used for fringes and quiver bottoms (ibid.: 48). The quiver was then

> sewn on only one side; the other side was formed by the fold. A round piece of dressed buckskin was sewn into the bottom. To keep the quiver extended, a stick or unworked arrow shaft was attached to the outside of the side seam and laced in place with buckskin. The quiver was about two feet high and open at the top. The bow case when cut from a small skin was sewn on both sides and the bottom with either mountain lion skin or buckskin thongs. A large skin was so cut that each case could be made with a single seam. (Ibid.: 46)

For the quiver, the fur of the mountain lion was almost always placed inside. On the bow case, the fur was always on the inside with the exposing flesh side usually painted with yellow dye. The legs of the animal were left hanging, attached to either the bow case or the quiver. For ornamentation, the tail was allowed to hang free with buckskin, ribbon, beads, and the feathers of a turkey or eagle sometimes providing additional decoration. It is generally believed that only men were allowed to make mountain lion quivers. Certain rituals were also to be performed during the manufacture of these quivers. The most highly prized quivers were made during the course of an Enemyway ceremony (ibid.: 46–49).

Another interesting use of mountain lion skin was in the making of the Navajo hunting or war cap. The preparation of these caps is described as follows:

> The head skin of the lion was severed just below the eyes; about six inches of neck were left attached. The skin was placed over the rounded end of a log to prevent shrinking while it dried. It was occasionally removed, worked, and stretched over the knee to produce the desired shape. Then it was dressed. First it was buried in damp earth; then brains were rubbed on it; and finally it was pounded with a stone or stick. (Ibid.: 279)

After the cape was completed, various kinds of ornamentation were added. Often a strip of bayeta decorated with abalone shell discs was placed on the rim above the forehead. Tufts of eagle and owl feathers were placed on top and a skin strap was attached to hold the cap in place. The neck skin of the cougar made a flap in the back, presumably to keep out rain (ibid.: 279–280). Quite possibly the privilege of wearing these skin caps was reserved for certain clans. If other clans were to wear them, bad luck would befall the wearer. In addition, as in the case of the mountain lion quivers, only men could make and wear these caps (bid.: 275, 428).

A photograph taken before 1894 of a Navajo man wearing such a cape shows a cap complete with eye holes, ears attached, and the cape extending down the neck (ibid.: 187). The wearer of such a cap would take on a decidedly "lionlike" appearance. This would provide a degree of power during a hunt or in time of war. This, however, brings up the question of witchcraft and the well-known Navajo fear of so-called skinwalkers—witches who wear the skins of animals and thus are able to transform into those animals for the purpose of bringing harm to others. While witchcraft and skinwalkers are most commonly associated with members of the canine family, usually coyotes and wolves, they have also been known to take the shape of mountain lions (Morgan: 3, 29). Will Tsosie offers the view that traditionally the wearing of animals skins for hunting and warfare was common, and that the entire concept of skinwalkers did not exist prior to the coming of Christian missionaries, who considered certain animals, such as wolves, snakes, and lions, to be inherently evil. Tsosie believes that such Christian fears transferred to Navajo culture and over time became mistakenly viewed as being traditional Navajo beliefs (Tsosie). It is interesting to note that Polly Schaafsma has recorded the presence of Spanish crosses carved on boulders in conjunction with earlier carved Anasazi images of lions and snakes, in the West Mesa area near Albuquerque, New Mexico. This, along with other written documentation, reveals an attempt by the Spanish to exorcise, or at least neutralize, what they perceived to be signs of evil or devil worship among the Native people (Schaafsma: 148–149).

Mountain lion skin is also used to make hair ties for girls during their puberty ceremony, the *kinaalda.* The type of skin used for this item—either deer, mountain sheep, otter, or cougar—is determined by the personality of the girl as she is growing up or by the personality her family wishes her to adopt. If a girl appears to be tough or athletic—a tomboy, so to speak—or if her family wishes her to develop into a cunning, aggressive, and forceful young woman, the skin of the mountain lion is used. In such cases, a strip of hide, "two fingers" wide, is cut from the nose to the tail of the cat skin. These ties are often used repeatedly and handed down through the family. Will Tsosie's grandmother, the matriarch of her family, possesses a six-foot-long mountain lion hair tie used, worn apart, repaired, and used again for generations (Tsosie).

There are a number of other uses of mountain lion parts that relate to Navajo religion and to various specific ceremonies. A mountain lion skin, for example, is sometimes used as a rug during a Blessingway ceremony (Tsosie). Navajo medicine bundles, or *jish* as they are called, must be sewn together with a particular type of sinew as determined by the ceremony it has been made for. Mountain lion sinew is often used for this purpose, including for making Flintway and Shootingway *jish* (Haile, 1943: 54; Frisbie: 31, 56). Cougar sinew is also used as the string for the miniature bows used in the Evil Way ceremony (Wyman and Kluckhohn: 32). Medicine bundles, along with the masks and the wrappings on the hoof rattles used in the Flintway ceremony, are always made of unwounded or "sacred" buckskin—a hide that possesses no unnatural holes or tears. The hide of a deer killed by a cougar qualifies for such a characterization (Frisbie: 93). In addition, the shoulder pouches worn by men during ceremonies and other special occasions have reportedly been made of mountain lion skin (ibid.: 39). The gall of the cougar, along with that of other animals, has been used as medicine to cure dizziness and fainting. The rendered fat of the mountain lion is sometimes mixed in combination with other tallows, including that of buffalo, otter, wildcat, wolf, antelope, elk, deer, and mountain sheep, and then with red ocher and glittering iron ore to produce a body paint for the patient during a Flintway ceremony (Hill: 168; Haile, 1943: 51). The "death blood" and fur of the mountain lion is also used in the Flintway ceremony (Haile, 1943: 54).

Mountain lion claws are used to split the yucca used to tie together the hoops employed in the Big Star ceremony (Wheelwright and McAllester: 90). They are also attached to the bandoliers and wristlets worn by singers of the Upward-Reaching Way or Evil Way. This ritual is the fundamental "ghostway" ceremony used specifically for the treatment or prevention of disease, illness, and misfortune caused by ghosts. Mountain lion claws are used because, as one early Navajo source stated, "Ghosts are scared of Mountain lions" (Wyman and Bailey: 14). Mountain Lion is also said to be the only power feared by witches. Wristlets made of cougar claws were also worn in earlier times by Navajo warriors in battle to give them power and strength (Hill: 9).

Closing Thoughts

No one knows how many mountain lions currently inhabit Navajo Country. The last "official" lion on the reservation was killed in 1978. I have talked to ranchers and sheepherders who graze their livestock in the Chuska and Lukachukai Mountains. Several have told me that they occasionally see the great cat, but sightings are rare. My guess is that a few cougars exist in the most remote and wildest corners of the mountains. Interestingly, when Chris Bolgiano, who wrote an excellent book entitled *Mountain Lion: An Unnatural History of Pumas and People,* interviewed a Navajo Fish and Game official in the mid-1990s—an individual who was herself a tribal member—she was told, "We know we have lions but we don't know much about lion populations. I'd like to see a research project to determine whether we could have a sport hunting season, which would bring income from licenses" (Bolgiano: 13).

Navajo or white, the bottom line seems always to be the almighty dollar.

In past times when food was scarce, Navajos often found themselves turning to the mountain lion for their very survival. In these times of hardship, Navajos would seek out the remains of mountain lion kills, which they then would feast upon. The Navajos who used this source of meat believed that the mountain lion purposefully made these kills and left them behind for the people to find and use. In such cases, it was proper etiquette to respect the lion's generosity by not taking all of the meat, but rather to leave some behind for later use by the lion. The Navajo term for this meat translates, appropriately I believe, to "pity portion"—a gift from a fellow being that possesses far greater power, and certainly far greater compassion, than is often shown by its human counterpart (Tsosie).

Today it is the mountain lion who depends on man to ensure its survival. Unlike man, however, the mountain lion does not need pity, but rather needs only our understanding and respect. Throughout their range, mountain lions, like most predators, are under siege—feared and hated by humans who have not taken the time to learn about them, or from them. They are slaughtered by ranchers not for the livestock they kill, but rather for the livestock they might kill. Wildlife departments hunt them down in a mistaken belief that fewer lions will mean more deer and elk for license-buying hunters. They are chased by hounds and shot defenseless out of trees for no other reason than for a sport hunter to prove his supposed manhood. And all the while, we are destroying their habitat and thus forcing these great cats into urban areas where they are then killed in the interest of so-called "public safety" (see Pavlik, 2011).

The traditional Navajo–mountain lion relationship is one we can all learn from.

References

Baldwin, Stuart J. 1986. "The Mountain Lion in Tompiro Stone Art," in *By Hands Unknown: Papers on Rock Art and Archaeology in Honor of James G. Bain*, edited by Anne V. Poore. Albuquerque, NM: Archaeological Society of New Mexico.

Bolgiano, Chris. 1995. *Mountain Lion: An Unnatural History of Pumas and People*. Mechanicsburg, PA: Stackpole Press.

Cushing, Frank H. 1883/1966. *Zuni Fetishes*. Flagstaff, AZ: K.C. Publications.

Frisbie, Charlotte J. 1987. *Navajo Medicine Bundles or Jish: Acquisition, Transmission, and Disposition in the Past and Present.* Albuquerque: University of New Mexico Press.

Gunnerson, James H. "Mountain Lions and Pueblo Shrines in the American Southwest," in *Icons of Power: Feline Symbolism in the Americas,* edited by Nicholas J. Saunders. New York: Routledge, 1998.

Haile, Father Berard. 1943. *Origin Legend of the Navaho* Flintway. Chicago: University of Chicago Press.

Haile, Father Berard. 1981. *The Upward Moving and Emergence Way*. Lincoln: University of Nebraska Press.

Hill, Willard W. 1938. *The Agricultural and Hunting Methods of the Navajo Indians.* New Haven, CT: Yale University Publications in Anthropology, No. 18.

Jones, Bernard M., Jr. 1994. "The Symbolic Image of Mountain Lion: Recreating Myth in Rock Art," *Rock Art Papers, Volume 11*: 157–170, San Diego Museum Papers, No. 31.

Jones, Bernard M., Jr. 1995. "The Heart at the Center of the Circle: Mountain Lion Symbolism and Solstice Ritual," *Rock Art Papers, Volume 12*: 45–54, San Diego Museum Papers, No. 33.

Kluckhohn, Clyde, Willard W. Hill, and Lucy Wales Kluckhohn. 1971. *Navaho Material Culture*. Cambridge, MA: Belknap Press of Harvard University.

Luckert, Karl W. 1975. *The Navajo Hunter Tradition*. Tucson: University of Arizona Press.

McCreery, Patricia and Ekkehart Malotki. 1994. *Tapamveni: The Rock Art Galleries of Petrified Forest and Beyond.* Petrified Forest, AZ: Petrified Forest Museum Association.

Morgan, William. 1936. *Human-Wolves among the Navajo*. New Haven, CT: Yale Publications in Anthropology, No. 11.

Newcomb, Franc J. 1939. "Origin Legend of the Navajo Eagle Chant," *Journal of American Folk-Lore*, 53(207): 50–78.

O'Bryan, Aileen. 1956/1993. *Navaho Indian Myths*. New York: Dover Publications.

Pavlik, Steve. 2007. "The Sacred Cat: The Role of the Mountain Lion in Navajo Mythology and Traditional Life-way," in *Listening to Cougar*, edited by Cara Blessley Lowe and Marc Bekoff. Boulder: University of Colorado Press: 91–103.

Pavlik Steve. 2011. "Who Is the Beast? Perspectives on Mountain Lions and Mankind," *Three Coyotes*, 1(1): 84–115.

Reichard, Gladys A. 1939/1977. *Navajo Medicine Man Sandpaintings*. New York: Dover Publications.

Roessel, Robert A. 1983. *Dinétah: Navajo History, Volume III.* Chinle, AZ: Navajo Curriculum Center.

Roessel, Ruth. 1971. *Navajo Studies at Navajo Community College*. Many Farms, AZ: Navajo Community College Press.

Rohn, Arthur H. and William and Lisa Ferguson. 1989. *Rock Art of Bandelier National Monument*. Albuquerque: University of New Mexico Press.

Schaafsma, Polly. 1992. *Rock Art in New Mexico*. Santa Fe: Museum of New Mexico Press.

Tsosie, Will. 1996. Personal conversation. March 9.

Tyler, Hamilton A. 1975. *Pueblo Animals and Myths*. Norman: University of Oklahoma Press.

Wardwell, Lelia. 1991. *American Historical Images on File: The Native American Experience.* New York: Facts on File.

Wheelwright, Mary C. 1958. *Myth of Willa-Chee-Ji De-ginnh-Keygo Hatral.* Santa Fe, NM: Museum of Navajo Ceremonial Art.

Wheelwright, Mary C. and David P. McAllester. 1956/1988. *The Myth and Prayers of the Great Star Chant and the Myth of the Coyote Chant.* Tsaile, AZ: Navajo Community College Press.

Wyman, Leland C. 1965. *The Red Antway of the Navaho.* Santa Fe, NM: Museum of Navajo Ceremonial Art.

Wyman, Leland C. 1970a. *Blessingway.* Tucson: University of Arizona Press.

Wyman, Leland C. 1970b. *Sandpaintings of the Navajo Shootingway and The Walcott Collection.* Smithsonian Contributions to Anthropology, Number 13. Washington, DC: Smithsonian Institution.

Wyman, Leland C. and Flora L. Bailey. 1943. "Navajo Upward-Reaching Way: Objective Behavior, Rationale, and Sanction," *University of New Mexico Bulletin* 389, Anthropological Series 4.

Wyman, Leland C. and Clyde Kluckhohn. 1938. "Navaho Classification of Their Song Ceremonials," *Memoirs of the American Anthropological Association,* Supplement 50: 3–38.

Zintgraff, Jim and Turpin A. Solveig. 1991. *Pecos River Rock Art: A Photographic Essay.* San Antonio, TX: Sandy McPherson Publishing Company.

 # Chapter Five
Mysteries of the Spotted Lion

This chapter is an adaptation of a paper that was originally presented to the Jaguar Conservation Team at their biannual meeting held at Animas, New Mexico, on January 22, 1998. That paper was later published as "Rohonas and Spotted Lions: The Historical and Cultural Occurrence of the Jaguar, Panthera onca, *among the Native Tribes of the American Southwest" in* Wicazo Sa Review, *Spring 2003.*

Stalking along the winding and twisting trails of the Navajo creation stories, and making cameo appearances in various traditional ceremonies, is the most intriguing and mysterious of the Animal People, Spotted Lion. Some anthropologists state emphatically that this personage is wholly mythical. Other anthropologists state with equal conviction that Spotted Lion is in fact Jaguar.

The Jaguar in the American Southwest

To most people the very word *jaguar* conjures up visions of a magnificent spotted cat stalking through the dense jungles of Brazil, Costa Rica, or perhaps Mexico. Few would associate this animal with the forests, woodlands, and especially the deserts of the American Southwest. Yet this land too is jaguar country. The historic range of the jaguar, *Panthera onca,* extended well into the United States; jaguars have been documented throughout the state of Arizona as far north as the Grand Canyon. In all, at least eighty-four jaguars are known from the state of Arizona alone since 1848. Jaguars have also been recorded in southern California, New Mexico, Texas, and perhaps even Colorado (Brown, 1991: 22; see also Brown, 1997a; Mahler).

Unfortunately, jaguars, like all other large predators, were killed whenever and wherever they appeared. Never plentiful, the jaguars that were native to the American Southwest were soon all but extirpated. Although some animals continued to enter the United States from the Mexican states of Chihuahua and Sonora, the great cat was not listed under the Endangered Species Act (ESA) of 1973. Between 1970 and 1996, many jaguars were reportedly sighted, especially in Arizona, but only two were "official"—that is, they were killed and their skins collected. Then, in 1996, two different jaguars were brought to bay by lion hounds belonging to two separate hunting parties two hundred miles apart in southern Arizona. The first cat was photographed, the second cat photographed and videotaped. Both were then given their freedom. The jaguar had returned to the American Southwest (Brown, 1997b).

The appearance of the two jaguars galvanized the conservation community to action. Lawsuits and threatened lawsuits resulted in the US Fish and Wildlife Service (FWS) belatedly listing the jaguar under the ESA in 1997. Meanwhile, the states of Arizona and New Mexico, along with a dozen other federal, state, county, and local agencies, developed a Jaguar Conservation Agreement with the FWS. Initially put together to prevent the listing of the jaguar, the coalition remained together after the cat was listed. The purpose of this group—a partnership of various government, public, and private interests calling itself the Jaguar Conservation Team (JCT)—was to develop and implement conservation practices beneficial to the jaguar. This group was disbanded in 2009 following a tragic incident in which what was perhaps the last borderlands jaguar in the United States was killed by the Arizona Game and Fish Department.

Rohonas *and Possible Pueblo Origins*

The jaguar has long been recognized as being the single most powerful and important animal icon in Indigenous Central and South America (Saunders). In addition, jaguars appear in the creation stories and culture of numerous North American tribes, including the Navajos (Pavlik, 2003). But before there were the Navajos as we know them, there were the historic Pueblos. And before there were Pueblos, there were their prehistoric Anasazi and Mogollon ancestors. It was with these earliest people that jaguar beliefs and related ceremonial practices probably began.

One definite prehistoric location that documents the jaguar is the Anasazi site, Pottery Mound. This site consists of a collection of ruins located in central New Mexico in the valley of the Puerco River, a major tributary of the Rio Grande. Pottery Mound, which is dated AD 1300 to 1475, is unusual among Anasazi sites in that it has produced evidence of Mexican influence, specifically as to pottery types, clay bells, and the presence of parrot and macaw feathers. The most distinguishing characteristic of Pottery Mound is its magnificent kiva art, paintings that cover the walls of many of the site's seventeen ceremonial rooms. One of the most spectacular paintings is of a jaguar. This animal is well drawn and unmistakable—light brown with dark spots. It is depicted reaching for a bird, possibly an eagle. Anthropologist Frank C. Hibben believed this image might be a reflection of the eagle-jaguar cult of Mexico. In the same fresco are depictions of mountain lions and seated human figures. Many of these figures, including the jaguar, wear quivers with arrows. Hibben notes that among the Anasazi, the mountain lion was usually linked with the war society, and these figures could represent a council of war (Hibben: 65; see also Crotty; Schaafsma). This association between the mountain lion and the jaguar, not only as warriors but as hunters, continues with the descendants of the Anasazi, the historic Pueblo Indians. At least one other excellent painting of a jaguar was found at the Pottery Mound site. Unfortunately, this painting was partially destroyed by pot hunters prior to archaeological excavation (Hibben: 110).

Another long-tailed spotted feline appears in a smoke-blackened cave on the Pajarito Plateau in northern New Mexico. A question arises if such paintings depict jaguars or mountain lion cubs, but as Schaafsma notes, "Although mountain lion cubs are spotted, it seems unlikely that juveniles would be selected as metaphors of power" (Schaafsma: 65). In all likelihood, then, this figure is indeed a jaguar. The rock art from this plateau dates between AD 1325 and 1550.

Two other impressive prehistoric sites that include jaguar rock art are found near El Paso, Texas. One is at Fort Hancock and is attributed to the Jornada branch of the Mogollon culture, AD 450 to 1400. This site includes a rock shelter called Jaguar Cave, its walls covered with pictographs of various animals. These paintings are in white and include what has been identified as a three-foot-long jaguar wearing a collar. Numerous other animals and kachinas are painted on this same panel, including an eight-foot-long plumed serpent also depicted wearing a collar. A series of parallel dots begin at the serpent's collar and continue on to form the end of the jaguar's tail. The painting in this shelter reflect an obvious Mesoamerican influence. A pictograph of a jaguar wearing a collar, for example, can be found in the Temple of Tlahuizcalpantecuhtli in Tula, Mexico. It is speculated that the plumed serpent might represent the Aztec god Quetzalcoatl (Sutherland and Steed, Jr.: 3–4, 39–40, 44–45; see also Wellman: 82, 85, and figure 361).

Another jaguar rock art site is located at Hueco Tanks State Park, Texas. This site, the Cave of the Masks, is also attributed to the Jornado branch of the Mogollon culture and contains a yellow and red painting of a spotted jaguar wearing a curving, conical "shaman's cap." Also found in this rock shelter is a painting of what has been called a "kachina blanket" and a number of beautifully painted mask designs. Again, the motifs and the style are considered to provide evidence of possible Mesoamerican influence (Davis and Jones: 81).

The historic Pueblo Indians are generally divided into two groups: the Eastern Pueblos, who live along the Rio Grande River in New Mexico, and the Western Pueblos—the Hopis of Arizona and the Acoma, Laguna, and Zuni tribes of west-central New Mexico. Both groups include tribes that were familiar with the jaguar.

In her definitive study of Pueblo religion, Elsie Clews Parsons wrote of a *rohona*, an "unidentified, perhaps mythic animal" that exists in the stories of the various Keresan-speaking Pueblo groups (Parsons: 187). Leslie A. White took up the challenge of identifying this creature and concluded "that it is a real animal and, furthermore, that it is a jaguar." Although among some Pueblos the *rohona* does appear to be another species—a weasel, mountain lion, coyote, or wolf—White found sufficient evidence to support his theory. Most Pueblos, he found, identified the animal as being a large cat. Since mountain lions are common in Navajo Country and play an important role in every Pueblo culture, they are clearly identified and can be ruled out as being the *rohona.* The wildcat or bobcat can probably be eliminated from consideration for the same reason. This leaves the lynx, a historic inhabitant of the northern limits of Pueblo Country, and the jaguar, which is already documented in the Anasazi and Mogollon record (White, 1944: 440). At the Pueblo of Santa Ana, White was told that the *rohona* was a "big cat with spots" and, along with the mountain lion, is talked of during ceremonies held by the tribe's hunting society. In this role, these two cats represent spirit hunters who bestow their power on the tribal hunters. These spirit hunters are associated with directions, and the jaguar is considered the spirit hunter of the west (White, 1942:

283; White, 1947: 231). A similar tradition exists at the Pueblo of Zia (White, 1944: 441)

At the ancient Hopi village of Awatovi and at nearby Kawaika-a site—the so-called Jeddito sites, several kiva murals depict elongated quadrupeds with short legs, long horizontal tails, and pointed ears and snouts. Watson Smith discusses the possibility that these animals might be the fabled *rohona.* He goes on to speculate that Keresan immigrants from the Eastern Pueblos might have brought knowledge of the jaguar to their Hopi relatives. In the end, Smith makes the questionable determination that these animals are most likely mountain lions since they resemble the mountain lion paintings found at Zuni (Smith: 210–211; see also Schaafsma: 91–93). The several reproductions he offers of the Jeddito creatures show spotted animals that are feline in appearance. One of the Kawaika-a paintings is especially interesting. It shows only the rear half of an animal, white with black spots and with a black-banded tail passing through a shield with an eagle and a star motif on it. The immediate impression is that it is an African cheetah. I am confident that it is a jaguar (see Smith: figure 56b). Another painting found at Awatovi deserves mention. This is a blue and white feline-like animal with a bearlike foot, also passing through a shield. The white portion of this figure is spotted like a jaguar. Polly Schaafsma speculates that this figure might be a jaguar (Schaafsma: 93). With regard to the mountain lion paintings at Zuni, which probably are indeed mountain lions, it must be noted that the Zuni did possess knowledge of jaguars as well. In 1540, the Spanish explorer Francisco Vasquez de Coronado visited Zuni and recorded the presence of both "tigers" and "leopards" in the area. One or both of these animals were certainly jaguars (Hammond and Rey: 172–173).

The Hopis also possessed knowledge of the jaguar. A 1908 photograph shows the full stretched-out skin of a jaguar killed by Hopi hunters from Second Mesa. The author of the book in which this picture appears, M. W. Billingsley, states that he took the photograph as the Hopis were dressing out the skin. He further notes that the skin showed no arrow marks and that the Indians claimed to have killed the jaguar "by hand" (Billingsley: 84). If true, this might reflect a ceremonial killing in which the animal was first captured and then smothered with corn pollen. This jaguar might be the same animal reportedly killed in 1907 or 1908 "by a group of Indians" four miles south of the rim of the Grand Canyon (Hoffmeister: 85).

On June 28, 1998, I attended a kachina dance held at the Hopi village of Shungopavi on Second Mesa. One of the *Siyangephoya* kachinas, or left-handed kachinas as they are commonly called in English, wore a magnificent arrow quiver made of jaguar skin. I was able to approach within a couple of feet of this dancer to make a clear identification of the pelt. The rosette-patterned markings were unmistakably jaguar. Another *Siyangephoya* wore a quiver of some kind of cloth made to represent a spotted cat. The other two *Siyangephoya* dancers wore quivers made of bobcat skin. Barton Wright describes *Siyangephoya* as one of the hunter kachinas (Wright: 110–111). I was unable to identify the source of the jaguar pelt used to make the quiver, though it might have come to the dancer through trade from Mexico. It is also possible that this skin was handed down from the jaguar killed by Hopi hunters at the turn of the century.

The Emergence of Spotted Lion in Navajo Culture

In the Navajo hunter tradition as recorded by Karl Luckert, reference is made to "Tiger," who, along with Wolf, Lion, and Bobcat, is a hunter of deer and was "present from the beginning" (Luckert: 40). Luckert believes that his Navajo collaborator's Tiger was exactly that, the Asian tiger. He theorizes that this animal was added to the story as its existence became known to the Navajo. This identification seems unlikely, since a second Navajo collaborator of Luckert's also makes reference to Tiger as being one of the leaders of the Hunter People (ibid.: 41). It seems much more probable that the Navajos adopted the word *tiger* from the Spanish and Mexicans with whom they had contact for more than three hundred years and who used the word *tigre* in reference to the jaguar. In addition, a third Luckert collaborator provided the anthropologist with another version of the Navajo hunter tradition in which the great hunters were identified as Wolf, Mountain Lion, Wildcats, and "spotted cats" (ibid.: 115). Just as he did with the term *tiger,* Luckert strangely does not seem to even consider the possibility that these spotted cat animal-gods his informant told him of were jaguars. Instead, he inexplicably concluded that these animals must be "cougars," despite the fact that the mountain lion, which most Navajos refer to as being a cougar, had already had been listed as a different entity by his informant. Perhaps Luckert simply did not know that mountain lions and cougars are the same animal. Perhaps he misinterpreted what his collaborators were telling him. In the end, it seems clear that Luckert's tigers and cougars were in reality jaguars.

The Franciscan Fathers also provide a somewhat confusing identification for the felines the Navajos were familiar with. In their ethnographic dictionary of the Navajo language, they list Navajo terms for five different cats: wildcat, lynx, mountain lion, puma, and leopard (Franciscan Fathers: 110–111). Similarities in the terms for puma and leopard suggest that the Navajo saw a close relationship between the two animals, or possibly—as I believe, based on the later writings of the most eminent of the Franciscan Fathers, Berard Haile—they were the same animal, namely the jaguar, considered within different contexts. Three other cats listed by the Franciscans, the canyon lynx, grass lynx, and meadow lynx, were thought to be mythical. The Franciscans also provided "sacred names" or ceremonial names for the mountain lion, wildcat, and puma, the latter of which they also referred to as being a "meadow wildcat" (ibid.: 175). Again, I believe this last animal to be the jaguar.

The story of Navajo creation is one of a progression of "emergences" from one world to the next. In his work on the Upward Moving and Emergence Way ceremony, recorded in 1908, Haile describes the Seventh World of the Navajo people as also being the home of the Cat People or Feline people—Mountain

Lion, Wildcat, Puma, and the Wildcat of the Canyons (Haile: 11). Again, since Mountain Lion and Puma are listed as separate entities, Puma must be a jaguar, or more accurately, Jaguar. The Cat People were anthropomorphic beings or deities who could talk, behaved like men, and possessed supernatural powers. In time, these beings transformed into the animal forms we recognize today. Thus Puma, the anthropomorphic being, became jaguar the animal. One other indication that Puma is in fact Jaguar is that in the Emergence story he lives in a "spotted house," quite possibly a symbolic reference to the spotted skin of the jaguar (ibid.: 11).

Haile goes on to describe the creation of two other pumas, one from the south and one from the north, who along with two wildcats stand in protection of the house of First Man. At one point in the story, the Wolf People, and then later the Mountain Lion, Kit Fox, and Badger People, launch an attack on the house of First Man, shooting arrows of turquoise, white shell, abalone, and jet that Puma and Wildcat catch and shoot back at their enemies. Later Puma and Wildcat of the North also attack First Man (ibid.: 11–13).

Haile also mentioned Puma (or Jaguar) in his narrative of the story leading to the first Beadway ceremony. Near the end of this ceremony, a "Wildcat" sandpainting was made. This sandpainting consisted of eight figures, including two of Mountain Lions, two of Wolves, two of Badgers, one of a Gray Wildcat, and one of "Spotted Puma" (ibid.: 92). Again, the inference is strong that Spotted Puma is Jaguar.

Gladys A. Reichard published a collection of sand-paintings—including from the Beadway—that were part of the John Frederick Huckel Collection. These sand-paintings were made by the medicine man Miguelito in 1924. In her narrative of the Beadway story, Gladys Reichard uses the name Spotted Lion instead of Puma. She goes on to identify Spotted Lion as being a "Mexican jaguar" (Reichard: 34). She reproduces three sand-paintings from Beadway, each of which includes two Spotted Lions dancing. In the first, called *The Exchange of the Quivers*, one Spotted Lion, in the company of Wolf, is shown holding a dark bow and wearing a blue quiver made of lynx skin. The second Spotted Lion, in the company of Mountain Lion, is shown holding a dark bow and wearing a quiver that Reichard describes as being of wolverine skin (ibid.: plate v.).

In the second sandpainting, also titled *The Exchange of the Quivers,* Mountain Lion, Wolf, and the two Spotted Lions are joined in their dance by two Badgers, two Lynx, and two Bobcats, but only Mountain Lion and Wolf have bow and quivers. In the third sandpainting, *The Hunting Animals with Corn Packs*, the same ten participants are dancing, but Mountain Lion and Wolf have given up their bows and quivers, and all are wearing packs on their backs laden with corn (Ibid.: plate vii.). This sandpainting is especially interesting in that it shows Spotted Lion, or jaguar, in an agricultural role and not simply as hunter and warrior.

In all three of the sandpaintings reproduced by Reichard, the figures of Spotted Lion—like Mountain Lion and Wolf—are elongated anthropomorphic depictions with straight tails. Badger's tail is shorter; Lynx and Bobcat have shorter curving "bobbed" tails. What is most interesting is that the Spotted Lion's are black with white spots. Perhaps this is meant to represent the black or melanistic phase of the jaguar, a color phase in which the rosette markings faintly show through the animal's dominant black coat. All jaguars reported from the American Southwest, however, have been of the typical orange coat variety. The black color phase appears to be limited to cats from South America. Yet the black color scheme in Navajo sandpaintings is common. Perhaps Navajo sandpainters, or at least an initial early Navajo sandpainter from whom others would copy, originally saw a photograph of a black jaguar, or maybe even saw one in a zoo where they are relatively common. Since most of the other figures in these sandpaintings also lack natural color depiction, it is also possible that the black coloring of the jaguar represents no more than the individual creativity of the sandpainter. Another interesting aspect of Spotted Lion in this sandpainting is that he is the only figure shown with stripes at the tip of his tail. In the standard orange color phase of the jaguar, the rosettes come together to form a circle against what becomes a white background at the tip of the tail, almost "raccoon like." Clearly Navajo sandpainters were familiar with the physical attributes of the jaguar, and clearly the identification of Spotted Lion as Jaguar is undeniable.

Leland C. Wyman also described two of these three Huckel sandpaintings; he too reached the conclusion that Spotted Lion is Jaguar (Wyman, 1960: 83–84) or Mexican jaguar (Wyman, 1983: 128, 130).

The Wheelwright Museum of the American Indian in Santa Fe, New Mexico, has in its collection two other Beadway sandpaintings that are very similar to the ones described above but are of an earlier provenance. In the first of these paintings, *Exchange of the Quivers*, two black Spotted Lions are shown with two Mountain Lions, one yellow, the other white. This painting is a 1925 copy of a 1904 original by medicine men Speech Man and Old Man's Son. The documentation accompanying the painting identifies the Spotted Lion as being a jaguar and explains that he was taught the Beadway by his brother Scavenger. The second Wheelwright Beadway sandpainting is titled *Hunting Animals with Cornpacks*. This 1929 painting by Husteen Ayonandeel shows two black Spotted Lions in the company of two Mountain Lions and two other figures who are presumably Wildcat or Lynx. Again, as in the Beadway sandpaintings, the Spotted Lions are black with white spots (Hevey).

Jaguars are also mentioned in a number of other Navajo sources. In the origin story of the Eagle Chant, a ceremony closely related to the Beadway, reference is made to Spotted Lion who, along with his fellow hunters Mountain Lion, Wolf, and Lynx, is one of the animal helpers to the great Navajo deity Monster Slayer (Newcomb: 66). Reference to the jaguar is also made by Leland C. Wyman and Flora L. Bailey in describing the paraphernalia used by Navajo medicine men or singers who practice the Evil Way ceremony, a ritual used to prevent diseases and misfortune caused by ghosts. Among the ceremonial items they list are two shoulder bands or bandoliers made of "spotted big wildcat skin," which they say was taken from a wildcat or jaguar, and wristlets made of "spotted skin." They conclude by noting that "the skin of a weasel may be used if jaguar is unavailable" (Wyman and Bailey: 13–14).

The Historical Jaguar in Navajo Country

I have had the opportunity to talk to a number of wildlife officials—scientists—on their thoughts regarding Navajo jaguar stories, and every scientist I talked to categorically dismissed such stories as being a case of "mistaken identity." The animal I was investigating, they told me, was most certainly a mountain lion. Scientists usually dismiss oral tradition because it cannot be supported with so-called hard scientific facts. As I think I have clearly demonstrated in this chapter, there is solid evidence to support the idea that Spotted Lion was indeed Jaguar, and that the physical, earthly manifestation of this deity—the jaguar itself—also played an important role in Navajo lifeway. While there have been no documented cases of jaguars appearing within the confines of what is today the Navajo Reservation, Navajo Country within a broader context was indeed also jaguar country, and Navajos undoubtedly came into actual physical contact with the great cat.

Beyond the rock art and their own oral traditions, many of the tribes the Navajo routinely associated with were people who had firsthand jaguar knowledge. In turn, Navajo jaguar knowledge might have come from contact with these people. Navajos, for example, have had a long and intimate relationship with the Hopis. The Hopis, if you remember, actually killed a jaguar near the rim of the Grand Canyon in 1907 or 1908. This jaguar was undoubtedly seen by Navajos who frequented this area; others might have traveled there specifically to view the animal as news of this important event most certainly spread quickly. Navajos also routinely traveled to the Hopi mesas to attend ceremonies held there and undoubtedly would have seen jaguar skins used in these rituals.

A few miles south of the current Navajo Reservation is the Zuni Pueblo. Jaguars have been historically documented in this area. In 1540, Spanish explorer Francisco Vasquez de Coronado visited Zuni and reported the presence of both "tigers" and "leopards" there. One or both of these animals were most certainly jaguars (Pavlik, 2003: 162).

Jaguars appear throughout the historical literature of the western Apaches—linguistic relatives of Navajos—who live in the mountain ranges farther south. Navajos traded with, and occasionally warred against, these people as well. As late as 1963–1964, two jaguars were killed on or near the Fort Apache Reservation (ibid.: 166).

In 1864–1868, the Navajo tribe was incarcerated along with the Apaches at Fort Sumner on the Bosque Redondo Reservation along the Pecos River in southern New Mexico. John C. Cremony, an officer in the Second Calvary of the California Volunteers stationed at Fort Sumner, 1862–1868, wrote that he frequently hunted with the Apaches there, and that "even jaguars were by no means uncommon" (ibid.: 166). Navajos might have had contact with jaguars at Fort Sumner. I could provide other examples, but these will suffice to illustrate my point that Navajos most certainly knew the jaguar.

Postscript

As noted in the beginning of this chapter, in 1996 two jaguars were recorded in southern Arizona. These sightings led to jaguars being "listed" under the Endangered Species Act the next year. The first of these jaguars would never be seen again, but the second one, an animal named Macho B by his admirers, remained in the public eye and became a symbol for environmentalists and others who saw him as proof that the American Southwest could remain a homeland for these magnificent cats. Jack Childs, the lion hunter who first videotaped Macho B, immersed himself in the study of borderlands jaguar conservation, eventually setting up strings of remote sensor cameras throughout the mountain ranges of southeastern Arizona. In 2003, Macho B reappeared in one of Childs's photographs. Over the next six years he appeared in fifty other photographs, proving without question he was a "resident" animal and not simply a transient jaguar as some biologists previously thought. During this time, the Arizona Game and Fish Department (AZGFD) made clear its desire to capture Macho B and put a radio collar on him to track his movements. Many people questioned the wisdom of this plan, especially as the animal reached an advanced age. On February 18, 2009, Macho B was captured—supposedly inadvertently—in a leg snare set by a private contractor working for the Arizona Game and Fish Department, a jaguar specialist reportedly trapping mountain lions for the department. Macho B was tranquilized, and as had long been desired, he was fitted with a radio collar and released. But things went horribly wrong. The radio signals emitted from his collar revealed that the aged animal retreated into a dense area near his capture site and never left. On March 2, AZGFD personnel returned to the area to find Macho B weak and unable to even escape. They again tranquilized him and flew him by helicopter to the Phoenix Zoo, where a team of veterinarians proclaimed he was suffering from acute kidney failure. That same day, Macho B, the jaguar who had meant so much to so many people, was euthanized. It was estimated that the jaguar was sixteen to twenty years old. The previous oldest jaguar on record had died at the age of thirteen.

Shortly after the death of Macho B, a young woman who had voluntarily assisted the biologist in trapping the jaguar, came forth and admitted that she had been instructed by him to bait the snare with female jaguar scat that he had provided her. AZGFD and the biologist had apparently lied about the circumstances of Macho B's capture. Since the capture of Macho B was a violation of the Endangered Species Act, a federal investigation was launched. It was determined that Macho B had been wrongly and criminally captured without the proper federal permits. Moreover, it was determined that the biologist who had trapped Macho B, along with at least one other AZGFD employee, had conspired to cover up what had happened. In the end, AZGFD was—wrongly, in my opinion—exonerated of any wrongdoing. The biologist who had orchestrated the entire tragedy was fined and given a five-year probation from working with any big cats in the United States—though he quickly found employment in Spain. And in one of the more bizarre developments of this case, the courageous woman who played the role of whistle-blower was charged with conspiracy and received one year probation from working with big cats in the United States (see Brun).

The story of the life and death of Macho B well illustrates the way western society—and especially western science—looks upon and treats the Animal People. Western man sees other forms of life as being mere objects over which he has complete dominion. For over thirteen years Macho B willingly *chose*—on his own terms—to teach and share his secrets, to give all of us a glimpse into his private life. He did so in a manner that maintained his freedom and dignity. But for AZGFD, those who directly had a hand in his death, and the western value system they represent, it was not enough. It is never enough.

Vine Deloria Jr. notes that a great gulf exists between how western science and tribal people handle knowledge. Western science *forces* secrets from nature, whereas Native Americans have always accepted secrets from the rest of creation (Deloria Jr. and Wildcat: 64). Western science answers to no higher power. It sees no limit to its quest for knowledge and arrogantly believes it is entitled to know the most intimate details of everything. In contrast, Native people accept the unknown and unexplained with reverence. They know that some things cannot, and should not, be explained. In the tribal world, some things are better left a mystery. It is those mysteries that keep Native people—including the Navajos—humble and respectful toward powers greater than themselves. This is the foundation of Native traditional ecological knowledge. It is a foundation that Western society would be well advised to turn to as it seeks to understand and live in harmony with the natural world.

References

Baird, Spencer F. 1859. *Special Report upon the Mammals of the Mexican Boundary*. Washington, DC: Smithsonian Institution.

Billingsley, M. W. 1971. *Behind the Scenes in Hopi Land*. Private printing.

Brown, David E. 1991. "Revival for El Tigre?" *Defenders,* 66(1): 27–35.

Brown, David E. 1997a. "Jaguars Known and Reported Killed or Photographed (in Arizona) since 1890." Unpublished paper.

Brown, David E. 1997b. "Return of El Tigre," *Defenders,* 72(4): 12–15.

Brown, David E. and Carlos A. Lopez. 2001. *Borderland Jaguars.* Salt Lake City: University of Utah Press.

Brun, Janay. 2011. "Truth and Consequences," *Three Coyotes* 1(2): 13–21.

Cremony, John C. 1868/1970. *Life among the Apaches.* Glorietta, NM: Rio Grande Press.

Crotty, Helen K. 1995. *Anasazi Mural Art of the Pueblo IV Period, AD 1300–1600: Influences, Selective Adaptations, and Cultural Diversity in the Prehistoric Southwest*. PhD dissertation. Los Angeles: University of California.

Davis, John V. and Kay S. Jones. 1974. "A Rock Art Inventory at Hueco Tanks State Park, Texas," *El Paso Archaeological Society Special Report*, No. 12.

Deloria, Vine, Jr. and Daniel R. Wildcat. 2001. *Power and Place: Indian Education in America*. Golden, CO: Fulcrum Publishing.

Fragua Hevey, Janet. 1998. Personal conversation. April 10.

Franciscan Fathers. 1910. *An Ethnologic Dictionary of the Navajo Language.* St. Michaels, AZ: St. Michaels Press.

Goodwin, Grenville and Keith H. Basso. 1971. *Western Apache Raiding and Warfare.* Tucson: University of Arizona Press.

Haile, Father Berard. 1981. *The Upward Moving and Emergence Way*. Lincoln: University of Nebraska Press.

Hammond, George P. and Agapito Rey. 1940. *Narratives of the Coronado Expedition,* 1540–1542. Albuquerque, NM: Coronado Cuarto Centennial Publications.

Hibben, Frank C. 1975. *Kiva Art of the Anasazi at Pottery Mound.* Las Vegas, NV: K.C. Publications.

Hoffmeister, Donald F. 1971. *Mammals of the Grand Canyon.* Chicago: University of Illinois Press.

Luckert, Karl W. 1975. *The Navajo Hunter Tradition.* Tucson: University of Arizona Press.

Mahler, Richard. 2009. *The Jaguar's Shadow: Searching for a Mythic Cat.* New Haven, CT: Yale University Press.

Newcomb, Franc J. 1940. "Origin Legend of the Navajo Eagle Chant," *Journal of American Folk-Lore*, 53(207): 50–78.

Parsons, Elsie Clews. 1939/1966. *Pueblo Indian Religion.* 2 volumes. Lincoln: University of Nebraska Press.

Pavlik, Steve. 2003. "Rohonas and Spotted Lions: The Historical and Cultural Occurrence of the Jaguar, *Panthera onca*, among the Native Tribes of the American Southwest," *Wicazo Sa Review*, 18(1): 157–175.

Pavlik, Steve. 2009. Guest Commentary: "Western Scientists: Macho B Died for Your Sins," *Tucson Weekly*. August 6.

Pavlik, Steve. 2010. "Macho B Died for Your Sins: Western vs. Indigenous Perspectives on the Killing of the Last Borderlands Jaguar," *Red Ink*, 16(1): 40–45.

Reichard, Gladys A. 1939/1977. *Navajo Medicine Man Sandpaintings.* New York: Dover Publications.

Saunders, Nicholas J., ed. 1998. *Icons of Power: Feline Symbolism in the Americas.* New York: Routledge.

Schaafsma, Polly. 2000. *Warrior, Shield, and Star: Imagery and Ideology of Pueblo Warfare.* Santa Fe, NM: Western Edge Press.

Smith, Watson. 1952. *Kiva Mural Decorations at Awatovi and Kawaika-a.* Cambridge, MA: Peabody Museum of American Archaeology and Ethnology.

Sutherland, Kay and Paul Steed, Jr. 1974. "The Fort Hancock Rock Art Site Number One," *The Artifact*, 12(4): 1–64.

Wellman, Klaus F. 1979. *A Survey of North American Indian Art.* Graz, Austria: Akademische Druck-u Verlagsanstalt.

White, Leslie A. 1942. "The Pueblo of Santa Ana, New Mexico," *Memoirs of the American Anthropological Association*, Supplement 60: 1–360.

White, Leslie A. 1944. "'Rohona' in Pueblo Culture," *Papers of the Michigan Academy of Science, Arts, and Letters*, Vol. 29: 439–443.

White, Leslie A. 1947. "Ethnozoology of the Keresan Pueblo Indians," *Papers of the Michigan Academy of Science, Arts, and Letters*, Vol. 31: 223–243.

Wright, Barton. 1977. *Hopi Kachinas: The Complete Guide to Collecting Kachina Dolls.* Flagstaff, AZ: Northland Press.

Wyman, Leland C. 1960. *Navaho Sandpainting: The Huckel Collection.* Colorado Springs, CO: Taylor Museum.

Wyman, Leland C. 1983. *Southwest Indian Drypainting.* Albuquerque: University of New Mexico Press.

Wyman, Leland C. and Flora L. Bailey. 1943. "Navajo Upward-Reaching Way: Objective, Behavior, Rationale, and Sanction," *University of New Mexico Bulletin* 389, Anthropological Series 4.

Chapter Six
Children of the Monster Bird

This chapter was originally presented as a paper at the Western Social Science Association Conference held in Las Vegas, Nevada, April 11, 2003.

The birds of prey—the raptors—are the winged carnivores of Navajo Country. Eagles, hawks, owls, and vultures all play important roles in the stories and culture of the tribe.

No animal or bird is associated more with Native Americans than the eagle. In Navajo Country, there are two species of eagles, the golden eagle (*Aquila chrysaetos*) and the bald eagle (*Haliaeetus leucocephalus*). The golden eagle is a year-round resident, whereas the bald eagle is generally seen only in the winter. Unlike many other tribes, Navajos—at least traditional Navajos—hold only the golden eagle in great esteem. To the Navajos the golden eagle is everything that is to be admired—a proud and fierce bird that soared high in the clouds and could easily be admired as a great hunter and warrior. In contrast, the bald eagle is not as graceful as its golden brethren. Its heavy wingbeats make it appear slow. Nor is the bald eagle much of a hunter. Instead it feeds mostly on fish and carrion and often robs other weaker birds of their catches. In addition, bald eagles do not display the power or courage of golden eagles. Consequently, Navajos traditionally regarded the bald eagle as a "junk bird" and the lowest of the raptors in terms of status. The Navajo word for eagle, *asta*, is said to specifically mean the golden eagle (Tsosie, 2003).

In addition to the true eagles, the hawk species that inhabit Navajo Country are sometimes also traditionally identified as "eagles." Among these species are the osprey, red-tailed hawk, Cooper's hawk, northern goshawk, Swainson's hawk, ferruginous hawk, rough-legged hawk, sharp-shinned hawk, northern harrier, American kestrel, peregrine falcon, and prairie falcon. It is one or the other of these hawks and falcons that Navajos are referring to when they speak of "black eagle," "white eagle," "gray eagle," or "white back eagle" (see Franciscan Fathers: 158). This ambiguity in Navajo terminology is somewhat problematic. Sometimes these raptors are called eagles; sometimes they are more accurately called hawks. Navajos also have species names for each of these birds.

Navajo Country is also home to the turkey vulture and more recently is a destination for visiting California condors that have been reintroduced into the Grand Canyon by the US Fish and Wildlife Service and the Arizona Game and Fish Department. These visitations might very well be considered a homecoming, since condors historically inhabited the red rock cliffs of the Navajo Reservation. Vultures and condors, although categorized by western science as being birds of prey, are viewed somewhat differently by Navajos than the eagles and hawks. Although they are said to be sacred and are not molested, as carrion eaters they are associated with death and uncleanliness.

And finally there are the owls. As with the vultures, western science considers them birds of prey, but Navajos see them far differently. As denizens of the night, owls are associated by Navajos more with nighthawks and poorwills than with other raptors. Almost a dozen species of owls inhabit the Navajo Reservation, including the great-horned owl, barn owl, spotted owl, Western screech owl, flammulated owl, northern pygmy owl, burrowing owl, short-eared owl, and northern saw-whet owl.

For the Navajos, the eagle is truly a sacred bird, with an origin that traces far back into the creation stories. Eagle ceremonies are an important part of the Navajo traditional religious system, and the use of eagle body parts is an integral aspect of these ceremonies. Consequently, the hunting of eagles once held a vital place in Navajo life and, as might be expected, was surrounded by much ritual. In recent times, eagle parts are acquired by means other than hunting, but the eagle itself has not lost its meaning and power to the Navajo people. Indeed, the protection of eagles is, at least on the surface, a major cause of friction between the Navajos and their neighbors the Hopi—the only Indian tribe legally permitted to capture and kill eagles, which they do on Navajo land.

Origin of the Eagles

In the Navajo stories, the world was once inhabited by terrible monsters who ate people. Among these monsters were Yeitso, Monster-Who-Kicked-People-Off-The-Cliff, Monster-That-Killed-With-His-Eyes,

Horned Monster, Rolling Rock, Crushing Rock, Moving Sand, Wandering Stone, Tracking Bear, and the Twelve Running Antelopes. In addition, there existed a pair of Monster Birds that lived atop Shiprock, the geographic formation the Navajos also know as the Winged Rock.

The job of killing these monsters fell to the two hero twins, Monster Slayer and Child Born of Water. These brothers were the offspring of Changing Woman—the most beloved of the Navajo Holy People—and the Sun. Armed with magical weapons and flint armor given to them by their father, the twins began to destroy the monsters that plagued the Earth.

The actual task of killing the Monster Birds fell to the elder brother, Monster Slayer. The following account is adapted from *Navaho Legends* by Washington Matthews. A somewhat different version can be found in *Navaho Indian Myths* by Aileen O'Bryan.

Monster Slayer set out to hunt the Monster Birds. He walked down the backs of two great snakes until he arrived near Shiprock, where they had their nest. In this nest were two young. Monster Slayer was attacked by the male bird, who on the fourth attempt picked up the young hero in his talons. Flying over its nest, the male bird dropped Monster Slayer in order to kill him on the rocks near the nest. Instead, Monster Slayer floated down, clinging to a life feather given to him as a gift by Spider Woman. Upon landing, Monster Slayer released a bowel of blood to make it look as if he had smashed on the rocks. Entering the nest, he cautioned the young birds to be silent and positioned himself where the nestlings told him their parents would land. In due time, the male bird arrived, and Monster Slayer killed it with a lightning arrow given to him by his father, the Sun. A short time later the female bird arrived with the lifeless body of a Pueblo woman it had captured. Monster Slayer killed the female bird as well with a second lightning arrow. "Will you slay us too?" cried the baby birds. Monster Slayer replied that he would not. He would spare their lives, and they would be useful to man. To the elder baby bird, he said, "You shall furnish plumes for men to use in their rites, and bones for whistles." He then grasped the baby bird by its legs and swung it four times in the air. As he did this, the baby Monster Bird changed into a beautiful eagle with strong wings. Monster Slayer released this newly created eagle into the sky to fly away. He then repeated this act with the younger of the two baby birds, saying, "In the days to come men will listen to your voice to know what will be their future. Sometimes you will tell the truth; sometimes you will lie." And as Monster Slayer swung this younger bird around, its head grew large and round, and its eyes grew big, and it became an owl. Monster Slayer then threw this bird into a hole in the side of a cliff that became its home. In such a manner the first eagle and owl were created—the ancestors to all present-day eagles and owls.

In still another version of this story, an unnamed collaborator told Kluckhohn and Wyman that Monster Slayer gave the following instructions to the Rock Monster Birds:

Don't kill Navahos any more. Now you must just eat the rabbit and prairie dog. But you've got to be of some use. The Navahos will get feathers from you and use them in chasing away evil spirits. You are going to be just like my children from now on, so the evil spirits will be afraid of you and your feathers. (Kluckhohn and Wyman: 36–37)

The collaborator went on to add:

That's why eagles today fly away from Navahos and don't talk to them. That's why ever since then the evil spirits have been afraid of eagle feathers. Whenever an evil spirit sees an eagle feather moving, he runs about ten feet away. If he sees it move some more, he gets scared and runs away. (Ibid.)

The story of Monster Slayer killing the Monster Birds explains why Navajos believe that eagles and their feathers possess the power to ward off the evil influences of witchcraft. It is for this reason that traditional Navajos always carry an eagle feather on their person and use eagle feathers in all Evil Way ceremonies, a ceremony that is used against witchcraft.

Two interesting aspects of the Monster Bird story are the origin of the story itself and the biological identity—if any—of the Monster Birds.

As noted throughout this book, Navajos are descendants of Pueblos and Athabaskans. Most of the Navajo stories and resulting ceremonial system are, however, products of their Pueblo heritage. It should not be surprising then that the Pueblos have a Monster Bird tradition. *Kwatoko* is the "monster eagle" in Hopi myths. He was "as high as a man and the spread of his wings was as wide as a large house. He swooped down and carried off men, women, and children" (Tyler: 80). Again it should come as no surprise that both the male and female versions of *Kwatoko* were destroyed with lightning by the Hopi hero twins. It seems quite clear that the Navajo story traces its origin to the Pueblo story. But what were the Monster Birds?

One very plausible explanation is that the Monster Birds were California condors, which historically occupied Navajo Country. If the stories go back further, these birds might have been Pleistocene or Holocene (1.8 million to 8,000 years ago) condors or teratorns that inhabited the American Southwest during that time period (Mayor: 162; see also the writings of Steven D. Emslie). A somewhat more imaginative theory—but plausible, if one factors in the metaphysical view of time and space—is that the Monster Birds might have been pterosaurs or some other type of prehistoric flying animals from the Mesozoic period. There is a pictograph attributed to the Anasazi that is located at Black Dragon Wash in an area known as the San Rafael Swell in Utah. This image has widely been interpreted as being that of a pterosaur. It is interesting to note that not far away from this pictograph site, the University of Ohio quarried a fossil pterosaur. Certainly there are far more questions than answers in this mystery.

Eagle Mythology and Ceremonialism

Anthropologists Leland C. Wyman and Clyde Kluckhohn in their definitive classification of Navajo ceremonials list fifty-eight distinct rituals, not counting the various huntingways. Wyman and Kluckhohn consider nine of these ceremonials to be extinct. (Wyman and Kluckhohn: 36). In addition, most of these ceremonials have multiple branches or sub-ceremonials. The origins of these ceremonies are found in the Navajo stories. Eagles make cameo appearances throughout the Navajo stories. Two stories, however, the Eagle Way (also called the Eagle Catching Myth), and the Beadway myth, focus on eagles. Both chants are used to cure headaches and head diseases, boils and sores, inflamed throat, swollen legs, itching, loss of appetite, and vomiting (Reichard, 1950: 122). It is to these two stories that we now turn our attention.

In the story of the Eagle Way Chant, White Shell Woman and Turquoise Woman, daughters of Changing Woman, go on a journey. Along the way they meet Monster Slayer, who helps them by advising them how to avoid monsters and telling them where to locate food. In time he wins their trust, and they go to live with him. After some time of living together, two other maidens visit them. Unable to choose between the two pairs of women, Monster Slayer proposes a grinding contest to determine which pair will become his wives. The two maidens, through trickery, win the contest. Monster Slayer goes with them to their hunting camp. Initially, the father of the maidens, Cornsmut Man, objects to having an Earth person as a son-in-law. Monster Slayer, however, demonstrates his supernatural power by rendering Cornsmut Man unconscious, then ritually restoring him.

Monster Slayer and his two wives are sent ahead to construct a new shelter each time the hunting camp moves. In time, they enter the land of the Eagle People and their headman, Hair Turning White. This headman also opposes the presence of Monster Slayer, and the hero must again demonstrate his power by rendering Hair Turning White unconscious and then restoring him ritually. There follows a series of four trials and attempts to destroy Monster Slayer by Cornsmut Man and Hair Turning White. The pair attempt to kill Monster Slayer by using a cannibal eagle, a huge rattlesnake, a tracking bear, and poison. Each time, much to the amazement of the conspirators, Monster Slayer prevails by using his supernatural powers. Finally Cornsmut Man agrees to the marriage of Monster Slayer to his daughters. First, however, Monster Slayer must learn all of the songs and prayers of the Eagle Chant.

Cornsmut Man shows Monster Slayer the ritual of capturing eagles by building an eagle trapping pit, using a live rabbit as bait, and the proper method of then distributing the eagle feathers to the gods. Hair Turning White belittles this method and offers to show Monster Slayer another method to trap eagles. Cornsmut Man warns his soon-to-be son-in-law that Hair Turning White is a witch and that his method of catching eagles will result in the Earth people getting diseases. Monster Slayer elects to learn from Cornsmut Man.

The Eagle Chant myth continues with Monster Slayer experiencing a number of other adventures, including coming down with an illness back at the camp of the eagles—an event from which he is saved by his three brothers, Child Born of Water, Reared Within the Earth, and Changing Grandchild. The three brothers then convince Monster Slayer that he should return to his original wives back on the Earth.

Monster Slayer returns to the Earth, where he demonstrates to the Dove People how to trap eagles. He initially uses a squirrel as bait but is advised that he must use a rabbit. Following the successful hunt, he distributes the eagle feathers to the Holy People. The story ends with Monster Slayer and his two wives again parting company. The women travel to the sacred mountains, while he travels to the Shining Water (Spencer: 189–194).

In the story of the Beadway Chant, a Navajo boy, who is best known as Scavenger, is hunting for seeds near Pueblo Bonito and is captured by the Pueblos. The Pueblos take him to the village of Aztec, where he is kept as a prisoner for four days. They then take him to a cliff overlooking the San Juan River where the eagles nest. They tell him that they will lower him in a basket to the eagles' nest, where there are two young eagles. He is told that he is to place the two nestlings in the basket and lower them to the bottom of the cliff to where the Pueblos' fellow tribesmen are waiting. After he has accomplished this task, they will give him food, water, and freedom. Scavenger agrees. After he is lowered to the nest, however, he is told by Wind, "Do not take the little eagles." He is then told by Dragonfly, "Do not take them, or you will stay here forever and turn to dust." Now knowing that the Pueblos meant to trick him, Scavenger refuses to place the baby eagles in the basket, but now he is also stranded on the cliff. He spends a cold night huddled among the baby eagles.

At dawn the father eagle returns to the nest to find Scavenger with his children. Pleased that the Navajo did not send his children to the waiting Pueblos, the father eagle feeds cornmeal to the hungry boy. He then flies away, saying that he will return in four days and will decide then what to do. The next day, the mother eagle arrives at the nest. She too is pleased that Scavenger did not give her children to the Pueblos. She also feeds him cornmeal and then flies away, promising to return in three days.

Meantime, the Pueblos have vowed to shoot the boy with arrows. One of the baby eagles comes to the edge of the cliff and flaps its wings vigorously, releasing clouds of powder that blind the Pueblos, some falling off the cliff to their deaths. On the fourth day, the mother and father eagles return with a plan to help the boy escape. They wrap him in magical robes and give him a crystal to light up the inside of the robes. Then other eagles appear and, holding the robes in their beaks, lift the boy and fly him to safety. At one point, it becomes apparent that the boy is too heavy and they call upon the Blue and Black Racer Snakes (Arrow Snakes), who wrap their tails around Scavenger and pull him through a hole in the clouds to the home of the eagles.

Upon arriving at the home of the eagles, Scavenger—now called Eagle Boy in some versions of this story—watches as the eagles step out of their feathery clothing to reveal themselves to be people.

During his stay with the eagles, his hosts always tell him to stay while they go about their business. Scavenger never listens to their advice and constantly gets himself into trouble, often nearly meeting death. Each time, the eagles return home to save him, often through various ceremonies. In this way Scavenger learns about ceremonies and medicine.

Eventually Scavenger asks Spider Woman where the eagles travel to each day. Spider Woman replies that they go to battle their enemies the Bumble Bees and the Tumbleweeds. Scavenger wants to help his friends, so Spider Woman gives him a life feather for protection and a black cane to use against the enemies of the eagles. In return, Spider Woman asks Scavenger to bring her new feathers from the bodies of the fallen eagles to replenish her four hoops. When the eagles leave on their next war party, Scavenger follows them. He witnesses a terrible fight in which many eagles are killed. He then joins in the battle. Going among the Tumbleweeds, Scavenger gathers them up harmlessly with his black cane and burns them. Then he destroys the Bumble Bees by spitting the juice of a magical plant on them that stuns them and renders their stings harmless. He then clubs them to death using rabbit brush as a whip. Finally he fulfills his promise to Spider Woman by collecting the feathers from the bodies of the dead eagles.

The eagles are thankful for Scavenger's help defeating their enemies and reward him by offering two of their young girls for marriage, an offer he accepts. During the remainder of his stay with the eagles, he learns the songs and procedures for the Beadway ceremony. In time, he returns to the Earth for a short period in which he passes this ceremonial knowledge on to the people. Eventually he returns to live among the eagles (Matthews: 195–208; Spencer: 195–201).

What I have provided is the briefest possible discussion of these two myths. Both are far more complicated, with many details. Every detail in these stories is important, for every detail reveals some aspect of the story that must be properly demonstrated when the ceremony is conducted. Consequently, each ceremony includes the use of ritual equipment that is accounted for in the myth itself. Not surprisingly, much of the ritual equipment from the Eagle Chant and Beadway Chant—and most other Navajo ceremonies as well—are made of or include the body parts of eagles.

Ceremonial Utilization of Eagles

Except for ritual consumption, eagles are not eaten by Navajo people. Consequently, the use of eagle body parts is reserved almost entirely for ceremonial purposes.

As noted earlier, there were at least fifty-eight distinct traditional Navajo ceremonies with numerous subgroups. Almost all of these ceremonies were—and are—healing ceremonies conducted by a trained practitioner called a medicine man or, more properly, a singer. Most Navajo singers tend to be specialists. In other words, they often know and practice one, perhaps only a few, ceremonies. In order to successfully perform a ceremony, a singer must use a multitude of medicines and ceremonial items that anthropologists usually refer to as his or her "equipment." This equipment falls into two general categories, that which can be used for any ceremony, and that which is specific to a particular ceremony. Every item of ceremonial equipment traces its origin and use back to the creation story that explains the illness and the remedy for it. Not surprisingly, a disproportionate amount of this ceremonial equipment is made completely of or includes parts of eagles. Below is a brief description of some of these items.

Feathers are the main item taken from an eagle carcass. All feathers are utilized, but especially desirable are the tail and wing feathers, plumes, and the down or fluff feathers.

Navajos distinguish between two general categories of feathers, living and nonliving. Living feathers—or life feathers, as they are also called—are those that are taken from a living bird. Sources of these feathers are birds that are captured alive, or feathers that fall from a living bird—a rare gift. Ideally these are feathers that have never touched the ground. Unlike the Hopis, Navajos never keep live eagles as a source of feathers and other body parts.

One use of a life feather is for personal protection, especially against witchcraft. Small plume or fluff feathers are used for this purpose. Men often keep them in their billfolds. Most traditional Navajos generally carry a life feather. Most eagle feathers are used as required components of ceremonial equipment. The following list describes some of the uses for eagle feathers.

- The staff or stick that is carried to announce an Enemyway is adorned by two tail feathers.

- A bundle of wing feathers is used as an exorcism wand in the Windway ceremony.

- A single plume feather is used as a hair tie or chant tokens for a patient during most ceremonies.

- Plume feathers are used as part of prayer shafts (reeds).

- The six main *Yei* dancers in a Nightway ceremony each wear two tail feathers.

- The Hunch-Back *Yei* wears a row of wing feathers down his back.

- Talking God's headdress is made of twelve tail feathers—said to be the "rays of predawn" (Reichard, 1950: 188).

- Live feathers are used as "dancing feathers" as part of a specialty act in the Fire Dance portion of the Shootingway ceremony.

- Plume feathers are attached to many talking prayer sticks. Navajo talking prayer sticks are called *ketohs*—this probably means "place where it is feathered, or place of feathering" (ibid.: 301). These talking prayer sticks are used in the Mountainway, Beautyway, Nightway, and Navajo Windway.

- Miniature arrows are adorned with tail feathers. This is for the Evil Way ceremony.

- Feathers play a role in the ash blowing (blackening) rite (ibid.: 517).

- Unraveling strings are made of wool or cotton and one or more live feathers are tied to them (ibid.: 642).

- Down is tied on to the yarn of an aspergill or medicine stopper (ibid.: 638).

- Hoops (used in Shootingway) have feathers attached to them.

- Both hide and gourd rattles have plumes attached.

- Eagle feathers were used to decorate the "war caps" of Navajo warriors (Hill, 1936: 9)

- A live feather was part of every Navajo war bundle (ibid.: 10).

- Two feathers were attached to the war lance at the juncture of the handle and point (ibid.: 10).

- Feathers were also attached to the war shield for protection and success in fighting (ibid.: 11).

- Jewel offerings: plumes included in bags.

- Wide Boards: paddle-shaped boards with life feathers attached. Used in a number of ceremonies including Male Shootingway, Windway, Hailway, and Waterway.

- For Beadway and Eagle Way, a special whistle is made of a femur from a rabbit killed by an eagle.

- Bundle prayer sticks have live plumes attached at their top ends by loops of buckskin or cotton strings. These prayer sticks are stuck in the ground around a sandpainting.

In addition to feathers, other parts of the eagle's carcass are also utilized for ceremonial or religious purposes.

Eagle talons are used to decorate the bandoliers and wristlets worn by Shootingway singers; they are also used to rip the yucca used to tie spruce branches together in the making of collars for *Yei* dancers.

Eagle gall (or bile) was used as part of an antidote against witchcraft. A bitter-tasting grass was ground up into a powder. To this powder a small mixture of liquid eagle, wolf, and mountain lion gall was added. Will Tsosie reports that this is a very expensive medicine; a few drops of this liquid—enough to fill the *tip* of a teaspoon—costs over one hundred dollars. This mixture is then carried in a small buckskin pouch. Again, as in the case of the life feather, a traditional Navajo, according to Tsosie, "Does not leave home without it" (Tsosie, 2003).

The eye water—tears—of the eagle is used in the star-gazing ritual. A "star gazer" would grind up some crystal and "mirage stone" and mix this dust with the eye water from an eagle and rub it under his own eye. The he would fix his gaze on a star until a vision came to him (Hill, 1938: 165).

Eagle bones were used to make whistles that are blown to attract the Holy People in the Mountainway and Beadway ceremonies.

In closing this section, a word needs to be said regarding the use of eagle parts in Native American

Church (NAC) ceremonies. As I have noted elsewhere, the NAC is now the dominant religion on the Navajo Reservation, with perhaps 75 percent of tribal members participating. This work is restricted to a discussion of orthodox traditional religion only. The NAC does use some eagle parts, most notably for whistles and fans, in their ceremonies. NAC requests to the National Eagle Repository far outnumber traditional requests. Aberle's definitive work on the peyote religion among the Navajos (1966) does not shed any additional light on the use of eagle feathers or body parts.

Navajo Eagle Hunting

Traditionally, the Navajos hunted eagles and other birds of prey in a manner as prescribed by the Eagle Way or Eagle Catching myth. The following information is from Willard W. Hill (1938: 161–166).

Eagles were considered—along with deer, antelope and bear—"holy human beings," and thus the hunting of eagles was considered to be a ritual hunt with a strict adherence to the sanctions found in the eagle myths. The hunt itself took place from late November until January and was placed under the supervision of a singer who knew the eagle rites. Indeed, in most cases the singer was the actual hunter, joined by one special assistant who might have been an apprentice. In addition to the leader and his assistant, others accompanied the hunters to provide nonritualistic assistance. The hunt itself generally lasted for twelve days.

The hunt began with the building of two shelters. One shelter, composed of brush and with the entrance facing east, primarily served as a temporary home for the assistants. The second shelter was the eagle pit from which the capture of the eagles would take place. This pit was dug the night before the hunt.

The eagle pit was a hole in the ground about six feet long, three feet wide, and four feet deep—large enough for the eagle hunter to lie down in. Poles were laid across the excavation and covered with bark and earth to camouflage its presence. A small hole was left open at one end, just large enough to pull an eagle through. Occasionally a second "room" was attached as a place to keep the eagles that were to be captured.

When the pit was completed, all of the participants returned to the brush shelter to spend the night singing eagle hunting songs. Just before dawn, the lead hunter and his special assistant entered the eagle pit.

A live rabbit was tied near the pit to serve as bait. Another stake was set up near one end of the pit to which the first eagle caught would be tied to later serve as a decoy. The hunters were said to be naked except that they were colored with white clay and spotted with corn smut—quite possibly to acknowledge the role of Cornsmut Man, who taught Monster Slayer the Eagle Way ceremony and hunting method. Then the wait began. Time was passed by singing eagle songs and praying for good luck in the hunt.

If all went well, eagles and hawks would soon begin to come to the bait. When an eagle swooped down to grab the rabbit, the hunter would reach up through the hole, grab the bird by the legs, and pull it into the pit.

The first eagle to offer itself was always then used as a decoy. Each successive eagle or hawk was pulled in, bound, and placed to the side or in the adjoining room. When night fell, the hunt came to an end. The captured eagles were then strangled or clubbed to death. The hunters returned to their camp.

Once back at the brush shelter, the eagles were skinned in a special manner as prescribed by the Eagle Catching Myth. The head and legs were left attached to the carcass. The eagles were then roasted, and a feast followed. Everyone who would eat the eagle's flesh would have eagle hunting songs sung over them and were given a special "eagle medicine" of some unspecified herbs.

After the hunting party had feasted, the feathers and remaining parts of the eagle carcasses that were not to be used were taken outside, where a Blessingway ceremony was held for the eagle. The next day, or perhaps after the conclusion of the hunt, the eagle feathers were distributed among all of the participants.

With the close of the hunt, the rabbit that had been used as bait was released. For a reward, a turquoise bead or white shell bead was attached to the rabbit's leg. In addition, the first-caught eagle was also released. Again, a turquoise or white shell bead was attached to its leg or around its neck.

Occasionally, a captured eagle was not killed, and plume feathers were pulled from it before it was released. This was one source of the life feathers mentioned earlier.

According to Hill, members of the Coyote Pass clan—a clan with Pueblo origins—were allowed to capture eagles and raise them for feathers. Will Tsosie, a member of the Coyote Pass clan himself, disputes this (Tsosie, 2003).

Upon returning home from the hunt, the participants held one additional evening ceremony.

It is difficult to determine when the ritualistic way of hunting eagles came to an end. Will Tsosie talked of his father killing two eagles for feathers shortly before the passage of federal laws designed to protect the birds. In this case, his father shot the eagles with a rifle but dusted the bullets with ash beforehand. The dead birds were then gently beaten with a clump or fistful of snakeweed to "chase off bad spirits" or to "remove bad intentions." These birds were plucked, not skinned, and some of the feathers were left on each wing to "allow the eagle to return home." Tsosie states that Navajos for the most part stopped killing eagles after federal laws were passed to protect them. However, he believes that some Navajos undoubtedly continue to kill eagles illegally (ibid.).

The Navajo-Hopi Eagle Dispute

In general, raptors are protected by state and federal laws that make it illegal to kill, capture, possess, harass, or harm any bird of prey or possess any bird of prey part without a valid permit. For untold years, Americans had indiscriminately killed birds of prey, which they considered to be vermin. Eagles did receive some measure of protection under the Migratory Bird Treaty Act, but this protection was not adequate. Under this act, killing an eagle was only a misdemeanor unless it could be proved the killing was done for commercial reasons. Then, in 1940, the United States government passed the Bald Eagle Protection Act, which prohibited "the take, possession, sale, purchase, barter, offer to sell, purchase or barter, transport, export or import, of any bald or golden eagle, alive or dead, including any part, nest, or egg, unless allowed by permit." But a greater threat to the eagle's survival began during the same period as the chemical pesticide (dichlorodiphenyltrichloroethane) (DDT) came into widespread use to destroy mosquitoes and agricultural pests. DDT-tainted runoff from farm fields polluted rivers and lakes and infected fish, the primary food of bald eagles. The chemical entered the bloodstream of the eagles and interfered with the repro-ductive cycle of the female birds. Specifically, DDT made it impossible for the birds to produce adequate calcium for eggs. Consequently, eagles produced eggs that were too soft and crushed easily under pressure. Entire gener-ations of eagles were lost; also hard hit were peregrine falcons. In 1892, it was estimated that there were 50,000 nesting pairs of bald eagles in the continental United States; by 1963 the number had been reduced to 417.

In 1962, Rachel Carson published her monumental book *Silent Spring*, in which she alerted the nation to plummeting bird populations, including that of bald eagles. With its national symbol on the brink of extinc-tion, the United States government decided to act. In 1972, the turning point in saving the eagle came when the Environmental Protection Agency (EPA) banned the use of DDT. The following year the Endangered Species Act (ESA) was passed. The ESA protected two classifications of wildlife species: endangered, meaning a species or subspecies "on the brink of extinction," and threatened, a species or subspecies "likely to become endangered within the foreseeable future." The southern bald eagle had been listed as endangered under a precursor to the ESA in 1967; the northern bald eagle was listed as endangered in 1978. In sum, bald eagles were given complete protection as an endangered species in forty-three states and as a threatened species in five additional states. Only in Alaska, which had a robust and seemingly healthy population, were bald eagles left unprotected.

The banning of DDT and the listing of the bald eagle under the ESA, as well as a renewed interest and support to continue such conservation measures, had the desired effect of saving the bald eagle—and a number of other raptors, including the peregrine falcon and California condor—from extinction. By 1999, the number of breeding pairs of bald eagles in the lower United States climbed to 5,748. In 2001, the bald eagle's status under the ESA was downgraded from endangered to threatened.

Meanwhile, golden eagles were also benefiting from the efforts to save the bald eagle. In 1962, golden eagles were included under the Bald Eagle Protection Act because it was difficult to distinguish young bald eagles from young golden eagles. Because they were never considered either endangered or threatened, golden eagles never were listed under the ESA.

Recognizing the importance of golden eagles in Native American ceremonialism, when the Bald Eagle Protection Act—now simply known as the Eagle Act—was amended to include the golden eagle, a provision was added that allowed Indians to harvest golden eagles for religious purposes. Specifically, the amended act said:

> Whenever, after investigation, the Secretary of the Interior shall determine that it is compatible with the preservation of the bald eagle or the golden eagle to permit the taking, possession, and transportation of specimens thereof for the . . . religious purposes of Indian tribes . . . he may authorize the taking of such eagles.

The act went on to say:

> Provided further, that bald eagles may not be taken for any purpose unless, prior to taking, a permit to do so is procured from the Secretary of the Interior.

In order to receive a permit, the following information must be submitted to the appropriate regional US Fish and Wildlife Service office:

1. Species and number of eagles proposed to be taken.
2. State and local area where the taking is proposed to be done.
3. Name of the tribe with which the applicant is associated.
4. Name of the tribal religious ceremony for which required.
5. A certificate of enrollment from a federally recognized tribe.

The federal government also established the National Eagle Repository (NER) in the early 1970s to provide Native Americans with feathers of both bald and golden eagles for religious purposes. The NER serves as a collection point for dead eagles. Many of these birds have died as a result of electrocution, vehicle collisions, unlawful shooting, trapping, poisoning, or from natural causes, and most are sent to the NER by federal and state wildlife personnel. The NER provides Indians with whole carcasses or specific parts on a first-come, first-served basis. While it is not within the scope of this book to provide a detailed analysis of the NER, one complaint commonly heard about the organization is the long wait—two and a half years—required before an applicant receives his order. The problem is one of supply and demand: currently, there are more than four thousand people on a waiting list for the approximately nine hundred eagles the NER receives each year.

Since 1962, only one tribe has received a permit from the Secretary of the Interior to harvest live eagles, the Hopi. In the case of the Hopi, the permit is issued in the name of the tribal chairman. This permit, first issued in 1986, is renewed annually.

Again, it is not within the scope of this work to provide any detailed analysis of Hopi ceremonial use of eagles or eagle-gathering methods. In brief, nesting eaglets are collected in late May or early June for use in the Niman ceremony. The baby eagles are taken from their nests and brought back to the villages to be kept on their rooftops for approximately two months. The young eagles are supposedly treated like family members, being fed well and offered a multitude of gifts and offerings. On the second day of the Niman ceremony, held in late July, the young eagle is then sacrificed—smothered in corn meal. The feathers are removed except for a primary feather left on each wing that allows the eagle's spirit to soar away to deliver messages of thankfulness and goodwill to the gods. The downy feathers are used primarily to make *pahos*, or prayer sticks. Other feathers are used to make additional ceremonial objects to be used in various ceremonies. Carcasses are interred in a graveyard created expressly for that purpose.

The Hopi practice of gathering and sacrifice of young eagles has many critics. Some environmental groups consider this event a barbaric activity. An article written by Ted Williams for *Audubon magazine* in 2001 accused the Hopis of mistreating the eaglets, claiming among other things that tribal members sew the birds' eyelids shut (Williams: 32).

Another criticism concerns the number of eagles and other raptors being taken by the Hopis. From 1986 to 2009, the tribe has captured and killed—according to the reports that they must file each year with the Department of the Interior—466 golden eagles and 166 red-tailed hawks. Moreover, the number of birds taken each year continues to increase. In 1986, the tribe took 11 total birds. In 2008, they took 38 eagles and 6 red-tailed hawks. In 2009, they took 23 eagles and 6 red-tailed hawks.

Another concern is where the eagles are coming from. Over the years, the Hopis have depleted the eagles from their own small reservation. Consequently, they are seeking to expand their hunting territory. Since 1999, the Hopis have sought to collect eaglets from several national parks or monuments, in particular Wupatki National Monument. And increasingly they have sought to hunt for eagles on Navajo land.

Navajos have long opposed the Hopi gathering of eagles on their land. For Navajos who know the stories, this opposition is simply a modern-day continuance of the Beadway legend, in which Eagle Boy saved the baby eagles from the Pueblos and in return was rewarded various powers and gifts. In a very real sense, traditional Navajos recognize a timeless and reciprocal bond between themselves and eagles—including the duty of protecting them from others. Some Navajos have even spoken out against what they perceive as the Hopi ceremonial mistreatment of eagles.

Over the years, Navajos living in the areas where the Hopis gather the eagles have offered quiet opposition to the practice. Some gather the baby eagles and hide them from the Hopis. Attempts to stop the collecting through legal means have failed. In 1999, the US District Court in Phoenix granted a Hopi request to collect baby eagles on Navajo land. A year later the same judge again granted the Hopis permission. The next day, Navajo police arrested eleven Hopi eagle gatherers and escorted them to the reservation boundary. This event took place at Indian Wells—fifty miles south of Keams Canyon, the boundary of the Hopi Reservation. Hopi eagle gathering on Navajo land continues today. Since 2007, the federal government has limited the number of eagles the Hopis can collect on Navajo lands to eighteen. It should be noted that the Hopis claim that they have been collecting eagles on this same land for thousands of years—long before the official establishment of the Navajo Reservation boundaries. There is no way to prove or disprove such claims. Obviously the Navajo-Hopi eagle controversy is only one part of a much broader and complicated land dispute issue. Some might argue that it is only an issue of preserving and asserting tribal sovereignty. But it is often the most visible and personal element of the dispute. Both tribes have also openly criticized and demeaned the religious practices of the other—something generally unheard of in Indian Country. There is no end in sight in this struggle to win the spiritual favor of the eagles.

In 2013, the US Fish and Wildlife Service authorized the Hopi tribe to collect forty nesting golden eagles. For the first time, however, the number of eaglets that could be collected on the Navajo Reservation was limited, to five (Fonseca).

The Owls of Navajo Country

Owls are one of the most complex and misunderstood creatures in contemporary Navajo culture. If one were to ask most Navajos today what they know about owls, the first response would probably be that they are harbingers of death, that the sound of a nearby owl means that someone will soon die. This item of "traditional knowledge," however, seems to have no basis in the Navajo stories.

In the Navajo stories, owls almost always appear as benevolent or positive beings. The powerful Navajo deity Talking God is associated with and often appears in the form of an owl (Tsosie, 2009). Owls also commonly come to the aid of the heroes—like Rainboy in the Hailway story and the Visionary in Nightway—by providing them with food, blankets, medicine, and knowledge (Reichard, 1950: 456). In the Mountainway as told by River Junction Charley to Father Berard Haile, a baby is found and raised by Owl Man and Owl Woman (Wyman: 250–251).

Owls provided for the Navajo people in historic times as well. Stories from the Long Walk period, for example, tell of owls who lead to safety people who were being hunted by soldiers (Roessel: 88). Owls also gave tribal members various other gifts and powers, including songs and medicine. Their feathers were historically used to decorate Navajo war caps and to provide warriors with protection and to acquire power (Hill, 1936: 9). Often owls were credited with having warned the Navajos of an approaching enemy.

The power that is most associated with owls, however, is the one given to them by Monster Slayer at the time of their creation, the power to look into the future. This power of premonition and the mandate to inform the Navajo people of the future applies to both the good and the bad. In other words, in Navajo orthodox traditional thought, owls are simply messengers, not necessarily messengers of death.

Owls are creatures of the night and are most comfortable when humans are most vulnerable. Humans fear the night and subsequently fear the creatures of the night. In addition, darkness is the realm of ghosts, witches, and consequently of death itself.

It is perhaps quite natural that many cultures view the owl with fear and suspicion. But if the traditional Navajo concept of the owl was largely positive, where did contemporary tribal fears originate?

The Navajo belief that the owl is the messenger of, or associated with, death might very well come from Pueblo tradition. On the Hopi mesas, owls are associated with the multidimensional deity Maasaw. This, the most powerful of Hopi kachinas, is, among other things, the god of death. Among the Rio Grande Pueblos, owls are commonly seen as being aligned with witches and witchcraft (Tyler: 156–157, 169–170).

As in the case of the defamation of wolves, coyotes, and snakes, it is possible that the relationship seen by contemporary Navajos between owls and death might be derived from the Christian tradition of the Spanish and Mexicans—also the probable source of Pueblo witchcraft beliefs (see Parsons, 1927). In his book *Witchcraft in the Southwest: Spanish and Indian Supernaturalism on the Rio Grande*, Marc Simmons makes numerous references to owls, which, along with black cats, he describes as being the "ancient and universally feared heralds of witchcraft" (Simmons: 59). Simmons also notes the strong presence of witchcraft beliefs within Mexican folk culture. Navajo contact with the Spanish came early—perhaps four hundred years ago—and was often intimate and intense. In addition to trading with the Spanish and later the Mexicans, Navajos also adopted countless Hispanos into the tribe, many of whom were captured as slaves. Indeed, there are a number of Navajo clans that are of Mexican origin. Quite possibly, Navajo witchcraft beliefs, as well as the related concept of owls being messengers of death to be feared, were products of the long history of contact with the Spanish and Mexicans.

It should again be noted that in Navajo tradition, animals such as owls *can* be messengers that forecast bad events, such as an impending death. Orthodox traditionalists know that owl visitations must be viewed within a certain context. An owl that appears outside your window and hoots is doing exactly what it is supposed to be doing, being an owl. An owl that returns night after night might very well be bringing a message, good or bad. If one wanted to be on the safe side and not hear the message, Will Tsosie states that preventative action could be taken by making an offering to the owl. A turquoise bead is held between the thumb and the pinky finger and then flung to the North with a prayer that the owl takes back its message (Tsosie, 2009).

In the 1990s, a misinterpretation—and attempted abuse—of culture emerged in a political and economic struggle between traditional Navajo environmentalists organized as Diné CARE; the Navajo Forest Products Industries (NFPI), a tribal enterprise; and the Bureau of Indian Affairs (BIA). At the center of the controversy was the spotted owl (*Strix occidentalis*). NFPI operated what had once been the largest lumber mill in the Southwest. Over the years, an overharvesting of the old-growth forests and mismanagement had resulted in the company greatly scaling down in size and incurring almost $8 million in debt. When NFPI announced plans to log the Chuska Mountains, Diné CARE, led by its cofounder Leroy Jackson, moved to stop them, arguing in part that the mountains were the habitat of the endangered spotted owl and that an Environmental Impact Statement (EIS) should be required before the federal government approved any new tribal logging plan. NFPI and the BIA countered that since the Navajo tribe was a sovereign entity, it was exempt from developing an EIS. Moreover, in its exemption request, NFPI and the BIA argued that because owls are "symbols of death" to the Navajo people, the extirpation of the bird from tribal forests would be legally justified on religious and cultural grounds. Jackson spoke out publicly at hearings against the tribal logging plan and what he interpreted as being a perverted and racist view of Navajo traditional culture. His remarks resulted in telephone death threats, and he was hung in effigy by Navajo loggers fearing the loss of their jobs. NFPI executives also threatened him with legal action and at least one veiled threat that "someone was going to get hurt." Jackson was scheduled to fly to Washington, DC, to meet with government officials in another attempt to lobby against the tribal logging program when he disappeared on October 1, 1993. Eight days later his body was found inside a parked van near Chama, New Mexico. A state police investigation determined that Jackson died of a methadone overdose, although he was not known to be a drug user. His family and friends remain convinced to this day that he was murdered. Shortly after Jackson's death, the Navajo

Tribal Council agreed to drop any opposition to an EIS, and the US Fish and Wildlife Service has also ruled that the tribe was not exempt from the Endangered Species Act. Today NFPI has all but ceased to exist (see Atencio; Gabriel; LaDuke; St. Clair).

References

Aberle, David F. 1982. *The Peyote Religion among the Navajo*. Chicago: University of Chicago Press.

Atencio, Ernie. 1994. "After a Heavy Harvest and a Death, Navajo Forestry Realigns with Culture," *High Country News*. October 31.

Fonseca, Felicia. 2013. "Permit Lets Hopi Take 40 Golden Eagles," *Associated Press*. April 10.

Franciscan Fathers. 1910. *An Ethnologic Dictionary of the Navajo Language.* St. Michaels, AZ: St. Michaels Press.

Frisbie, Charlotte J. 1987. *Navajo Medicine Bundles or Jish: Acquisition, Transmission, and Disposition in the Past and Present.* Albuquerque: University of New Mexico Press.

Gabriel, Trip. 1994. "A Death in Navajo Country," *Outside Magazine*. May.

Hardeen, George. 1996. "Two Tribes, Two Religions Vie for Place in the Desert," *High Country News*. August 5.

Hill, Willard W. 1936. *Navaho Warfare.* New Haven, CT: Yale University Publications in Anthropology, No. 5.

Hill, Willard W. 1938. *The Agricultural and Hunting Methods of the Navaho Indians.* New Haven, CT: Yale University Publications in Anthropology, No. 18.

Hill, Willard W. and Dorothy W. Hill. 1943. "The Legend of the Navajo Eagle-Catching Way," *New Mexico Anthropologist*, 6, 7(2): 31–36.

Kelley, Matt. 2000. "Federal Officials Block Hopis from Taking Eagles for Religious Ceremonies," *Seattle-Post Intelligencer.* July 22.

Kiefer, Michael. 1994. "Death of an Ecowarrior," *Phoenix New Times.* January 6.

Kluckhohn, Clyde. 1944/1962. "Notes on Navaho Eagle Way," in *Culture and Behavior: The Collected Essays of Clyde Kluckhohn*, edited by Richard Kluckhohn. New York: Free Press of Glencoe: 123–133.

Kluckhohn, Clyde and Leland C. Wyman. 1940. "An Introduction to Navajo Chant Practice," *Memoirs of the American Anthropological Association*, Supplement 53: 1–204.

LaDuke, Winona. 1994. "The Dilemma of Indian Forestry," *Earth Island Journal.* Summer.

Matthews, Washington. 1897/1994. *Navaho Legends.* Salt Lake City: University of Utah Press.

Mayor, Adrienne. 2005. *Fossil Legends of the First Americans.* Princeton, NJ: Princeton University Press.

Newcomb, Franc J. 1940. "Origin Legend of the Navajo Eagle Chant," *Journal of American Folk-Lore*, 53(207): 50–78.

O'Bryan, Aileen. 1956/1993. *Navaho Indian Myths*. New York: Dover Publications.

Page, Jake. 1990. "Hyeouma," *Native Peoples (Summer)*: 31–36.

Parsons, Elsie Clews. 1927. "Witchcraft among the Pueblos: Indian or Spanish?" *Man*, 27: 106–112.

Peterson, Roger Tory. 1990. A *Field Guide to Western Birds* (Peterson Field Guides). Boston: Houghton Mifflin Company.

Ramirez, Anthony. 2000. "Die Like an Eagle: Indian Rights vs. a National Sanctuary," *New York Times*. November 19.

Reichard, Gladys A. 1939/1977. *Navajo Medicine Man Sandpaintings.* New York: Dover Publications.

Reichard, Gladys A. 1950. *Navaho Religion: A Study of Symbolism*. New York: Bollingen Foundation.

Roessel, Ruth. 1973. *Navajo Stories of the Long Walk Period*. Tsaile, AZ: Navajo Community College Press.

Simmons, Marc. 1974. *Witchcraft in the Southwest: Spanish and Indian Supernaturalism on the Rio Grande*. Flagstaff, AZ: Northland Press.

Spencer, Katherine. 1957. "Mythology and Values: An Analysis of Navaho Chantway Myths, *American Folklore Society Memoirs*, Vol. 48.

St. Clair, Jeffrey. 2008. *Born Under a Bad Sky: Notes from the Dark Side of the Earth*. Petrolia, CA: AK Press/CounterPunch.

Tsosie, Will. 2003. Personal conversation. March 28.

Tsosie, Will. 2009. Personal conversation. November 16.

Tyler, Hamilton A. 1979/1991. *Pueblo Birds and Myths.* Flagstaff, AZ: Northland Publishing Company.

US Fish and Wildlife Service. 1998. *National Eagle Repository: Denver, Colorado*, pamphlet, 10 pp. No printing information provided.

Wheelwright, Mary C. 1962. *Eagle Catching Myth and Bead Myth*. Santa Fe, NM: Museum of Navajo Ceremonial Art.

Williams, Ted. 2001. "Golden Eagles for the Gods," *Audubon,* 103(2): 30–32; 33–39.

Wyman, Leland C. 1975. *The Mountainway of the Navajo.* Tucson: University of Arizona Press.

Wyman, Lyman C. and Clyde Kluckhohn. 1938. "Navaho Classification of Their Song Ceremonials," *Memoirs of the American Anthropological Association*, Supplement 50: 3–38.

 # Chapter Seven
A Serpent's Tale

This chapter was originally presented as a paper at the Western Social Science Association Conference held in Reno, Nevada, April 21, 2001.

Snakes in the Ladies Room

Long before the actor Samuel L. Jackson encountered his worst nightmare in *Snakes On a Plane*—arguably one of the worst movies ever made in Hollywood—the Navajo Nation had experienced its own worst nightmare in what could have been a prequel entitled *Snakes in the Ladies Room.*

On July 25, 1994, an elderly Navajo woman was surprised by a snake in a bathroom stall of Navajo Tribal Administration Building No. 2 in Window Rock. In the days that followed, tribal officials tried unsuccessfully to keep the snake out by plugging holes under a commode and in an adjoining wall. Despite their best efforts, the snake, which was identified as being either a gopher snake or a garter snake, reappeared, causing clients of the tribal health and social services divisions to become "hysterical." Eventually the building was closed as officials sought to remedy the situation. Medicine men were brought in who proclaimed the appearance of the snake (or snakes) to be not only a health hazard, but an omen. They offered prayers, performed a ceremony inside the building, and placed herbs around the outside of the building to determine the message brought by the snakes and to counteract the influence the snakes might exert on the people who used the building. In a less publicized move, officials also contacted the Navajo Tribal Zoological Park to see if ferrets could be secured for release into the building to kill the snakes. Unfortunately, the zoo did not have any ferrets in its collection. The entire incident made front-page headlines not only in the *Navajo Times* and the *Gallup Independent*, but also in a number of Southwest state and regional newspapers. That a wave of snake phobia had swept the entire Window Rock community was best illustrated when word leaked out that at the local high school, a Navajo biology teacher had taken the extreme measure of cutting out, or taping over with pieces of paper, all of the pictures of snakes in textbooks she used in her class so as not to frighten or offend her students! Clearly, snakes were on the minds of the Navajo people during the summer of 1994 (see Becenti; Shebala; Schwartz).

The reaction—in some cases overreaction—of tribal members to the snake sightings reflects a far deeper and more significant issue than that of simple ophidiophobia, or fear of snakes, that many Euro-Americans experience. It was a response born from legitimate cultural concerns over the spiritual power of snakes. And in some cases it was a response to what I believe to be a misinterpretation of traditional beliefs about snakes—one more example of the defamation of one of the Animal People brought on by the encroachment of Judeo-Christian values and beliefs, and perhaps even by the prejudices of at least one misinformed anthropologist.

Snakes have always fascinated humankind for a multitude of reasons. Their general physical appearance—long, slender, and having no extremities or eyelids—immediately catches our attention. The characteristics and habits of snakes also make them unique: the fact that they travel without legs—often very rapidly and sometimes with a distinctive s-shaped movement; that they swallow prey much larger than themselves whole by way of hinged jaws—after first killing it through constriction or the use of venom; that they hibernate for the winter to emerge miraculously—often in mass—each spring; and that several times a year they shed their skins. In addition, while some snakes lay eggs, others exhibit live birth. In every way imaginable, snakes are indeed different.

Snakes' uniqueness have given them a special place in human cultures. Some cultures, including those that are Christian-based, hate the snake and have aligned it with the forces of evil. Other cultures, including many Eastern and most American Indian cultures, hold the snake in the highest regard.

The Identity of Snakes in Navajo Country and Tribal Tradition

From a review of the Peterson Field Guide *Western Reptiles and Amphibians* (Stebbins, 1985)—pretty much the standard field bible for southwestern herpetologists—it appears that at least seven species of snakes inhabit the Navajo Reservation.

The Hopi subspecies of the western rattlesnake (*Crotalus viridis nuntius*) is a common reptile found throughout Navajo Country. This is the only venomous snake found on the Navajo Reservation, and as far as rattlesnakes go, it is a relatively small animal, rarely more than two and a half feet in length. This rattlesnake, which feeds mainly on small mammals, is the snake most commonly used in the famous Hopi Snake Dances.

The Great Basin gopher snake (*Pituophis catenifer deserticola*) is the largest snake found in the American Southwest, reaching a length of nine feet. This impressive animal is also commonly called bullsnake and kills its prey, usually rodents and rabbits, by constriction.

The striped whipsnake (*Masticophis taeniatus*) is a common, sleek and slender snake measuring up to five feet in length. This alert, fast-moving snake feeds predominantly on lizards, other snakes, small mammals, young birds, and insects.

There are two species of garter snakes found in Navajo Country, the black-necked garter snake (*Thamnophis cyrtopsis*) and the "wandering" subspecies of the western terrestrial garter snake (*Thamnophis elegans vagrans*). These small snakes seldom exceed three and a half feet in length and eat a wide variety of prey items including frogs, tadpoles, fish, earthworms—pretty much anything they can catch and swallow. Although the western terrestrial, as its name suggests, is most often found on land, both species are aquatic by nature and are seldom found far from water.

The remaining species of snakes found on the Navajo Reservation are the glossy snake (*Arizona elegans noctivaga*) and the night snake (*Hypsiglena torquata*). Both are nocturnal animals and thus are rarely encountered. Both feed on lizards and small snakes.

Navajo identification and classification of the various species of snakes is a much more complicated and problematic issue.

Father Berard Haile, the Franciscan priest who worked among the Navajos for over fifty years and who is considered the foremost authority in the field of Navajo anthropology, writes that snakes first appeared in the Yellow Underworld of the Navajo creation stories. In his work entitled *The Upward Moving and Emergence Way*, which he finished in 1908 (published in 1981), Haile states that in the beginning there were Big Snake, the Endless Snake, Bullsnake, Arrowsnake, Flying Snake, Snapping Snake, Stubby Rattler, and Watersnake, in addition to the Black Snake, and the Blue, Yellow and White Snakes, the Glittering (pink) Snake, and "Snake People" who were spotted with all colors. Haile goes on to note that "some of the snakes mentioned here are probably mythical" (Haile: 17).

In 1910, the Franciscan Fathers, foremost of whom was Haile, published an *Ethnologic Dictionary of the Navajo Language* that came to be the definitive source in Navajo ethnographic literature. In this book, reference is made to rattlesnakes, bullsnakes (which are also referred to as copperheads) arrowsnakes, and track-snakes. The work also provides "sacred" or ceremonial names for rattlesnakes, bullsnakes, arrowsnakes, copperheads, tracksnakes, watersnakes, and sidewinders.

Other ethnographic sources make reference to flying snakes, slender snakes, crooked snakes, grinding snakes, red-headed snakes, twined snakes, and racers.

Confused yet?

To the best of my knowledge, no anthropologist or biologist has made any serious effort to match the Navajo names of snakes, actual or mythological, with western scientific names. What follows is my attempt to do so—admittedly largely educated guesswork on my part.

Big Snake plays a major role in the Navajo stories and consequently in Navajo traditional culture. Gladys Reichard has stated that Big Snake is a "mythical creature" that "cannot be equated with any known biological species." Karl W. Luckert identifies Big Snake as being the bullsnake (Luckert: 173). I think both are wrong. I am of the opinion that Big Snake—which might be the same creature as the Endless or Never-ending Snake—is in reality the rattlesnake. In the Navajo stories, Big Snake is said to be poisonous and clearly possesses a rattle. Moreover, Haile notes that the stubby rattlesnake is called *tliish bicho ii*, the Grandmother of snakes (Haile: 17). Other references to Big Snake refer to it as being the Grandfather of snakes. In addition, when represented on sandpaintings, Big Snake is almost always depicted as being somewhat short in stature but thick in girth, and usually with a rattle—the perfect image of a rattlesnake. Consequently, the evidence leads me to conclude that Big Snake was so-named because of his power rather than his size. In all likelihood, then, Big Snake is in fact the Hopi rattlesnake.

Arrowsnakes are also called flying snakes or "racers" in the Navajo stories. I believe that arrowsnakes are striped whipsnakes. Washington Matthews, in his 1897 publication *Navaho Legends*, cited the noted naturalist and US cavalry surgeon Henry Crecy Yarrow, who was of the opinion that the Navajo arrowsnake was the coachwhip snake *(Bascanium flagelliforme)*. Coachwhips, however, are not found on the Navajo Reservation. Striped whipsnakes, a closely related species, are. Both snakes are long, slender, and especially fast-moving animals that give the impression of "flying" across the ground in a movement that might be described as being "straight as an arrow." Consequently, I have no doubt that the arrowsnake that appears in the Navajo stories is a whipsnake.

An additional note on the idea of "flying snakes": Nick Sucik, who has a degree in anthropology from Northern Arizona University and whose work falls in the category cryptozoology—the search for animals that supposedly do not exist—has written a fascinating piece in which he expresses his opinion that flying snakes may very well be a yet-unidentified species of snake that actually inhabits the Navajo Reservation (see Sucik).

Watersnakes are also mentioned in the Navajo stories. Quite likely such references are to either the black-necked or wandering garter snakes. The two species are so similar in appearance that they cannot easily be recognized as different species. Moreover, both species are commonly found in and around water sources. Consequently, I strongly suspect that the Navajo watersnake is a garter snake.

Bullsnakes are also commonly mentioned in the Navajo stories. These snakes are undoubtedly Great Basin gopher snakes. The name bullsnake is a common colloquial name for the gopher snake throughout its range, including the Navajo Reservation.

Big Snake and His Kin in the Garden of Good and Evil

It is difficult to determine exactly when snakes became associated with the concept of evil in contemporary Navajo thought. Indeed, traditional Navajos do not possess the concept of true evil, at least not as it is used in Christian philosophy—that is, to mean a purposeful wickedness of supernatural origin. In Christianity, the evil of snakes can be traced to the first book of the Old Testament, where the snake is portrayed as the tempter, Satan. He is said to have tricked Adam and Eve into eating forbidden fruit from the tree of knowledge. By eating the apples, they committed original sin, causing their exile from Paradise. For its part in the fall of humankind, the snake is cursed by God to a life of crawling on its belly and eating dust. In time, snakes came to be associated as the servants of evil and even accomplices of witches. A strong witchcraft tradition among the Spanish along the Rio Grande with whom the Navajo had contact for hundreds of years might well be the source of contemporary tribal views of snakes (Simmons: 89). In traditional Navajo thought, however, snakes are generally viewed as being rather benevolent—sometimes dangerous, perhaps, but certainly not evil.

The pioneer anthropologist Washington Matthews is the only scholar to specifically examine the role of snakes in Navajo culture. In an 1898 article entitled "Serpent Worship among the Navajos," Matthews writes:

I have sought assiduously among the Navajos for examples of snake worship, and I have found that they exist. . . . The Navajo shows his reverence for the serpent in various ways; but the most obvious evidence of this reverence is the fact that under no circumstance will he kill a snake. If he comes across a coiled serpent in his path, he will either pass to one side or, lifting it gently with a stick, will throw it away (Matthews: 229–230).

Matthews goes on to say:

Like races of the Old World, of whom we have record, these Indians regard the snake as possessed of extraordinary wisdom. They think he is a great listener, that he hears and understands the language of man, and that he might make evil use of the knowledge learned from men. For this reason it is that their sacred myths may be told only in the winter season; that their most sacred rites may only then be performed; for at that time the earthly snakes are hidden in the earth and at that time too (by a strange coincidence) the celestial serpents (the flashes of crooked lightning) are hidden. (Ibid.: 230)

It should be noted that while Matthews credits snakes with making "evil use of the knowledge of men," he does not believe them to be evil themselves.

Indeed, they are "worshipped." As for the origin of this worship, Matthews writes:

> But among the Navajos, at least, I am inclined to think that the principal reason for snake worship is that the snake is a symbol for lightning. In fact I suspect it is more than a symbol and that it is in a certain way, to the Navajo mind, identical with the lightning; that the difference between the serpent and the crooked lightning is the same as that which exists between man and the anthropomorphic gods. (Ibid.: 233)

Foremost among the snakes that are or were once prayed to or culturally held in high esteem is Big Snake. The Navajo name for Big Snake is *Klishtso*, or the Great Snake. Matthews refers to Big Snake as being the "god of the serpents." Nowhere does Matthews use the word *evil* to describe Big Snake, but he does make it clear that this god of the snakes is a powerful figure and that its power is closely associated with lightning. Later anthropologists, including Haile—a Catholic missionary—also do not appear to associate Big Snake, or any snake, with evil. The idea seems to have been popularized by the anthropologist Gladys A. Reichard, who wrote on Navajo topics from 1928 until her death in 1978—fifty years of generally good scholarship. Reichard's specialty was Navajo religion. In 1950, she published her monumental book *Navaho Religion: A Study in Symbolism.* This book remains the only general work on Navajo religion. Since its publication, many have looked upon it as being something of the "bible" on this topic—an accolade not at all undeserved. Reichard, however, is from time to time guilty of misinterpretation and oversimplification. A case in point is her treatment of snakes in Navajo religion.

Reichard seems obsessed with labeling Big Snake—and snakes in general—as being evil. Consider the following passages from *Navaho Religion:*

> Thus evil may be transformed into good: things predominantly evil, such as snake, lightning, thunder, coyote, may even be evoked. (Reichard: 5)

> Perhaps one reason that three are prescribed is to give an odd number of snakes, since they are evil. (Ibid.: 185)

> The black Endless Snake symbolizes all snakes, their origin and the inevitable struggle against evil. (Ibid.: 197)

> Songs, like other forms of wealth, may be exchanged. At an impasse an evil power—Star, Thunder, Snake. (Ibid.: 290)

> Bear allied himself with evil. . . . The details given above seem to refer largely to bears and snakes as a class. (Ibid.: 385)

> Never-ending snake . . . is wholly evil and destroys the mind and consciousness by coiling around and squeezing his victim. (Ibid.: 454)

Reichard defines evil as being "that which is ritually not under control." Yet she readily admits that snakes can be controlled. "Destructive rather than constructive powers are more commonly ascribed to Thunders, Wind, and Snakes, yet with great effort they may be persuaded to aid man" (Ibid.: 51). Later she also writes:

> The belief that wild animals are helpers of human beings has not been laid aside now that game has been supplanted by the more easily obtained sheep, goat, and steer. If a few, such as Bear and Snake, are difficult to persuade, the

Navaho puts himself out a little more than usual so he will not incur their wrath (Ibid.: 142).

If snakes can be persuaded, albeit with great difficulty or by "putting oneself out a little more than usual," does this make them any more evil than other species?

In Navajo thought, if there is to be good, there must also be bad. One cannot exist without the other. Light is simply the reverse of darkness. Consequently, every living thing, deity, man, or animal, possesses both a good and bad side and is capable of displaying both tendencies. Snakes are no different.

But are some animals, such as the snake, more bad than good? Not really. Instead, what they possess is more power and consequently the capability of demonstrating toward humans a higher degree of potential danger. Traditionally Navajos dealt with such powerful animals by showing them a greater measure of respect and by keeping their distance from them. As noted by Matthews, Navajos simply avoided snakes. He also stated that Navajos traditionally did not kill snakes. While people of other cultures, most notably those that are Christian-based, attempt to kill or destroy what they fear, Navajos felt no need to do so.

Anthropologists and popular writers other than Reichard also inadvertently contributed to the defamation of the snake. In 1940, Franc C. Newcomb published *Navajo Omens and Taboos.* This book seems to have started the unfortunate tradition of looking at Navajo culture and religion as a shopping list of dos and don'ts—an aspect of Navajo life that seemed to fascinate some white outsiders. Many of Newcomb's negative taboos dealt with snakes. In 1946, Clyde Kluckhohn and Dorothea Leighton published their influential work *The Navaho*. In a chapter entitled "The Supernatural: Things to Do and Not to Do," the authors continued the practice of explaining Navajo religion as a series of taboos. Without question, more people—including Navajos—have read this book than all other books written on Navajo culture combined. Certainly when I first arrived on the Navajo Reservation in 1976, everyone seemingly had a copy.

In 1972, Ernest L. Bulow published another extremely popular booklet, *Navajo Taboos*. Bulow's work took the concept of understanding Navajo life as a series of taboos and omens to a new level. This book, which was published by the Navajo tribe, included no fewer than twenty-seven taboos that dealt specifically with snakes.

I believe that in time these publications and others like them came to replace the traditional knowledge that had been handed down through generations by tribal medicine men and elders. Taboos—if one insists on calling them that—that were once meant to warn the uninitiated of the *power* of natural forces and entities, such as the snake, came to be misinterpreted in Christian form to mean *evil.* Navajo religion itself came to be oversimplified, rather than understood as an intricate web of stories and teachings. Consequently, Navajo respect for snakes was replaced by fear as people were indoctrinated to a new and distorted view of the role of the snake in their culture.

It is hard to imagine how a creature that provides for the people—and indeed ensures their very survival—can be deemed evil. Snakes in Navajo culture, as in many cultures, are closely associated with life-giving rain. Their S-shaped or zigzag movements are the very earthly embodiment of thunder, lightning, and moisture. Will Tsosie knows snakes as being the "earthbound lightning people" (Tsosie, 2009). Consequently, snakes are associated with crop fertility and agriculture—gifts to the Navajo people as explained in the Beautyway. Snakes are also credited with bringing to the Navajo the gift of "ground crawling" plants or vines, such as pumpkins and melons.

Perhaps the strongest evidence available to us that Navajos did not historically consider the snake to be evil is the fact that snake imagery and symbolism is everywhere in the traditional tribal culture. In the Holy Land of the Navajos—Dinétah—snakes are a common rock art motif. One particularly spectacular petroglyph located in Blanco Canyon depicts a very realistic and fully coiled rattlesnake (Roessel, 1983: 121). Most significantly, snakes are the single most common image found on that most sacred of Navajo religious icons, sandpaintings. One could publish an entire book on Navajo snake symbolism as represented in sandpaintings. Snakes of all kinds are found as curing symbols on the sandpaintings of most major Navajo ceremonies, especially for Beautyway, Windway, and Shootingway—all of which will be discussed next. In the case of Windway, for example, snakes are found on 66 of the 133 recorded sandpaintings (Wyman, 1962: 209).

In regard to the tribal snake scare of 1994, two cultural concerns were most frequently cited. The first was the belief held by some that snakes negatively impact the urinary and reproductive organs of humans, and especially females. This knowledge traces to the Beautyway story, which describes snake infection as manifesting itself as "rheumatism, sore throat, stomach trouble, kidney and bladder trouble, and skin disease or sores" (Haile, Oakes, and Wyman: 17–18). Considering that the snake or snakes appeared in a tribal ladies room, women, and especially pregnant women, were justifiably worried that they could become infected. I should add, however, that I found no anthropological reference for snakes negatively impacting a woman's reproductive system, and Will Tsosie doubts that such a relationship exists (Tsosie, 2009).

The second concern expressed in 1994 was that the appearance of the snakes might represent a bad omen of some kind. In Navajo culture, all animals—including snakes—are potential messengers of either good or bad. They are generally regarded to be so when they appear "out of context," or away from their natural environment. In the case of the snake appearances, the weather had been unusually hot and dry, and it would not have been uncommon for snakes to have entered a building seeking shade, water, and perhaps even rodents as a source of food. In all likelihood, the concern that the snake in the ladies room was an omen of some sort appears to have been exaggerated.

One final addition to the idea that snakes are evil and must be avoided at all costs: a newspaper article later appeared in the *Arizona Republic* stating that Navajos were offended by a newly released Oliver Stone movie, *Natural Born Killers,* because it depicted a Navajo medicine man handling a rattlesnake. A Navajo and former president of the Native American Church of North America reportedly turned down the role because of such scenes, citing cultural objections (Donovan).

Interestingly, none other than Reichard herself in *Navaho Religion* stated that "a Shooting Chanter once told me that the snake sandpaintings of his chant were a substitute for real snakes which the Navaho previously used as the Hopi do in their Snake Dance" (Reichard: 116). Once again this passage takes us back to this theme that a close relationship—perhaps even a physical one—between snakes and a handful of orthodox Navajo spiritual practitioners able to control and channel their power existed prior to the introduction of Christian biblical doctrine and the influence of the prejudicial writings of some scholars and other uninformed popular writers. As a result, the snake, as surely as Adam and Eve themselves, experienced its own fall from grace in the Navajo Garden of Eden.

The Snake in Navajo Oral Tradition

Snakes play an integral part in many, if not most, of the Navajo creation stories. Consequently, it is within these stories that we find proof of the positive role of snakes in traditional Navajo culture.

In Sandoval's version of the origin story, Big Snake—along with Mountain Lion, Bear, and Otter—appears as one of the four "chiefs" of the Third World who originally serve as advisors to First Man and the other Animal People. Big Snake makes many contributions to the Navajo people, including introducing the pumpkin, watermelon, cantaloupe, and muskmelon—"plants that all crawl on the ground" (O'Bryan: 6). In the Gishin Biye' version of the origin story, Big Snake is one of the "pets" given by Changing Woman to the people to hunt for them and protect them. It seems that Big Snake proves somewhat unsuccessful in carrying out these responsibilities. Unlike the other animal protectors—Bear, Mountain Lion, Weasel, and Porcupine—Big Snake cannot walk and so has to be carried. Eventually he gets too heavy and is left behind under a rock at a place called Water-in-rock (Haile: 167, 170). In another version of the origin story, a bullsnake is said to have been given to the *To' dich'ii'nii* clan (Roessel, 1971: 16).

In three particular stories (and consequently the ceremonies derived from them)—Beautyway, Shootingway, and Windway—Big Snake and the Snake People are central characters.

The following account of the role of snakes in the Beautyway story and ceremony was recorded from Singer Man by Father Berard Haile in 1932 and taken from *Beautyway: A Navaho Ceremonial* by Father Berard Haile, Maud Oakes, and Leland Wyman.

In a continuation of the Enemyway story, Big Snake and Bear Man, initially portrayed as two old men, are denied two beautiful young sisters even after they have successfully completed a series of challenges presented to them by her brothers. Consequently, Big Snake and

Bear Man camp near a site where the brothers, who have returned from a successful war against the Pueblos, are undergoing a cleansing ritual. As the two old men smoke a sweet-smelling tobacco that "robs one of your mind," they grow youthful in appearance and their tattered clothes become fine. Soon the two maidens, Older Sister and Younger Sister, appear from the nearby dance, enticed by the sweet smell of the smoke. The girls ask for a smoke and, after becoming intoxicated, spend the night, or marry, the two men. In the morning, they awaken to find themselves with Big Snake and Bear Man, who have returned to their former shriveled, disgusting shapes. Younger Sister, who has slept with Big Snake and who is said to be from Wide Rock, has been bound to him with an "endless snake. She awakes to the sound of the snake's rattle.

At dawn the girls escape their "husbands." The flight of Older Sister from Bear Man constitutes the Mountainway story, whereas the flight of Younger Sister from Big Snake becomes the Beautyway story. Because the two stories have a common origin and their plots are interwoven, they are said to be related. Beautyway is also called the Snake Chant. Younger Sister—in one version named Glishpah—becomes Snake Woman.

Big Snake follows Younger Sister through the use of his magical smoke, which directs him along her trail. Younger Sister flees over the hills and mountains with no apparent objective except to escape. Along the way, she is aided by a number of deities and various Animal People. At one point in the story, five Endless Snakes rear up and bar her way until Talking God subdues them by giving her their sacred names and sprinkling them with pollen so that she can step over them.

At another point, she is invited into the home of the Weasel People, who enlarge the entrance by blowing and causing a heavy smoke that Big Snake's smoke cannot penetrate. When the fog lifts, Big Snake continues his pursuit. In time, Younger Sister comes to drink at a pool, where she finds a strange young man. After telling her story to him, he allows her passage into the pool. "Down there people are living," he tells her. In the land below, she finds Mountain sheep, ruins, and gardens. Unknown to her, however, she has entered the home of her husband's people.

Big Snake himself soon arrives but apparently does not notice her. The people she encounters warn her that they are "just ugly in appearance" and that during the night she should not relight the fire. She does exactly that, however, and finds herself surrounded by snakes. She goes back to sleep, and in the morning she awakes to find that the Snake People have again taken human form. They scold her for having "showed no regard for anyone" in her stepping all over them during the night.

On each of the next five days, she is warned not to touch certain water jugs. She does so anyway and is scolded by the Snake People and told that it is no wonder "she goes about aimlessly."

On three successive days, she is told not to go to the east, south, and north. Again she disobeys and falls into trouble from which the Snake People must rescue her, after which they scold her for causing them unnecessary labor.

Younger Sister spends four winters with the Snake People. During this time, she is taught the songs and rituals for the Beautyway ceremony by Big Snake, who has reappeared as a handsome young man. She is happy to see him, despite being admonished by him for her having run away. After learning the Beautyway, she is instructed to return to the Earth People and teach them the ceremony, in particular her youngest brother. She does this, and upon completing this task she returns to the home of the Snake People, where she is placed in charge of clouds, rain, mist, and vegetation for the benefit of the people on Earth.

The Beautyway ceremony is used to cure snakebite and other forms of "snake sickness," which might manifest itself as sore joints, sore throat, stomach trouble, kidney and bladder trouble, skin disease or sores, swollen joints, and mental confusion or loss of consciousness (Haile, Oakes, and Wyman: 17–18).

The following information on the role of snakes in the Windway ceremony is taken primarily from *The Windways of the Navaho* by Leland C. Wyman.

In the Navajo Windway stories the hero becomes involved in a series of disastrous incidents in which he is rescued or restored through the intervention of various supernatural beings, including snakes. In the first of the Windway stories, the hero is stolen by the Snake People, quite possibly by Big Snake himself, who takes him to their home beneath a pool as described in the Beautyway story. Black God searches for him but is denied entrance four times by Big Snake. Finally Black God sets fire to the waters, and the Snake People are forced to give up their captive.

In a second incident, the hero and his family eat flag plants—another "test" from the Big Snake People—which prove to be poisonous. Dark Wind performs a ceremony that cures them.

In another Windway story, the hero, who is now called Older Brother, goes hunting in an area that he has been warned not to trespass. He kills a deer that belongs to Big Snake and roasts and eats the colon, which turns into a snake as he swallows it. The hero goes to sleep and awakes to find himself transformed into a Big Snake. Talking God tells Older Brother's family what has happened and why. The Wind People intervene and ceremonially restore him to his human form by passing him through hoops.

The remainder of Wyman's account of the Windway story is the hero's travels in search of additional ceremonial knowledge. Among the many people he visits are the Snake People, who are standing beside their shed garments. They ask him the purpose of his travels, and he replies that he is looking for prayer sticks. The Snake People tell him that the prayer sticks he seeks are in the possession of Big Snake Old Man and that he must have offerings of jet, turquoise, abalone, and white beads.

The Windway ceremony is used to treat any disease attributed to the influence of winds, snakes, lightning, or cactus (Wyman, 1962: 20–22).

The following information on the role of snakes in the Shootingway ceremony is taken primarily from *Sandpaintings of the Navajo Shooting Chant* by Franc C. Newcomb and Gladys Reichard. The information on the Shootingway story was provided to them by the singer Blue Eyes from Lukachukai. (There are two general branches of the Shootingway story, male and female. For the purposes of this chapter I will discuss only the male branch.)

The story of the Male Shootingway tells of the travels and adventures of the Twin Brothers, Monster Slayer and Child Born of Water, and their acquisition of ceremonial knowledge from various supernatural beings, including Big Snake and the Snake People.

Early in the story, while the twins are still infants, their mother, Changing Woman, leaves them for four days. In her absence, the twins refuse to eat the food left for them, and they weaken. Bear Man and Rattlesnake Man (Big Snake) feed them special food. Big Snake feeds them "the pollen of vegetation of all kinds." This food is initially too strong for them, but they survive, and ultimately this food makes them powerful.

Sometime afterward, the twins embark on an epic journey to visit their father, the Sun. After encountering a number of supernatural beings who present them with gifts, they arrive at the house of the Sun, guarded by Wind, Thunder, Bear, and Big Snake. Wind, their own protector, tells the boys the sacred names of these guardians, who then allow them to pass.

After first denying he is their father, Sun presents the twins with four tests, which they pass with help from various supernatural beings. At this point, Sun accepts them and makes every effort to give them the powers they will need to conquer the monsters that plague the Earth. One item that he gives them are rattles that he says are really big snakes. One is a black rattle he calls the Big Dark Snake rattle. The current wife of Sun becomes angry because her own child is bitten by a watersnake and swells up. Sun entrusts the care of this boy to his half-brothers, the twins, who cure him with their newly acquired powers.

After destroying most of the monsters of the world, Monster Slayer goes to live in a canyon. Changing Woman sends her personal guardians, Big Bear and Big Snake, to protect his new home.

In one Shootingway story, Monster Slayer travels to the home of Old Man Big Snake, who asks the young man if he has any tobacco. After first refusing him, Monster Slayer gives him poisonous tobacco that renders him unconscious. The wife of Old Man Big Snake begs Monster Slayer to restore her husband, giving him all of her husband's valuable possessions. When Old Man Big Snake is restored, he bargains with Monster Slayer for the return of some of his valuables, giving the young man knowledge of five sandpaintings in exchange. He then asks Monster Slayer to marry his daughter. Monster Slayer declines but is told by Old Man Big Snake of other Snake People who possess knowledge, though he warns Monster Slayer not to go there.

Monster Slayer ignores the advice of Old Man Big Snake and travels to the home of all of the Snake People, where he finds all types of snakes—Big Snakes, Arrow Snakes, and Crooked Snakes—all of the Snake People except for the Watersnakes. The leader of the Snake People tells Monster Slayer that Old Man Big Snake is a "tricky old fellow" who has withheld knowledge from him. At this point, the leader of all the snakes voluntarily teaches Monster Slayer important ceremonial knowledge, including sandpaintings.

Monster Slayer returns to the home of Old Man Big Snake, and the cycle of events is twice more repeated. Old Man Big Snake offers his daughter, whom Monster Slayer refuses, and he is told the location of other Snake People but warned not to travel there, advice that Monster Slayer ignores. In this manner, Monster Slayer travels next to the home of the Grinding Snakes and the Endless Snakes, then to the home of the Watersnakes and Arrow Snakes with striped bodies. With each of these visits, Monster Slayer acquires additional ceremonial knowledge and sandpaintings. Finally he returns to the home of Old Man Big Snake and accepts the marriage to his daughter.

Soon afterward, Red Coyote, who had wanted to marry the daughter of Old Man Big Snake, blows his own skin onto Monster Slayer, transforming him into a coyote, while he himself takes on the appearance of Monster Slayer. He then tries to move in with the daughter of Old Man Big Snake, but the girl had been forewarned by the Wind and rejects him. The Snake People, including his new wife, go out looking for Monster Slayer. They find him and perform a transformation ceremony over him using hoops that represent snakes. Monster Slayer is restored to his previous form but still lacks his senses. They then send for help to the leader of the Snake People, who restores his speech. Another trip to the Grinding Snakes and Endless Snakes restores his hearing. At the conclusion of this episode, Monster Slayer leaves his wife and her people.

The Shootingway ceremony is used to treat infection from lightning, snakes, and arrows. It is also used for colds, fevers, rheumatism, paralysis, and abdominal pain.

In looking at these stories, it appears that several lessons can be learned. First is that snakes, despite Reichard's claim, can be controlled. The Holy People, such as Talking God, Monster Slayer, and Black God, all possess the ability to subdue and manipulate snakes. Second, every bad act carried out by Big Snake, and the Snake People in general, is initially brought on by some transgression committed by man or other deities. Big Snake and his relatives react accordingly but are "bad" only in that they possess great power to counter with harm. Third is that emerging from these stories is the clear implication that when all things are considered, Big Snake and the Snake People ultimately do more good than harm. In most cases, they care for and watch over the heroes and heroines of the stories, instructing them in various prayers and rituals associated with each respective story, and providing them with gifts of prayer sticks, sandpaintings, and other knowledge before sending them on their way to benefit humankind. Often they offer their kindness and powers despite the arrogance, and even the stupidity, of the hero or heroine.

It should be noted that although Big Snake and the Snake People bring on certain illnesses, they also provide a remedy for that which they inflict. Again, they do not set out to maliciously harm people, but rather are only responding to transgressions committed against them. They use their considerable powers not only to harm, but also to cure. Most importantly, they are providing a lesson in how to keep the Earth in balance by treating that which is around you with the respect. It can be argued that nowadays the earthly descendants of Big Snake and the Snake People continue to teach those who break this natural law.

The Role of Snake as Hunter

Very little has been written about Big Snake as a hunter. Big Snake, although clearly identified as being a hunter deity, is not classified as being one of the "divine hunters" of the Deer Hunting Way as are Wolf, Mountain Lion, Spotted Lion, Bobcat, and Lynx (Luckert: 173). There is, however, a Big Snake huntingway in which hunters "attack like snakes from ambush" (Hill: 113–117). Will Tsosie states that hunters who know this way possess the ability to "seduce" or "take over the will" of game—usually deer—and draw them close for a kill (Tsosie, 2009). This hunting ritual follows closely after the Wolfway in terms of its procedures before and after the hunt.

Big Snake, as noted earlier, is also credited with being the "owner" of the deer. In the Windway story, the hero, Older Brother, "poaches" an animal belonging to him and is transformed into a snake himself (Wyman, 1962: 119–122).

A Personal Snake Story and Some Final Thoughts

Many years ago, I was exploring some Anasazi ruins in the Black Mesa area of the Navajo Reservation with my good friend Tony Salandro. I was walking by a clump of sage grass when I heard emanating from it a peculiar "buzzing" sound. I thought it must be some sort of an insect, possibly a cicada, and being curious I parted the brush with my hands and poked my head inside. To my surprise I found myself nose to nose with a rattlesnake. For a brief moment I froze, then I sprung into action—and I do mean sprung. With a move that would have shamed any black-clad ninja in the best of the Hong Kong martial arts movies, I leaped straight backward and without turning around landed perfectly erect ten feet from the bush! Grabbing my heart, I was able to utter only one brief panic-induced sentence: "It's a rattlesnake!" Tony hurried over to offer assistance, and after I regained my composure, we parted—with two very long sticks—the sagebrush to expose the object of my terror. There we found—all ten inches of him—a coiled and now very disturbed Hopi rattlesnake. I think Tony's next remarks were something like "You call THAT a rattlesnake?" Over the years he would retell this story a hundred times to anyone who would listen, and each time he would embellish the facts somewhat. The latest version I heard had me leaping fifty feet backward, and my poor little snake had now shrunk to a mere four inches!

That was my first meeting with a rattlesnake in the West—I had once seen a timber rattlesnake in my native Pennsylvania—and it inspired me to learn as much I could about these fascinating animals. Since then I have had hundreds of rattlesnake encounters, and I will readily admit that I have fallen hopelessly in love with these wonderful animals (see Pavlik). I have found them to be physically beautiful and spiritually awe inspiring. They are shy and gentle and always patient and forgiving. I have never had a rattlesnake strike unprovoked. I have learned that if I treat them with respect, they always return the favor. In the end, they are much like the rest of us, simply trying to survive in what is often a hostile world.

As a society, we desperately need to find a better way to relate to the natural world and to the other lifeforms—including snakes—with which we share the Earth. It is my hope that the New Traditionalism of the Navajo evolves to take on a greater share of the older orthodox knowledge, and especially the value system upon which it was based. If this happens, all of us will be more enlightened members of the family of related beings.

References

Becenti, Deenise. 1994. "Snakes Alive! Serpents Make Workers Squirm," *The Salt Lake Tribune*. August 6.

Bulow, Ernest L. 1972. *Navajo Taboos.* Gallup, NM: Buffalo Medicine Books.

Donovan, Bill. 1994. "Movie Snake Scene Offends Navajos," *Arizona Republic*.

Franciscan Fathers. 1910. *An Ethnologic Dictionary of the Navajo Language*. St. Michaels, AZ: St. Michaels Press.

Haile, Father Berard. 1981. *The Upward Moving and Emergence Way.* Lincoln: University of Nebraska Press.

Haile, Father Berard, Maud Oakes, and Leland C. Wyman. 1957. *Beautyway: A Navaho Ceremonial*. New York: Pantheon Books.

Hill, Willard W. 1938. *The Agricultural and Hunting Methods of the Navaho Indians*. New Haven, CT: Yale University Publications in Anthropology, No. 18.

Kluckhohn, Clyde and Dorothea Leighton. 1946. *The Navaho.* Cambridge, MA: Harvard University Press.

Luckert, Karl W. 1975. *The Navajo Hunter Tradition.* Tucson: University of Arizona Press.

Matthews, Washington. 1897/1994. *Navaho Legends.* Salt Lake City: University of Utah Press.

Matthews, Washington. 1898. "Serpent Worship among the Navajos," *Land of Sunshine*, 9(5): 228–235.

Newcomb, Franc J. 1940. *Navajo Omens and Taboos.* Santa Fe, NM: Rydal Press.

Newcomb, Franc J. and Gladys A. Reichard. 1975. *Sandpaintings of the Navajo Shooting Chant.* New York: Dover Publications.

O'Bryan, Aileen. 1956/1993. *Navaho Indian Myths*. New York: Dover Publications.

Pavlik, Steve. 2011. "For the Love of Rattlesnakes," *Three Coyotes*, 1.2: 129–157.

Reichard, Gladys A. 1950. *Navaho Religion: A Study in Symbolism.* New York: Bollingen Foundation.

Roessel, Robert A. 1983. *Dinétah: Navajo History, Volume III.* Chinle, AZ: Navajo Curriculum Center.

Roessel, Ruth. 1971. *Navajo Studies at Navajo Community College.* Many Farms, AZ: Navajo Community College Press.

Schwarz, Maureen Trudelle. 1997. "Snakes in the Ladies Room: Navajo Views on Personhood and Effect," *American Ethnologist*, 24(3): 602–627.

Shebala, Marley. 1994. "Snake Sightings Create Major Concern by All," *Navajo Times*. August18.

Simmons, Marc. 1974. *Witchcraft in the Southwest: Spanish and Indian Supernaturalism on the Rio Grande*. Flagstaff, AZ: Northland Press.

Stebbins, Robert C. 1985. *A Field Guide to Western Reptiles and Amphibians* (Peterson Field Guides). Boston: Houghton Mifflin Company.

Sucik, Nick. 2004. "Exploring the Prospect of an Unidentified Species of Reptile within the Navajo and Hopi Lands: In Search of *Tl'iish Naat'a'i* (Snake-That-Flies). www.azcentral.com/12news. April.

Tsosie, Will. 2006. Personal conversation. August 10.

Tsosie, Will, 2009. Personal conversation. August 2.

Wyman, Leland C. 1962. *The Windways of the Navaho.* Colorado Springs, CO: The Taylor Museum.

Wyman, Leland C. 1970. *Sandpaintings of the Navaho Shootingway and The Walcott Collection.* Smithsonian Contributions to Anthropology, Number 13. Washington, DC: Smithsonian Institution.

 # Chapter Eight
Notes on Other Hunting People

*This chapter was originally presented as a paper entitled
"Na'azheel—The Ones Who Hunt: The Role of Meso-carnivores
in Navajo Culture" at the Defenders of Wildlife Carnivore Conference, Denver, Colorado, November 14, 2000.*

In addition to the larger (some might say more char-
ismatic) hunters, a number of smaller carnivores play
important roles in Navajo culture.

Bobcats and Lynx

The identification of various members of the feline family in Navajo ethnozoology is often difficult. In their ethnographic dictionary, the Franciscan Fathers list Navajo
terms for five different cats: wildcat, lynx, mountain
lion, puma, and leopard (Franciscan Fathers: 110–111).
Three other cats listed by the Franciscans, the canyon
lynx, grass lynx, and meadow lynx, were thought to be
mythical. The Franciscans, foremost of whom was the
eminent scholar of Navajo religion Father Berard Haile,
also provided "sacred names" or ceremonial names
for the wildcat, mountain lion, and puma, the latter of
which is also referred to as a "meadow wildcat" (ibid.:

175). In another publication, Haile also makes reference to a meadow wildcat, cliff wildcat, and "cat of the valleys" (Haile, 1981: 29).

Three members of the cat family inhabit Navajo Country today: the bobcat or "wildcat" (*Felis rufus*), the lynx (*Lynx canadensis*), and the mountain lion (*Puma concolor*). A fourth cat, the jaguar (*Panthera onca*), is found throughout the Navajo stories—quite possibly via the Pueblo side of the Navajos' heritage. Historically jaguars were recorded in Navajo Country, and it is highly likely that the Navajos also encountered the jaguar while they were incarcerated at Fort Sumner, New Mexico, in 1864–1868. Jaguars were known to the Navajos as "spotted lions." Today only the bobcat remains common. Mountain lions exist in unknown numbers—certainly just a few—in the more remote mountain ranges on the Navajo Reservation. The lynx were also historically found in southeast Colorado, an area that is well within the traditional Navajo homeland.

Most Navajos simply refer to bobcats as being "wildcats." The Navajo name for the bobcat is *nashdolilbahi.* I have found no descriptive explanation for this word. Navajos know him as the "younger brother" of the mountain lion (Tsosie, 2001). Bobcats are found throughout the mountains and brush country of the Navajo Reservation. The population of this small predator appears healthy, and the Navajo Nation Department of Fish and Wildlife regulates hunting and trapping season on bobcats, which they officially consider to be furbearers.

It is doubtful that lynx ever inhabited any of the mountain ranges that are today found within the borders of the reservation. Lynx, however, inhabited the nearby San Juan Mountains in southwestern Colorado, an area that Navajos historically hunted and traveled through and told of in their stories. By the mid-1970s, the lynx had been extirpated in Colorado. In 1999 and 2000, approximately one hundred lynx were reintroduced into the San Juans; despite some initial setbacks, these cats are now doing well and expanding their range. It can be assumed that lynx from the San Juans will move into the mountain ranges within the Navajo Reservation itself.

An important aspect of Navajo mythology is the so-called Navajo hunter tradition, beliefs that trace back to the Athabaskan period of Navajo prehistory and were later elaborated and enriched by Pueblo elements. The Navajo hunter tradition includes stories of animal elders and tutelaries. In the Navajo Deer Hunting Way, for example, the deer gods themselves provided the "divine hunters," Bobcat, Wolf, Mountain Lion, Tiger (Jaguar), and "Cat" (Lynx?) with the knowledge necessary to hunt them. In time, men appeared and also acquired this knowledge and passed it down through the generations. Presumably the deer gods also taught man how to hunt them. In addition, man acquired more specific knowledge of hunting from the divine predators. In this account, Bobcat and the other animal hunters were "present from the beginning" (Luckert: 18, 40).

It is mostly from the Pueblo side of their heritage that the Navajos adopted the belief that their creation is the result of a series of "emergences" from one world to the next. In his work on the Upward Moving and

Emergence Way ceremony, recorded in 1908, Haile describes the Seventh World of the Navajo as being the home of the Cat People or Feline People—Mountain Lion, Wildcat, Puma, and "Wildcat of the Canyons"—a possible reference to Lynx. The Cat People were anthropomorphic beings or deities who could talk and behave like men and who possessed supernatural powers. In time, many of these beings transformed into the animal forms we recognize today. Thus, Wildcat the anthropomorphic being became the animal we now call the wildcat.

Wildcat, along with Puma, is initially seen as guardian of the house of First Man. These deities appear in pairs and represent the north and the south. Early in the story, the Wolf People, then later the Mountain Lion, Kit Fox, and Badger People, launch an attack on the house of First Man, shooting arrows of turquoise, white shell, abalone, and jet. These arrows are caught by Wildcat and Puma, who shoot them back at their enemies. Later, Wildcat and Puma of the north themselves attack First Man (Haile, 1981: 29).

Bobcats and lynx also appear in the stories behind a number of Navajo ceremonies. In the Beadway story, for example, reference is made to a "yellow" bobcat and a "blue" lynx (Reichard, 1939/1977: 32, 43). Also in the Beadway story, Lynx, along with his fellow hunters Mountain Lion, Spotted Lion, and Wolf, is said to be one of the helpers to the great Navajo deity Monster Slayer (Newcomb: 66).

Bobcat also makes something of a cameo appearance in the Beautyway myth. In this story, the heroine,

Younger Sister, is playing with the Rock Wrens, who bury her under a pile of large rocks. Bobcat is one of the hunters called in to rescue her. His attempt to dig her out from the west side of the rock pile fails, and it remains up to Badger to recover her bones. The story does, however, have a happy ending when she is restored to life (Haile, Oakes, and Wyman: 82).

Bobcat also finds himself the second main character in a number of the famous Navajo Coyote stories. These stories, which are usually separate from the creation stories, highlight the foolish misfortunes of Coyote. They serve to demonstrate socially unacceptable behavior while at the same time reinforcing the more positive moral norms of the tribe.

Bobcats and presumably lynx were hunted for their body parts and occasionally for their meat (Franciscan Fathers: 214). The most common method used to kill bobcats was a deadfall trap. Occasionally they were tracked down and killed in deep snow or treed by dogs and shot (Hill, 1938: 168, 170).

If a bobcat was fat, the animal was eaten. The Navajos reportedly made a sausage out of bobcat meat that was stuffed into casings made from the skin (Hill, 1938: 170; Johnson: 26). However, the primary objective for killing bobcats was to acquire their skins and claws.

Bobcat skins were used to make caps and mittens and were especially valued for scarves (Kluckhohn, Hill, and Kluckhohn: 414). War caps were also made of bobcat skin (Hill, 1936: 9). A photograph taken prior to 1894 shows a Navajo tribesman sitting in front of a very large robe made of bobcat skins (Kluckhohn, Hill, and Kluckhohn: 187). Bobcat claws were used for decorative purposes on various items of clothing (ibid.: 414). Bobcat skin was also used to make arrow cases, but reportedly not bow cases (ibid.: 414).

Bobcat sinew was used as string to sew the medicine bag, or *jish*, used in some Navajo ceremonies (Frisbie: 71).

Indeed, various parts of the bobcat, especially its claws, were used to make ceremonial items. The most common of these items are probably the bandoliers and wristlets used by medicine men that perform the Upward-Reaching Way ceremony, an Evilway ritual for the treatment or prevention of disease or misfortune caused by ghosts. The bandoliers for this ceremony, two of them, were made of strips of jaguar or bobcat skin. To these strips were attached the claw of a mountain lion or bobcat and various flint arrow points. These bandoliers were placed on the patient, one over each shoulder and crossing on the chest. Four wristlets of "spotted" skin, again either jaguar or bobcat, were also made and used in a similar fashion. Supposedly only the fore claws of the bobcat were used for this purpose. In the mythology, First Man reportedly made the first of these items and then gave the instructions for future production (Wyman and Bailey: 13–14).

Bobcat claws, mountain lion claws, and flint points also decorated straps of buckskin that were placed on a patient in the Enemyway ceremony. These straps were employed in a similar manner as the bandoliers, but differed in that they were braided and reportedly came from the blood-stained shirt of an enemy killed in battle. The first of these braided straps was said to be made by Monster Slayer (Tsosie, 2001).

Bobcat skin wristlets are also used by medicine men that practice the Mountainway ceremony, a ceremony prescribed for the treatment of bear sickness. Such wristlets are decorated with bear claws (Frisbie: 313). Bobcat claws are also used to decorate the eagle fan used in the Windway ceremony (ibid.: 68).

Bobcat gall, as well as the gall from other guardian animals, such as the mountain lion, wolf, and eagle, is ground up and added to an herbal powder that is taken as preventative medicine to ward off witchcraft. A traditional Navajo who finds himself entering an unfamiliar or threatening environment, a place in which the potential for witchcraft might exist, will take such medicine (Tsosie, 1999).

Bobcat fat is also added to the fat of other animals to create a lotion that is smeared over a patient in ceremonies designed to exorcise evil caused by ghosts and witches. Ashes are then placed over the lotion. This constitutes the "darkening rite" of such ceremonies and is thought to confuse or scare off the evil presence (ibid.; see also Haile, 1938: 195).

Bobcats themselves, as well as the common house cat, are said to be animals that possess the ability to "witch" people. They do this using their whiskers, which are said to have power. Quite possibly Bobcat acquired this power through his mythological association with First Man, who is also said to be the first witch (Tsosie, 1999).

The bobcat and lynx also appear in a number of Navajo sandpaintings, most notably in two belonging to the Beadway ceremony. In the first of these, entitled *The Exchange of the Quivers*, the most powerful of the hunters, Wolf and Mountain Lion, are shown exchanging arrow quivers in a dance. To the left and right of each are seen the other hunters, Bobcat, Lynx, Spotted Lion, and Badger. Bobcat and Lynx are very similar in appearance, both spotted and with short, curved tails. Lynx is blue, while Bobcat is yellow. Both are shown holding life feathers. The second sandpainting, entitled *The Hunting Animals with Cornpacks*, shows the same characters, but here each of the hunters wears a backpack on his back containing corn. In the myth, they secured this corn using supernatural powers that enabled them to plant, cultivate, and harvest the crop in just a few minutes (Reichard, 1939/1977: 33–35, plates VI and VII).

Two small wildcats also appear at the east side of a Feather Chant sandpainting (Reichard, 1950: 701–702).

Foxes

There are three species of fox on the Navajo Reservation: the kit fox (*Vulpes macrotis*), the gray fox (*Urocyon cinereoargenteus*), and the red fox (*Vulpes vulpes*). The first two, though seldom seen, are not rare and are found throughout the reservation in the habitats each prefers. The red fox, however, is found only in the extreme northeast portion of the reservation, and its very existence was a matter of scientific debate until it was finally confirmed in the 1920s. I have been fortunate to see a number of these beautiful canines near Many Farms Lake.

The Navajo creation story tells of a "Yellow Fox" springing up from yellow light in the west, while a "Blue Fox" originated from blue light in the south. The Yellow Fox would seem most certainly to be the red fox, while the Blue Fox possibly represents either or both the kit and the gray fox. The Navajo name for the red fox is *mai'ii itsooi*, or "orange coyote," while the word for both the kit and the gray fox is *mai'ii doot' izhi*, which means blue or gray coyote. It appears that little or no distinction is made between these two latter species. In the Navajo stories, reference is usually made only to Yellow Fox or Blue Fox.

The sacred or ceremonial names for each species of fox are also interesting. The Franciscan Fathers state that the sacred name for the kit fox—which I assume to be the same for the gray fox—translates to "the youthful chief of the bordered fields." The sacred name for the yellow or red fox translates to "the chief and youth created with the earth" (Franciscan Fathers: 175). While both of these names are beautifully descriptive, I have been unable to find any additional information behind their origins or meanings.

Fox skins and tails are worn by dancers in the Nightway ceremony. In addition, Coyoteway singers wear a fox skin (Hill, 1938: 170).

Kluckhohn, in his classic study of Navajo witch-craft, states that witches occasionally wear the skins of the "desert fox"—which I assume to be the kit fox—as were-animals or skinwalkers (Kluckhohn: 26)

The Weasel Family

The Mustelidae or Mustelids are more commonly known as the weasel family. It is a diverse family and the largest of the order Carnivora. The North American representatives include the "true" weasels, ferrets, minks, martens, fishers, otters, badgers, and wolverines. Until recently they also included the skunks, which are now classified as their own family, Mephitidae. Some biologists continue to see the weasels and the skunks as being of one family, and for the purposes of this chapter I will discuss them together.

Navajo Country was a land rich with Mustelids. Tribal members likely came in contact with long-tailed weasels, black-footed ferrets, pine martens, river otters, badgers, and wolverines. Striped skunks and spotted skunks were also common throughout the entire range of the Navajo people.

Not surprisingly, members of the weasel and skunk families played important roles in the Navajo stories and in the tribe's culture and traditions.

Weasels, Martens, and Ferrets

Long-tailed weasels *(Mustela frenata)*, pine martens *(Martes Americana)*, and black-footed ferrets *(Mustela nigripes)* are similar-looking animals that once inhabited much of the land traditionally claimed by the Navajos. Today only the long-tailed weasel lives on land within the borders of the main reservation, its range restricted to the mountainous areas. In November 1993, I observed one of these agile little predators in full white winter pelage—the ermine phase—in the Chuska Mountains. Martens (an animal that frequently climbs trees in pursuit of its favorite prey, squirrels) once might have existed in these same mountains but are today restricted to the San Juan Mountains of southwestern Colorado. The black-footed ferret, once common on the prairie lands of the reservation, is now considered extirpated from its historic Navajo home range. An effort is currently being made to reintroduce black-footed ferrets to the Aubrey Valley in northeastern Arizona. This land is now partly owned by the Navajo Nation, and the tribe is cooperating with the Arizona Game and Fish Department on the reintroduction program.

In the Gishin Biye' version of the Emergence story, Weasel—who is said to come from Big Adobe Incline—is one of the "pets" given by Changing Woman to the four original clans. Weasel helps by hunting for the people and then defending them from an attack by the Ute Indians. In doing so, Weasel, like the other protector animals, Bear, Mountain Lion, and Porcupine, becomes so mean that he is sent to live in the mountains. In appreciation, the *honágháahnii* clan is said to be kind to weasels (Haile, 1981: 167; 172).

In the Navajo stories, the above three members of the weasel family are usually described by, or associated with, color. Haile, for example, in describing the inhabitants of the White-Yellowish Underworld, makes reference to Dark Weasel, White Weasel, Blue Weasel, Pink Weasel, and Yellow Weasel (ibid.: 29). Wyman, in discussing the female branch of the Mountainway ceremony (a ceremony in which weasels appear throughout), tells of the heroine encountering a group of these animals on her journey:

> There was a small mountain in the distance. When she came to it a strange white something ran along, its breast was black. She learned that this was a weasel. Another yellow one ran along right behind the other. Then a blue one ran along again, then a black one again, and a spotted one again ran along. When that happened he said, "They call us all Weasel, we all have a prayerstick, no doubt. Which place are you bound for, my grandchild?" (Wyman: 207)

It is not surprising that in the stories weasels are described in a multitude of colors. I suspect that in some cases references to "dark" weasels might mean the standard color phase of the long-tailed weasel, which is a deep chocolate brown. "Black" weasels might refer to the black-footed ferret, whereas "yellow" weasel might mean the pine marten. "White" weasels are undoubtedly ermines, and "spotted" weasels might very well refer to the various white-and-brown color schemes a long-tailed weasel goes through on its way to becoming an ermine. All of this is admittedly speculation on my part.

Weasels are considered to be among the Mountain People and most commonly appear in the Mountainway and the closely related Beautyway stories. They are considered to be one of the "dangerous" animals in that they are thought to be one of the etiological factors behind the need for a Mountainway or Beautyway ceremony. Wyman's classic study on the Mountainway includes the following:

> Weasels may be killed for their skins to be used in ceremonial paraphernalia, but this should not be done by either par-

ent of an unborn child for fear of prenatal infection. Yucca Patch Man remarked in telling his myth that, "This disease is very dangerous and affects a person in this manner . . . it dries up a person in disease." (Ibid.: 21)

During the story of the female branch of the Mountainway, along her journey the heroine encounters Meal Sprinkler, who provides additional information on the Weasel People, including the fact that Dark Weasel is "their leader" and that the prayer stick each possesses has the power to help cure the diseases they can pass on to humans. "This disease is very dangerous and affects a person in this manner," he explains. "Whenever it dries up a person in disease, remember that these [weasels] are doing it. Whenever earth surface people suffer (in this manner), let these [prayer sticks] be cut for them," he explained. (Ibid.: 210)

In this story, we see a standard theme in the Navajo understanding of the natural world: that while a certain animal might have the power to cause disease due to the transgressions of humankind—in this case, the weasel bringing on a prenatal disease to the child of a parent who has violated natural law—it is also that very same animal that possesses the power and the tools to cure that disease.

Weasels are mentioned a number of times in the Mountainway stories. In one of the "specialty acts" of the Fire or Corral Dance held on the final night of the Mountainway ceremony, a stuffed skin of a weasel appears magically from a basket of spruce twigs (ibid.: 28–29).

In the Beautyway ceremony, the heroine is helped by the Weasel People, who are called Slim People Narrow in the Waist. They are said to live at Whirling Mountain—the Carrizo Mountains in Arizona. They also provide the pouch made of their own skin for this ceremony (Haile, Oakes, and Wyman: 138; 177).

Weasel body parts are used in various ways for both the Mountainway and Beautyway ceremonies. As noted, Beautyway pouches are made of weasel skin, and every pouch usually contains additional skins. A complete weasel skin is also ground up as medicine for this ceremony (ibid.: 87, 119).

Weasels appear in sandpaintings from the Mountainway and Beautyway ceremonies. In one Beautyway sandpainting, entitled *Big Snakes on Their House*, white and yellow weasels are depicted as eastern guardians (ibid.: 170). In other numerous Mountainway and Beautyway sandpaintings, various Holy People are shown wearing headdresses made of weasel skins (see, for example, Wyman: 91, and Haile, Oakes, and Wyman: figure x). In a Beautyway sandpainting made by Hastin Gani and entitled *People with Weasel Skins*, Holy People are shown with weasel skin pouches; also included are four weasel skins, two yellow and two white (Haile, Oakes, and Wyman: plate x).

The black-footed ferret does not appear to be singled out in the anthropological literature. As I noted earlier, mentions of "black" weasels might refer to this animal. Certainly black-footed ferrets were historically found on the Navajo Reservation and played an important role in Navajo ceremonialism. The Arizona

Game and Fish Department's black-footed ferret web-site includes information compiled by Debra A. Yazzie, a wildlife biologist with the Navajo Natural Heritage Program. Yazzie's source is a traditional education specialist, Earvin James. According to James, the gallbladder of the ferret is dried and ground into fine powder that is administered in an unnamed ceremony. The nails of the ferret are also ground up and used in the same manner. James also confirms that ferret pelts are used to make ceremonial pouches and are cut into strips that are wrapped around the patient. James also notes that ferret figures are used in some sand-paintings. I assume that all of these uses are part of the Mountainway or Beautyway ceremonies (Arizona Game and Fish Department).

James also describes the use of a live ferret in a birth ceremony:

> A live ferret is captured and placed on a sheepskin. Corn pollen is sprinkled on the ferret while a prayer is chanted by the medicine man. The corn pollen is then gathered and placed in a pouch and used to bless a newborn baby at a later time. The baby is blessed to be hardworking, full of energy, and brave. (Ibid.)

A number of years ago I had an opportunity to examine a Navajo medicine bag or *jish*. This bag, which I assumed to have belonged to a Mountainway or Beautyway singer, contained nearly a dozen black-footed ferret pelts. These pelts appeared to be very old and very well used. The individual who had this bag was unaware of who its prior owner was or of the origin of the pelts.

River Otters

The river otter was once found in the northern limits of Navajo Country along the Colorado and San Juan Rivers. Otters are now extirpated from these areas except for the Gunnison River in southwestern Colorado, where they were reintroduced in 1984.

The Navajo name for the otter is *tga'ba'astin*—probably from the words *tgaba*, which means "the shore," and *setgi'*, which means "it lies"—in sum, an animal that lies by the shore (Franciscan Fathers: 156). Otters are somewhat unique among the carnivores in that they are considered to be one of the Water Creatures and thus are more closely associated with beavers and frogs than they are with other meat-eating animals, including other similar-looking Mustelids.

In Sandoval's version of the creation story, Otter first appears in the Third World along with Mountain Lion, Bear, and Big Snake as the chiefs of the four directions, who serve as advisors to First Man and the other Animal People (O'Bryan: 6).

Otters are especially associated with the Beautyway ceremony. In this story, the heroine, Younger Sister, encounters the Otter People at Slim Water Lake, then again at Scattered Springs (Haile, Oakes, and Wyman: 139). Big Snake, the principle antagonist of Beautyway, possesses an otter skin quiver (ibid.: 57).

Otters and otter-related items also appear in numerous Beautyway sandpaintings. In a number of these, Big Otter—the "denizen of the rivers"—is depicted along with other "water creatures" (ibid.: figure 7; plate XIII). In another sandpainting, entitled *Snake People Who Make Medicine*, the arm streamers of the main figures are made of otter skin (ibid.: figure 5). In still another sandpainting, this one entitled *Mountain Gods*, the deities are shown wearing otter skin collars (ibid.: plate VIII).

Since otters appear in the Mountainway, they also appear in the sandpaintings of that ceremony. A brown otter appears in one Mountainway sandpainting, *People with Long Hair* (Wyman: 92). In at least two other Mountainway sandpaintings, *The Long Bodies* and *Whirling Rainbow People*, figures are shown wearing otter skin collars (ibid.: 99, 120).

Otters are not limited to Mountainway and Beautyway and in fact are found throughout the Navajo stories. In the story of the hero twins' journey to visit their father the Sun, Monster Slayer and Child Born of Water are tested by their father, who attempts to freeze them. They are saved by Beaver Man and Otter Woman, who give them their skins to keep them warm. This is the origin of the otter skin collars worn by many of the Holy People (Reichard, 1950: 386, 639). Beaver and otter skin collars are also considered to be "one of the most powerful pieces of equipment" and are worn by Shootingway singers (Frisbie: 70). In addition, a Shootingway singer must always possess at least a small strip of otter skin in his *jish* (Wyman: 78). A screen is erected during a Shootingway ceremony on which a male beaver collar is hung over the south end, while a female otter skin is hung over the north end (Reichard, 1950: 711).

In a number of Shootingway sandpaintings, including *Buffalo Never Dies*, the Holy People are shown wearing otter skin collars (ibid.: 704).

In another Navajo story, Self Teacher is stuck in a log at the falls on the San Juan River. Offerings are made to the Water People, including Otter, for his release. In the same story, Frog tells Self Teacher how to invoke himself with prayer sticks if any of the Water People, such as Otter, should ever give him disease. Otter prayer sticks are brown in color (Matthews: 168; Reichard, 1950: 438–439).

Both Calling God and Fringe Mouth wear otter tails as part of their dress (Tsosie, 1999).

In addition to its fur, other body parts of the otter are used in various ceremonies. Otter fat is used by singers to clean their *jish* (Frisbie: 110). Otter fat mixed with charcoal is also used to produce body paint for the "darkening rite" part of some healing ceremonies (Tsosie, 2001).

The gall of the otter was used as an antidote against witchcraft (Hill, 1938: 170).

To the Navajo, the otter represents playfulness and happiness. In a *kinaalda* (the puberty ceremony for young girls who have come of age), a girl who exhibits such traits and is well liked and one for whom things in life come easily uses a hair tie of otter skin. Otter skins, along with those of mountain lions, are also considered to be signs of wealth and are highly sought as possessions. In earlier times, otter pelts were valued trade items and were usually obtained from the Pueblos of the northern Rio Grande River valley (Tsosie, 2001).

Otter also plays a major role in one of the well-known Coyote stories of the Navajos. In this story, Coyote comes across a group of otters at play. The otters are betting their skins against one another on the results of the game. When one otter lost his skin, he would jump into the water and miraculously emerge with a new skin. After considerable pleading, Coyote is finally allowed to participate in the game—and soon loses his skin. Despite jumping time after time into the water, Coyote's skin will not return. Finally taking pity on him, the otters place him in a badger hole, which they then cover with earth. When Coyote emerges, he is again covered with fur, but not the beautiful glossy fur he once had. Instead, his fur is now coarse and rough. Coyote has worn his new skin ever since (Matthews: 97–99).

And finally, otters were considered by the Navajos to be "rare game"—an infrequent source of food to be used in hard times. The Navajos knew that when they faced starvation, the otter would take pity on them and allow itself to be caught and eaten in these times of need (Reichard, 1950: 66).

Badgers

The badger, *Taxidea taxus*, is a relatively common carnivore found in every habitat throughout the Navajo Reservation. Badger is also an important character in a number of the Navajo ceremonies.

In the Navajo creation story, the sky stooped down and the earth rose to meet it. The two bodies came in contact, and at that moment from the earth sprung Coyote and Badger. Coyote rose first, and for this reason he is considered to be the elder brother of Badger. While Coyote "skulked among the people," Badger entered a hole in the ground at the Place of Emergence that led to the lower world. Both Coyote and Badger are consequently said to be the "children of the sky" (Matthews: 71; Reichard, 1950: 422).

In the Emergence story, while the people were escaping from the Lower world, they sent Badger to enlarge the hole made by Locust. When he returned, his feet were stained black with mud, and they have remained that color ever since (Matthew: 76).

Also in the Emergence story, there comes a time when men and women argue with each other, resulting in a separation of the sexes, each believing it does not need the other. During the separation, Badger goes among the women and makes them mad with sexual desire (Reichard, 1950: 382).

Badger also plays an important role in the Mountainway stories. In the female branch of Mountainway, the heroine encounters Badger at Black Mountain (Wyman: 75). In the first Mountainway ceremony ever held, Badger danced in the corral with Porcupine and Jumping Rat (ibid.: 242–243). And finally in one "specialty" act of the Mountainway ceremony, a man washes his hands in a shower of burning pitch and is magically unharmed—a stunt first performed by Badger (ibid.: 29).

In the Beautyway story, Younger Sister encounters the Badger People, who are said to live at the east side of Black Mountain (Haile, Oakes, and Wyman: 138). The heroine later tries to play as the Rock Wrens do, but instead rolls rocks on herself and is crushed. Wolf, Mountain Lion, and Wildcat are all called upon to find and rescue her, but each fails. Finally it is Badger who succeeds in finding and recovering her bones, and she is subsequently restored to life (ibid.: 82). This same story appears in Beadway, except that in this case it is a boy—Scavenger—who is purposefully trapped under rocks by the Black-tailed Swallow People. The Hunting People—Wolf, Mountain Lion, Lynx, and Bobcat—try but fail to recover his bones, but Badger succeeds. Like the heroine in the Beautyway story, the hero is restored to life (Reichard, 1939/1977: 32).

Body parts of the badger are used in a number of ceremonies. Beautyway singers use a badger skin rattle (Haile, Oakes, and Wyman: 111). Skin from the paws of a badger is used to make wristlets worn during Mountainway (Hill, 1938: 170). Badger feet are used in the Nightway ceremony (Frisbie: 67). Badger gall is used as an antidote against witchcraft (Hill, 1938: 170). Arrowheads that have been disinterred by a badger are also used ceremonially (Frisbie: 383).

Interestingly, I found no reference to badgers appearing on either Beautyway or Mountainway sandpaintings. Badgers are, however, one of the Hunting People—along with Wolf, Mountain Lion, Spotted Lion, Bobcat, and Lynx—that appear in the Beadway story and consequently on a number of sandpaintings used in that ceremony (Reichard, 1939/1977: 33–35, plates VI, VII). Although Reichard states that Navajos considered the badger to be a "hunter par excellence," I found few anthropological references to support this. The Beadway story is also the only reference I found in which the badger is characterized as being a hunter. Karl Luckert does not mention the badger in his study of the early Navajo hunter tradition. Quite possibly the recognition and acknowledgment of the badger's hunting skills came later.

Body parts of the badger were used for nonceremonial purposes as well. The skin of the badger was used to make clothing items and was especially prized as a material for moccasin soles. Quivers and caps were also made of badger skin (Hill, 1938: 170).

Badgers are believed to have exceptional powers of hearing and the ability to see the future. Navajo war leaders rubbed the ear wax of a badger on the ears and under the eyes of their warriors to gain these abilities (Reichard, 1950: 257).

Wolverines

The most impressive and legendary of the Mustelids, the wolverine (*Gulo gulo*) was once found throughout the mountainous ranges of Navajo Country. Historical records of this animal's existence come from the San Juan Mountains of southwestern Colorado—where the animal might still exist—and even from northern Arizona and New Mexico (Nead, Halfpenny, and Bissell; Hash). In all probability, wolverines were never common.

It seems highly likely that the Navajos at least knew of the wolverine. There is, however, a surprising scarcity of references to this animal in the anthropological literature. In her description of a mountain lion in a sandpainting from the Beadway ceremony, Reichard writes that he is wearing a "brown quiver made of wolverine (?) skin" (Reichard, 1939/1977: 33). The fact that Reichard felt compelled to insert a question mark strongly suggests that she doubted the accuracy of her Navajo collaborator, the medicine man Miguelito, on this detail.

Skunks

There are two species of skunk found on the Navajo Reservation, the common striped skunk (*Mephitis mephitis*) and the rarer western spotted skunk (*Spilogale gracilis*). Skunks are found throughout Navajo Country, the striped skunk preferring the more mountainous and wooded areas, and the spotted skunk more commonly found in rocky desert areas.

One of the most interesting aspects of the Navajo view of skunks is that the animals represent not two species, but different sexes of what seems to be viewed as the same species. In the stories, Striped Skunk, or Big Skunk as he is called, is considered to be a male, whereas Spotted Skunk, or Small Skunk, is considered to be a female. Striped Skunk is referred to as the "chief of the mountains"; Spotted Skunk is called the "young woman chief of the mountains" (Wyman: 50–51, 217).

In the Emergence story, both Big Skunk and Spotted Skunk first make their appearance in the Yellow Underworld along with most other mammals (Haile, 1981: 29). In the first shoe game, Skunk received ashes as his winnings. It is for this reason that skunks are mostly black. One of the other animals wanted Skunk to look different and so took white paint and ran it down his back (McPherson: 63).

The most notable characteristic of skunks of course is their ability to discharge a strong, noxious scent when alarmed or threatened. This quality obviously did not go unnoticed by the Navajos. The generic name for all skunks is *wolizhi*, which translates roughly to "the one who urinates" (Franciscan Fathers: 142).

In commenting on how the Navajos view skunks, the Franciscan Fathers make an interesting observation that "the bite of a skunk is poisonous, and the animal is ordinarily avoided" (ibid.: 142). This undoubtedly represents knowledge by the Navajos nearly one hundred years ago that skunks are common carriers of rabies.

Skunks are frequently mentioned in the Mountainway stories. In the male branch, the hero is taught how to make prayer sticks by the Skunk People. In the female branch, the heroine encounters both Big Skunk and Spotted Skunk on her journey (Matthews: 26; Wyman: 15, 50–51, and 217).

Skunks, like most animals, are considered to possess power, and their body parts are used in various ways to heal. Tails and skins are hung in a hogan, and the meat is eaten to help cure tuberculosis and other diseases. The tail of the skunk is also burned to produce a healing smoke when people become unconscious. Skunk musk is used as an inhalant for colds and as a treatment for mouth sores (McPherson: 63–64; Haile, 1981: 106; Hill, 1938: 170). In addition, the bladder of the skunk is given as a drink to a patient who is a victim of witchcraft (Kluckhohn: 192).

Skunk skins were used to make various items of clothing, most notably headbands and caps. Skunk skins were also reportedly sold to traders (Kluckhohn, Hill, and Kluckhohn: 415; Hill, 1938: 170).

I found no reference in the anthropological literature to indicate that Navajos viewed skunks as being predators.

Raccoons, Ringtails, and Coatis

At least three members of the Procyonidae family inhabit Navajo Country: raccoons, ringtails, and coatis.

The raccoon *(Procyon lotor)* is found through the mountainous habitats of the current Navajo Reservation. I have seen these fascinating animals many times, often in broad daylight, in the Chuska Mountains. Interestingly, Theodore H. Eaton Jr. does not list the raccoon in his 1937 survey *Mammals of the Navajo Country.* Halloran and Taber state that "raccoons ascend the watershed of the Chuska Mountains along willow-lined streams that originate in the highest reaches of this mountain complex" (Halloran and Taber, 1965: 140). The fact that the raccoon does not seem to appear in any of the Navajo stories leads me to think that perhaps it is a recent arrival to Navajo Country.

Eaton does, however, list the ringtail (*Bassariscus astutus*) as being a Navajo resident. The information he provides on this animal is rather generic in nature, and he lists no particular areas on the reservation in which it exists. I have found no one who has ever seen or heard of a ringtail on the reservation; quite possibly it no longer resides there, if it ever did. Certainly ringtails do inhabit areas that were historically frequented by the Navajos, such as the Grand Canyon, however, and early Navajos must have been familiar with them. Still, ringtails do not seem to appear in any Navajo stories.

The coati *(Nasua nasua)* was originally a tropical animal of Mexico and Central and South America whose range did not extend into the United States. Over the years the coati has expanded northward, probably due to climate change, and today this animal is common in the mountains of southern Arizona and is even encountered as far north as the Painted Desert, part of which lies within the southern portion of the Navajo Reservation (Hoffmeister: 488–490). Interestingly, when I taught on the White Mountain Apache Reservation in the late 1990s, the tribal people there would occasionally encounter coatis, and because of their behavior or appearance, they referred to them as monkeys. Because the animals were new arrivals to the region, no Apache word existed to describe them. Without question, the presence of coatis in Navajo Country is a very recent phenomenon and this is why they do not appear in any Navajo stories.

References

Arizona Game and Fish Department. "Black-footed ferret." http://www.azgfd.gov.

Eaton, Thomas Hildreth, Dorothy Morris, and Ruth Morris. 1937. *Mammals of the Navajo Country.* Berkeley, CA: National Youth Administration.

Franciscan Fathers, 1910. *An Ethnologic Dictionary of the Navajo Language.* St. Michaels, AZ: St. Michaels Press.

Frisbie, Charlotte J. 1987. *Navajo Medicine Bundles or Jish: Acquisition, Transmission, and Disposition in the Past and Present.* Albuquerque: University of New Mexico Press.

Haile, Father Berard. 1938. *Origin Legend of the Navaho Enemy Way.* New Haven, CT: Yale University Press.

Haile, Father Berard. 1981. *The Upward Moving and Emergence Way*. Lincoln: University of Nebraska Press.

Haile, Father Berard, Maud Oakes and Leland C. Wyman, 1957. *Beautyway: A Navaho Ceremonial*. New York: Pantheon Books.

Haley, Delphine. 1975. *Sleek and Savage: North America's Weasel Family*. Seattle, WA: Pacific Search Books.

Halloran, Arthur F. and Freeman E. Taber. 1965. "Carnivore Notes from the Navajo Indian Reservation," *Southwest Naturalist*, 10: 139–140.

Hansen, Kevin. 2006. *Bobcat: Master of Survival.* New York: Oxford University Press.

Hash, Howard S. 1987. "Wolverine," in *Wild Furbearer Management and Conservation in America*, edited by Milan Novak et al. Toronto: Ontario Ministry of Natural Resources: 575–585.

Hill, Willard W. 1936. *Navaho Warfare.* New Haven, CT: Yale University Publications in Anthropology, No. 5.

Hill, Willard W. 1938. *The Agricultural and Hunting Methods of the Navaho Indians.* New Haven, CT: Yale University Publications in Anthropology, No. 18.

Hill, Willard W. and Dorothea W. Hill, 1945. "Navaho Coyote Tales: Their Position in the Southern Athabaskan Group," *Journal of American Folklore*, 58.

Hoffmeister, Donald F. 1986. *Mammals of Arizona.* Tucson: University of Arizona.

Johnson, Christie. 1977. *Southwest Mammals: Navajo Beliefs and Legends.* Blanding, UT: San Juan School District Media Center.

King, Carolyn. 1989. *The Natural History of Weasels and Stoats.* Ithaca, NY: Cornell University Press.

Kluckhohn, Clyde. 1944. *Navaho Witchcraft.* Boston: Beacon Press.

Kluckhohn, Clyde, Willard W. Hill, and Lucy W. Kluckhohn, 1975. *Navaho Material Culture.* Cambridge, MA: Belknap Press of Harvard University.

Luckert, Karl A. 1975. *The Navajo Hunter Tradition.* Tucson: University of Arizona Press.

Matthews, Washington. 1897/1994. *Navaho Legends.* Salt Lake City: University of Utah Press.

McPherson, Robert S. 1992. *Sacred Land, Sacred View: Navajo Perceptions of the Four Corners Region.* Salt Lake City, UT: Brigham Young University Press.

Nead, David M., James C. Halfpenny, and Steve Bissell. 1985. "The Status of Wolverines in Colorado," *Northwest Science*, 8(4): 286–289.

Newcomb, Franc J. 1940. "Origin Legend of the Navajo Eagle Chant," *Journal of American Folk-Lore*, 53(207): 50–78.

O'Bryan, Aileen O. 1956/1993. *Navaho Indian Myths.* New York: Dover Publications.

Pavlik Steve. 2003. "Rohonas and Spotted Lions: The Historical and Cultural Occurrence of the Jaguar, *Panthera onca*, among the Native Tribes of the American Southwest," *Wicazo Sa Review*, 18(1): 157–175.

Reichard, Gladys A. 1939/1977. *Navajo Medicine Man Sandpaintings.* New York: Dover Publications.

Reichard, Gladys A. 1950. *Navaho Religion.* New York: Bollingen Foundation.

Roessel, Robert A. and Dillon Platero. 1974. *Coyote Stories of the Navajo People.* Phoenix, AZ: Navajo Curriculum Center Press.

Tsosie, Will. 1999. Personal conversation. October 12.

Tsosie, Will. 2001. Personal conversation. August 4.

Wyman, Leland C. 1975. *The Mountainway of the Navajo.* Tucson: University of Arizona Press.

Wyman, Leland C. and Flora L. Bailey. 1943. "Navajo Upward-Reaching Way: Objective Behavior, Rationale, and Sanction," *University of New Mexico Bulletin* 389, Anthropological Series 4.

 References

Aberle, David F. 1982. *The Peyote Religion among the Navajo*. Chicago: University of Chicago Press.

Arizona Game and Fish Department. "Black-footed ferret." http://www.azgfd.gov.

Atencio, Ernie. 1994. "After a Heavy Harvest and a Death, Navajo Forestry Realigns with Culture," *High Country News*. October 31.

Bailey, Vernon. 1931. *Mammals of New Mexico*. Washington, DC: US Department of Agriculture, Bureau of Biological Survey.

Baird, Spencer F. 1859. *Special Report upon the Mammals of the Mexican Boundary*. Washington, DC: Smithsonian Institution.

Baldwin, Stuart J. 1986. "The Mountain Lion in Tompiro Stone Art," in *By Hands Unknown: Papers on Rock Art and Archaeology in Honor of James G. Bain*, edited by Anne V. Poore. Albuquerque, NM: Archaeological Society of New Mexico.

Bass, Rick. 1998. *The New Wolves: The Return of the Mexican Wolf to the American Southwest*. New York: The Lyons Press.

Basso, Keith. 1969. *Western Apache Witchcraft*. Tucson: University of Arizona Anthropological Papers, No. 15.

Becenti, Deenise. 1994. "Snakes Alive! Serpents Make Workers Squirm," *The Salt Lake Tribune*. August 6.

Bekoff, Marc. 2007. *The Emotional Lives of Animals: A Leading Scientist Explores Animal Joy, Sorrow, and Empathy—and Why They Matter*. Novato, CA: New World Library.

Berkes, Fikret. 1999. *Sacred Ecology: Traditional Ecological Knowledge and Resource Management*. Philadelphia, PA: Taylor & Francis Publishers.

Billingsley, M. W. 1971. *Behind the Scenes in Hopi Land*. Private printing.

Bolgiano, Chris. 1995. *Mountain Lion: An Unnatural History of Pumas and People.* Mechanicsburg, PA: Stackpole Press.

Brady, Margaret K. 1984. *Some Kind of Power: Navajo Children's Skinwalker Narratives.* Salt Lake City: University of Utah Press.

Brown, David E. 1991. "Revival for El Tigre?" *Defenders,* 66(1): 27–35.

Brown, David E. 1997a. "Jaguars Known and Reported Killed or Photographed (in Arizona) since 1890." Unpublished paper.

Brown, David E. 1997b. "Return of El Tigre," *Defenders,* 72(4): 12–15.

Brown, David E., ed. 1983. *The Wolf in the Southwest: The Making of an Endangered Species*. Tucson: University of Arizona Press.

Brown, David E. and Carlos A. Lopez. 2001. *Borderland Jaguars.* Salt Lake City: University of Utah Press.

Brun, Janay. 2011. "Truth and Consequences," *Three Coyotes,* 1(2): 13–21.

Bulow, Ernest L. 1972. *Navajo Taboos*. Gallup, NM: Buffalo Medicine Books.

Burbank, James C. 1990. *Vanishing Lobo: The Mexican Wolf and the Southwest.* Boulder, CO: Johnson Publishing Company.

Busch, Robert H. 1995. *The Wolf Almanac*. New York: The Lyons Press.

Cooper, Guy H. 1987. "Coyote in Navajo Religion and Cosmology," *The Canadian Journal of Native Studies,* VII(2): 181–193.

Cremony, John C. 1868/1970. *Life among the Apaches.* Glorietta, NM: Rio Grande Press.

Crotty, Helen K. 1995. *Anasazi Mural Art of the Pueblo IV Period, AD 1300–1600: Influences, Selective Adaptations, and Cultural Diversity in the Prehistoric Southwest.* PhD dissertation. Los Angeles: University of California.

Cushing, Frank H. 1883/1966. *Zuni Fetishes.* Flagstaff, AZ: K.C. Publications.

Darwin, Charles. 1872/1998. *The Expression of Emotions in Man and Animals.* New York: Oxford University Press.

Davis, John V. and Kay S. Jones. 1974. "A Rock Art Inventory at Hueco Tanks State Park, Texas," El Paso Archaeological Society Special Report, No. 12.

Deloria, Vine, Jr. 1969. *Custer Died for Your Sins: An Indian Manifesto*. New York: The Macmillan Company.

Deloria, Vine, Jr. 2004. "Philosophy and the Tribal People," in *American Indian Thought: Philosophical Essays,* edited by Anne Waters. Malden, MA: Blackwell Publishing Company: 3–11.

Deloria, Vine, Jr. and Daniel R. Wildcat. 2001. *Power and Place: Indian Education in America*. Golden, CO: Fulcrum Publishing.

Donovan, Bill. 1994. "Movie Snake Scene Offends Navajos," *Arizona Republic*.

Donovan, Bill. 1998. *Navajo Times*. December 12.

Donovan, Bill. 1999a. "Navajos May Close Zoo," *Arizona Republic.* January 8.

Donovan, Bill. 1999b. "Navajos Weigh Options to Keep Tribal Zoo Open," *Arizona Republic.* February 1.

Eaton, Thomas Hildreth, Dorothy Morris, and Ruth Morris. 1937. *Mammals of the Navajo Country*. Berkeley, CA: National Youth Administration.

Elmore, Francis H. 1953. "The Deer and His Importance to the Navajo," *El Palacio*, 60: 371–384.

Farmer, Malcolm. 1982. "Bear Ceremonialism among the Navajos and Other Apacheans," in *Papers in Honor of Leland C. Wyman*, edited by David M. Brugge and Charlotte J. Frisbie: 110–114. *Museum of New Mexico Papers in Anthropology*, 17. Santa Fe: Museum of New Mexico Press.

Fonseca, Felicia. 2013. "Permit Lets Hopi Take 40 Golden Eagles," Associated Press. April 10.

Fragua Hevey, Janet. 1998. Personal conversation. April 10.

Franciscan Fathers. 1910. *An Ethnologic Dictionary of the Navajo Language*. St. Michaels, AZ: St. Michaels Press.

Frisbie, Charlotte J. 1987. *Navajo Medicine Bundles or Jish: Acquisition, Transmission, and Disposition in the Past and Present*. Albuquerque: University of New Mexico Press.

Gabriel, Trip. 1994. "A Death in Navajo Country," *Outside Magazine*. May.

Goodwin, Grenville and Keith H. Basso. 1971. *Western Apache Raiding and Warfare*. Tucson: University of Arizona Press.

Griffin, Donald R. 1981. *The Question of Animal Awareness: Evolutionary Continuity of Mental Experience*. New York: The Rockefeller University Press.

Gunnerson, James H. 1998. "Mountain Lions and Pueblo Shrines in the American Southwest," in *Icons of Power: Feline Symbolism in the Americas*, edited by Nicholas J. Saunders. New York: Routledge.

Haile, Father Berard. 1938. *Origin Legend of the Navaho Enemy Way*. New Haven, CT: Yale University Press.

Haile, Father Berard. 1943. *Origin Legend of the Navaho Flintway*. Chicago: University of Chicago Press.

Haile, Father Berard. 1981. *The Upward Moving and Emergence Way*. Lincoln: University of Nebraska Press.

Haile, Father Berard. 1984. *Navajo Coyote Tales*. Lincoln: University of Nebraska Press.

Haile, Father Berard, Maud Oakes, and Leland C. Wyman. 1957. *Beautyway: A Navaho Ceremonial*. New York: Pantheon Books.

Haley, Delphine. 1975. *Sleek and Savage: North America's Weasel Family*. Seattle, WA: Pacific Search Books.

Halpern, Katherine Spencer and Susan Brown McGreevy, eds. 1997. *Washington Matthews: Studies of Navajo Culture, 1880–1894*. Albuquerque: University of New Mexico Press.

Hammond, George P. and Agapito Rey. 1940. *Narratives of the Coronado Expedition, 1540–1542*. Albuquerque, NM: Coronado Centennial Publications.

Hansen, Kevin. 2006. *Bobcat: Master of Survival*. New York: Oxford University Press.

Hardeen, George. 1996. "Two Tribes, Two Religions Vie for Place in the Desert," *High Country News*. August 5.

Hash, Howard S. 1987. "Wolverine," in *Wild Furbearer Management and Conservation in America,* edited by Milan Novak et al. Toronto: Ontario Ministry of Natural Resources: 575–585.

Hassell, Sandy. 1949/1972. *Know the Navajos*. Estes Park, CO: Vic Walker.

Hester, James J. 1962. *Early Navajo Migrations and Acculturation in the Southwest.* Museum of New Mexico Papers in Anthropology, No. 6. Santa Fe: Museum of New Mexico Press.

Hibben, Frank C. 1975. *Kiva Art of the Anasazi at Pottery Mound.* Las Vegas, NV: K.C. Publications.

Hill, Willard W. 1936. *Navaho Warfare.* New Haven, CT: Yale University Publications in Anthropology, No. 5.

Hill, Willard W. 1938. *The Agricultural and Hunting Methods of the Navaho Indians.* New Haven, CT: Yale University Publications in Anthropology, No. 18.

Hill, Willard W. and Dorothy W. Hill. 1943. "The Legend of the Navajo Eagle-Catching Way," *New Mexico Anthropologist*, 6,7(2): 31–36.

Hill, Willard W. and Dorothy W. Hill. 1945. "Navaho Coyote Tales and Their Position in the Southern Athapaskan Group," *Journal of American Folklore*, 58.

Hillerman, Tony. 1986. *Skinwalkers.* New York: Harper & Row.

Hoffmeister, Donald F. 1971. *Mammals of the Grand Canyon.* Chicago: University of Illinois Press.

Hoffmeister, Donald F. 1986. *Mammals of Arizona.* Tucson: University of Arizona Press.

Johnson, Christie. 1977. *Southwest Mammals: Navajo Beliefs and Legends.* Blanding, UT: San Juan School District Media Center.

Jones, Bernard M., Jr. 1994. "The Symbolic Image of Mountain Lion: Recreating Myth in Rock Art," *Rock Art Papers, Volume 11:* 157–170, San Diego Museum Papers, No. 31.

Jones, Bernard M., Jr. 1995. "The Heart at the Center of the Circle: Mountain Lion Symbolism and Solstice Ritual," *Rock Art Papers, Volume 12:* 45–54, San Diego Museum Papers, No. 33.

Kelley, Matt. 2000. "Federal Officials Block Hopis from Taking Eagles for Religious Ceremonies," *Seattle-Post Intelligencer*. July 22.

Kiefer, Michael. 1994. "Death of an Ecowarrior," *Phoenix New Times*. January 6.

King, Carolyn. 1989. *The Natural History of Weasels and Stoats*. Ithaca, NY: Cornell University Press.

Kluckhohn, Clyde. 1944. Navaho Witchcraft. Boston: Beacon Press.

Kluckhohn, Clyde. 1944/1962. "Notes on Navaho Eagle Way," in *Culture and Behavior: The Collected Essays of Clyde Kluck-hohn,* edited by Richard Kluckhohn. New York: Free Press of Glencoe: 123–133.

Kluckhohn, Clyde and Dorothea Leighton. 1946. *The Navaho*. Cambridge, MA: Harvard University Press.

Kluckhohn, Clyde and Leland C. Wyman. 1940. "An Introduction to Navajo Chant Practice," *Memoirs of the American Anthropological Association*, Supplement 53: 1–204.

Kluckhohn, Clyde, Willard W. Hill, and Lucy Wales Kluckhohn. 1971. *Navaho Material Culture*. Cambridge, MA: Harvard University Press.

LaDuke, Winona. 1994. "The Dilemma of Indian Forestry," *Earth Island Journal*. Summer.

Leopold, Aldo. 1949. *A Sand County Almanac*. New York: Oxford University Press.

Lopez, Barry H. 1978. *Of Wolves and Men*. New York: Charles Scribner's Sons.

Luckert, Karl W. 1975. *The Navajo Hunter Tradition.* Tucson: University of Arizona Press.

Luckert, Karl W. 1978. *A Navajo Bringing Home Ceremony: The Claus Chee Sonny Version of the Deerway Ajilee.* Flagstaff: Northern Arizona University Press.

Luckert, Karl W. 1979. *Coyoteway: A Navajo Holyway Healing Ceremonial.* Tucson: University of Arizona Press.

Lynch, Tom, ed. 2005. *El Lobo: Readings on the Mexican Wolf.* Salt Lake City: University of Utah Press.

Mahler, Richard. 2009. *The Jaguar's Shadow: Searching for a Mythic Cat.* New Haven, CT: Yale University Press.

Malotki, Ekkehart, and Michael Lomatuway'ma. 1994. *Hopi Coyote Tales: Istutuwutsi.* Lincoln: University of Nebraska Press.

Matthews, Washington. 1884. "Natural Naturalists," in *Washington Matthews: Studies of Navajo Culture, 1880–1894*, edited by Katherine Spencer Halpern and Susan Brown McGreevy. Albuquerque: University of New Mexico Press, 1997.

Matthews, Washington. 1887/1994. *Navaho Legends.* Salt Lake City: University of Utah Press.

Matthews, Washington. 1898. "Serpent Worship among the Navajos," *Land of Sunshine*, Vol. 29: 228–235.

Mayor, Adrienne. 2005. *Fossil Legends of the First Americans.* Princeton, NJ: Princeton University Press.

McCreery, Patricia and Ekkehart Malotki. 1994. *Tapamveni: The Rock Art Galleries of Petrified Forest and Beyond.* Petrified Forest, AZ: Petrified Forest Museum Association.

McPherson, Robert S. 1992. *Sacred Land, Sacred View: Navajo Perceptions of the Four Corners Region.* Salt Lake City, UT: Brigham Young University Press.

Mech, L. David. 1970. *The Wolf: The Ecology and Behavior of an Endangered Species.* Minneapolis: University of Minnesota Press.

Morgan, William. 1936. *Human-Wolves among the Navajo.* New Haven, CT: Yale University Publications in Anthropology, No. 11.

Murray, John A., ed. 1993. *Out among the Wolves: Contemporary Writings on the Wolf.* Anchorage: Alaska Northwest Books.

Nead, David M., James C. Halfpenny, and Steve Bissell. 1985. "The Status of Wolverines in Colorado," *Northwest Science*, 8(4): 286–289.

Newcomb, Franc J. 1940. "Origin Legend of the Navajo Eagle Chant," *Journal of American Folk-Lore*, 53(207): 50–78.

Newcomb, Franc J. 1940. *Navajo Omens and Taboos.* Santa Fe, NM: Rydal Press.

Newcomb, Franc J. and Gladys A. Reichard. 1975. *Sandpaintings of the Navajo Shooting Chant.* New York: Dover Publications.

O'Bryan, Aileen. 1956. *The Diné: Origin Myths of the Navaho Indians.* Washington, DC: Bureau of American Ethnology Bulletin No. 163.

O'Bryan, Aileen. 1956/1993. *Navaho Indian Myths.* New York: Dover Publications.

Opler, Morris E. 1941. *An Apache Life-Way: The Economic, Social, and Religious Institutions of the Chiricahua Indians.* Chicago: University of Chicago Press.

Page, Jake. 1990. "Hyeouma," *Native Peoples* (Summer): 31–36.

Parsons, Elsie Clews. 1927. "Witchcraft among the Pueblos: Indian or Spanish?" *Man*, 27: 106–112.

Parsons, Elsie Clews. 1939. *Pueblo Indian Religion, Volume I.* Lincoln: University of Nebraska Press.

Parsons, Elsie Clews. 1939/1996. *Pueblo Indian Religion.* 2 volumes. Lincoln: University of Nebraska Press.

Pavlik, Steve. 1992. Field notes.

Pavlik, Steve. 1992a. "Of Saints and Lamanites: An Analysis of Navajo Mormonism," *Wicazo Sa Review*, 8(1): 21–30.

Pavlik, Steve. 1992b. "The U.S. Supreme Court Decision on Peyote in Employment Division v. Smith: A Case Study in the Suppression of Native American Religious Freedom," *Wicazo Sa Review*, 8(2): 30–39.

Pavlik, Steve. 1995. "Navajo Orthodox Traditionalism." Paper presented at the Navajo Studies Conference, Farmington, New Mexico, March 12.

Pavlik, Steve. 1997. "Navajo Christianity: Historical Origins and Modern Trends," *Wicazo Sa Review,* 12(2): 43–58.

Pavlik, Steve. 1998. "The Role of Christianity and Church in Contemporary Navajo Society," in *A Good Cherokee, A Good Anthropologist: Papers in Honor of Robert K. Thomas,* edited by Steve Pavlik. Los Angeles: UCLA American Indian Studies Center: 189–200.

Pavlik, Steve. 1999. "San Carlos and White Mountain Apache Attitudes toward the Reintroduction of the Mexican Wolf to Its Historic Range in the Southwest," *Wicazo Sa Review*, 14(1): 129–145.

Pavlik, Steve. 2000a. "Will Big Trotter Reclaim His Place? The Role of the Wolf in Navajo Tradition," *American Indian Culture and Research Journal*, 24(4): 107–125.

Pavlik, Steve. 2000b. "The Navajo Nation Zoological Park Controversy: Cultural Implications for Wildlife Rehabilitators," in *22nd Annual International Wildlife Rehabilitation Council Conference Proceedings*, edited by Mary D. Reynolds. Suisun City, CA: 160–168.

Pavlik, Steve. 2000c. "It's All Happening at the (Navajo) Zoo: Divine Visitations, Sacred Animals, and Tribal Politics." Paper presented at the 42nd Western Social Science Association Conference, San Diego, California, April 28.

Pavlik, Steve. 2003. "Robert K. Thomas and the Taproots of Navajo Peoplehood." Paper presented at the Robert K. Thomas Symposium, Vancouver, British Columbia, Canada, July 23.

Pavlik, Steve. 2003. "Rohonas and Spotted Lions: The Historical and Cultural Occurrence of the Jaguar, *Panthera onca*, among the Native Tribes of the American Southwest," *Wicazo Sa Review*, 18(1): 157–175.

Pavlik, Steve. 2007. "The Sacred Cat: The Role of the Mountain Lion in Navajo Mythology and Traditional Life-way," in *Listening to Cougar*, edited by Cara Blessley Lowe and Marc Bekoff. Boulder: University of Colorado Press: 91–103.

Pavlik, Steve. 2009. Guest Commentary: "Western Scientists: Macho B Died for Your Sins," *Tucson Weekly.* August 6.

Pavlik, Steve. 2010. "Macho B Died for Your Sins: Western vs. Indigenous Perspectives on the Killing of the Last Borderlands Jaguar," *Red Ink*, 16(1): 40–45.

Pavlik, Steve. 2011a. "For the Love of Rattlesnakes," *Three Coyotes*, 1.2: 129–157.

Pavlik Steve. 2011b. "Who Is the Beast? Perspectives on Mountain Lions and Mankind," *Three Coyotes*, 1(1): 84–115.

Peterson, Roger Tory. 1990. *A Field Guide to Western Birds* (Peterson Field Guides). Boston, MA: Houghton Mifflin Company.

Ramirez, Anthony. 2000. "Die Like an Eagle: Indian Rights vs. a National Sanctuary," *New York Times*. November 19.

Reichard, Gladys A. 1939/1977. *Navajo Medicine Man Sandpaintings*. New York: Dover Publications.

Reichard, Gladys A. 1950. *Navaho Religion: A Study of Symbolism*. New York: Bollingen Foundation.

Robbins, Catherine. 1999. "A Zoo in Peril Stirs a Debate about Navajo Tradition," *New York Times*, March 28, 1999.

Robinson, Michael J. 2005. Predatory Bureaucracy: *The Extermination of Wolves and the Transformation of the West.* Boulder: University Press of Colorado.

Roessel, Robert A. 1983. *Dinétah: Navajo History, Volume III.* Chinle, AZ: Navajo Curriculum Center.

Roessel, Robert A. and Dillon Platero. 1974. *Coyote Stories of the Navajo People*. Phoenix, AZ: Navajo Curriculum Center Press.

Roessel, Ruth. 1971. *Navajo Studies at Navajo Community College*. Many Farms, AZ: Navajo Community College Press.

Roessel, Ruth. 1973. *Navajo Stories of the Long Walk Period.* Tsaile, AZ: Navajo Community College Press.

Rohn, Arthur H. and William and Lisa Ferguson. 1989. *Rock Art of Bandelier National Monument.* Albuquerque: University of New Mexico Press.

Royster, Judith V. and Michael C. Blumm. 2008. *Native American Natural Resources Law: Cases and Materials.* Durham, NC: Carolina Academic Press.

Saunders, Nicholas J., ed. 1998. *Icons of Power: Feline Symbolism in the Americas.* New York: Routledge.

Schaafsma, Polly. 1992. *Rock Art in New Mexico*. Santa Fe: Museum of New Mexico Press.

Schaafsma, Polly. 2000. *Warrior, Shield, and Star: Imagery and Ideology of Pueblo Warfare*. Santa Fe, NM: Western Edge Press.

Schwarz, Maureen Trudelle. 1997. "Snakes in the Ladies Room: Navajo Views on Personhood and Effect," *American Ethnologist*, 24(3): 602–627.

Selinger, Bernard. 2007. "The Navajo, Psychosis, Lacan, and Derrida," *Texas Studies in Literature and Language*, 49(1): 64–100.

Shebala, Marley. 1994. "Snake Sightings Create Major Concern by All," *Navajo Times*. August 18.

Simmons, Marc. 1974. *Witchcraft in the Southwest: Spanish and Indian Supernaturalism on the Rio Grande*. Flagstaff, AZ: Northland Press.

Smith, Watson. 1952. *Kiva Mural Decorations at Awatovi and Kawike-a*. Cambridge, MA: Peabody Museum of American Archaeology and Ethnology.

Spencer, Katherine. 1957. "Mythology and Values: An Analysis of Navaho Chantway Myths," *American Folklore Society Memoirs*, Vol. 48.

St. Clair, Jeffrey. 2008. *Born Under a Bad Sky: Notes from the Dark Side of the Earth*. Petrolia, CA: AK Press/CounterPunch.

Stebbins, Robert C. 1985. *A Field Guide to Western Reptiles and Amphibians* (Peterson Field Guides). Boston: Houghton Mifflin Company.

Steinhart, Peter. 1995. *The Company of Wolves*. New York: Alfred A. Knopf.

Sucik, Nick. 2004. "Exploring the Prospect of an Unidentified Species of Reptile within the Navajo and Hopi Lands: In Search of *Tl'iish Naat'a'i* (Snake-That-Flies)." www.azcentral.com/12news. April.

Sutherland, Kay and Paul Steed, Jr. 1974. "The Fort Hancock Rock Art Site Number One," *Artifact*, 12(4): 1–64.

Tsosie, Will. 1996. Personal conversation. March 9.

Tsosie, Will. 1999a. Personal conversation. July 30; September 26.

Tsosie, Will. 1999b. Personal conversation. October 12.

Tsosie, Will. 2001a. Personal conversation. August 4.

Tsosie, Will. 2001b. Personal conversation. October 19.

Tsosie, Will. 2003. Personal conversation. March 28.

Tsosie, Will. 2006. Personal conversation. August 10.

Tsosie, Will. 2009a. Personal conversation. August 16.

Tsosie, Will. 2009b. Personal conversation. August 2.

Tsosie, Will. 2009c. Personal conversation. November 16.

Tyler, Hamilton A. 1975. *Pueblo Animals and Myths.* Norman: University of Oklahoma Press.

Tyler, Hamilton A. 1979/1991. *Pueblo Birds and Myths*. Flagstaff, AZ: Northland Publishing Company.

US Fish and Wildlife Service. 1998. *National Eagle Repository: Denver, Colorado*, pamphlet, 10 pp. No printing information provided.

Wardwell, Lelia, 1991. *American Historical Images on File: The Native American Experience.* New York: Facts on File.

Wellman, Klaus. F. 1979. *A Survey of North American Indian Art.* Graz, Austria: Akademische Druck-u Verlagsanstalt.

Wheelwright, Mary C. 1958. *Myth of Willa-Chee-Ji De-ginnh-Keygo Hatral.* Santa Fe, NM: Museum of Navajo Ceremonial Art.

Wheelwright, Mary C. 1962. *Eagle Catching Myth and Bead Myth.* Santa Fe, NM: Museum of Navajo Ceremonial Art.

Wheelwright, Mary C. and David P. McAllester. 1956/1988. *The Myth and Prayers of the Great Star Chant and The Myth of the Coyote Chant.* Tsaile, AZ: Navajo Community College Press.

White, Leslie A. 1942. "The Pueblo of Santa Ana, New Mexico," *Memoirs of the American Anthropological Association*, Supplement 60: 1–360.

White, Leslie A. 1944. "'Rohona' in Pueblo Culture," *Papers of the Michigan Academy of Science, Arts, and Letters,* Vol. 29: 439–443.

White, Leslie A. 1947. "Ethnozoology of the Keresan Pueblo Indians," *Papers of the Michigan Academy of Science, Arts, and Letters*, Vol. 31: 223–243.

Williams, Ted. 2001. "Golden Eagles for the Gods," Audubon, 103(2): 30–32, 33–39.

Wilson, Edward O. 1984. *Biophilia.* Cambridge, MA: Harvard University Press.

Wright, Barton. 1977. *Hopi Kachinas: The Complete Guide to Collecting Kachina Dolls.* Flagstaff, AZ: Northland Press.

Wyman, Leland C. "Navaho Diagnosticians" (AA, 38, 1936, 236-46)

Wyman, Leland C. 1960. *Navaho Sandpainting: The Huckel Collection.* Colorado Springs, CO: Taylor Museum.

Wyman, Leland C. 1962. *The Windways of the Navaho.* Colorado Springs, CO: The Taylor Museum.

Wyman, Leland C. 1965. *The Red Antway of the Navaho.* Santa Fe, NM: Museum of Navajo Ceremonial Art.

Wyman, Leland C. 1970a. *Blessingway.* Tucson: University of Arizona Press.

Wyman, Leland C. 1970b. *Sandpaintings of the Navajo Shootingway and The Walcott Collection.* Smithsonian Contributions to Anthropology, Number 13. Washington, DC: Smithsonian Institution.

Wyman, Leland C. 1975. *The Mountainway of the Navajo.* Tucson: University of Arizona Press.

Wyman, Leland C. 1983. *Southwest Indian Drypainting.* Albuquerque: University of New Mexico Press.

Wyman, Leland C. and Clyde Kluckhohn. 1938. "Navajo Classification of Their Song Ceremonials," *Memoirs of the American Anthropological Association*, Supplement 50: 3–38.

Wyman, Leland C. and Flora L. Bailey. 1943. "Navajo Upward-Reaching Way: Objective Behavior, Rationale, and Sanction," University of New Mexico Bulletin 389, Anthropological Series 4.

Zintgraff, Jim and Turpin A. Solveig. 1991. *Pecos River Rock Art: A Photographic Essay.* San Antonio, TX: Sandy McPherson Publishing Company.

About the Author

Steve Pavlik teaches Native American Studies and Native Environmental Science at Northwest Indian College, Bellingham, Washington. He has more than thirty-five years of teaching experience in the field of American Indian education.

Mr. Pavlik holds a MA in American Indian Studies and a M. Ed. in American History from the University of Arizona. He is the author or editor of four books, including *Destroying Dogma: Vine Deloria, Jr. and His Influence on American Society* (edited with Daniel R. Wildcat) and more than 70 other published articles, essays, and reviews.

His academic specialty areas include Native American religion and spirituality, ethnozoology, cognitive ethology, and environmental ethics. Mr. Pavlik is also a naturalist and environmental activist.